15.00

Essential Woman

Essential Woman
Her Mystery, Her Power

Murry Hope

Mandala
An Imprint of HarperCollins*Publishers*

Mandala
An Imprint of GraftonBooks
A Division of HarperCollins*Publishers*
77-85 Fulham Palace Road,
Hammersmith, London W6 8JB

Published by Mandala 1991
1   3   5   7   9   10   8   6   4   2

A CIP catalogue record for this book
is available from the British Library

ISBN 1-85274 097 3

Typeset by Harper Phototypesetters Ltd.,
Northampton
Printed in Great Britain by
Biddles Ltd., Guildford

Contents

For Nancy B. Watson
who understands

Introduction

WE live in a world in which the word 'equality' is liberally bandied about in connection with colour, creed, race, and gender. But as far as the last is concerned, how equal is equal? Not very, I fear. Unfortunately, women are still viewed as an inferior form of creation by many of the world's major religions and social institutions, some of whom have the temerity to proclaim their credos publicly and with a degree of misplaced pride. While society occasionally allows a woman to rise to a position of authority this kind of acknowledgement is seldom shared by her sisters in the lower echelons of society, while there is no let-up in the efforts made by competing males to displace her.

From where did this myth of inequality originate, and what gave birth to these erroneous and totally unjust dogmas that perpetuate it? Or perhaps I should rephrase the question and ask: what errant energies implanted this insidious genetic programming and the taboos that followed in its wake? Over the centuries these have subtly filtered into the very fabric of our lives, and become so deeply embedded in the collective unconscious as to be blindly accepted as an essential dogma of earthly existence.

These and other metaphysical observations on the true nature and status of the feminine gender will be examined in the following pages, side by side with the manifestation of the psychological and physical suffering they have caused to countless millions of women over the centuries. Before my less militant readers withdraw, let me assure them that the battle of the sexes, which I view as a falsely engendered and subliminally programmed conflict that

should not exist in a civilized society, is not the exclusive
theme of this book. Both men *and women* have unconsciously contributed to the catalogue of evils that have
dominated society over the past centuries, each sex to some
extent playing into the hands of the other. Perhaps it is not
so much men and women who need liberating, but the
third, reconciling force or catalyst that connects them. In
other words, we must seek beyond the symptoms for the
cause of the blight — which will become apparent in the
following chapters.

The process of individuation, which involves the perfect
balancing of the anima and animus with each individual, is
believed to constitute part of the natural evolutionary process of the *Homo sapiens* experience. The more spiritually
mature a person is, the less accentuated the sexual polarity.
In a truly enlightened society men and women would live
harmoniously together, sharing each other's experiences,
burdens, sufferings and joys in full understanding, each
being able to 'relate' partially, if not totally, to the experiences of the other.

Objective examination of the subject matter does, however, call for a multidimensional overall view, from the
logical reasoning of sociology to the scientific and metaphysical exposure of the error of entrenched beliefs and the
harmful by-products of past *convenience conditioning*. Do
these assumed sexual attitudes, for example, constitute
part of a legitimate growth experience in accordance with
basic cosmic law? Or is there, in fact, an intelligence behind
it all, one that feeds from the energies of conflict, competition and the denigration of human dignity? If the latter,
then that element of chaos that has ruled this planet for so
long, which appears to have chosen the female experience
as its sacrificial scapegoat or laboratory mouse, must be
sought out, exposed for what it is and its chains broken once
and for all. And if the immolation of women is simply a
natural stage in the growth experience of *Homo sapiens*,
then is it not time that we shed the ragged robes of a
transcendentally impoverished childhood and the garish
regalia of rebellious adolescence and assume the individuated mantle of spiritual adulthood?

As I see it, the problems that face women are but one
symptom of a far more serious malaise that has afflicted our

planet for many centuries, and continues to do so in spite of the efforts made by serious and enlightened reformers, psychologists, sociologists and metaphysical teachers to effect a liberal and fair adjustment.

It has been suggested by some esoteric schools that when a spirit or psyche enters the feminine mode it does so specifically in order to undergo the experience of subjugation. Therefore, the sexual status quo should not be interfered with. This is rather like saying we must not seek to overcome those diseases that send thousands to their death each year, because in so doing we would be denying many souls the experience afforded by that particular type of suffering. However, whereas the latter battle is viewed as legitimate and ethically correct, the feminine cross is still seen by many as necessary to the balanced functioning of the social order.

What utter nonsense! By making this planet a happier and more secure place for women, where they could live without fear of the mental and physical abuses to which they are subjected at all levels of society, and by acknowledging their spiritual equality and full right of expression in all fields of human endeavour, those undergoing the male experience would attain their own spiritual maturity. But then there are always those souls or psyches who choose to remain in the 'child' mode, refusing to accept the full physical, mental, and spiritual responsibilities of adulthood. Until more powerful forces choose to intervene and Gaia decides once again to chastise her unruly brood, such spirits will, no doubt, continue to incarnate either in the masculine gender, or in female bodies that will afford them an easy ride at the expense of those males who adhere to obsolete religious and sociological dogmas.

The following chapters, which contain the beliefs and hopes as well as the stories and experiences of women over the ages, will, I trust, serve to clarify my point. These are not limited to the sagas of the famous, or those who have left some impression, no matter how small, on the communities in which they have lived. Included are the feelings, views, perplexities, resentments and sacrifices of 'ordinary' women who are faced with the complexities and rapidly changing values of today's world — those quietly voiced moans and laughs that we, as woman, share among ourselves, which afford us temporary relief from the tensions of day-to-day existence, and give us the strength to carry on the fight.

Part I
The Past

Chapter 1
Ouroboros

I ASK my readers to embark with me on a journey along
the corridors of time that will take us back through the
pages of recorded history to those prehistoric epochs whose
cobwebbed shrouds conceal the truth behind the strange
stories of lost continents and vanished civilizations that
have come down to us via the mythic channels of legend and
folklore. The subject matter of our investigation is WOMAN:
her past, present, and ultimate future on this planet. Myth
and legend — where is the reality in that, you may ask, and
how can it affect us in this day and age? However, as we shall
see, several answers to our present-day problems lie concealed within the fables of the past, many of which also
hold the key to the inner workings of the feminine psychology. Professor Efremov of the Soviet Union recently
accused Western scientists of a certain snobbishness when
it comes to the tales of the common people: 'Historians
must pay more respect to ancient traditions and folklore,' he
insisted. In view of the many so-called 'myths' that have
since been proven to be historical facts (Troy, for example),
we would be well counselled to heed his advice.[1]

Feminism, and women's studies in general, have given
birth to a new set of semantics. The American writer Riane
Eisler, for example, has coined the term *androcracy* in
preference to patriarchy to define a system ruled through
force or the threat of force by men. Her alternative term is
gylany (from the Greek roots *gyne* (woman) and *andros*
(man)). 'The letter *l* between the two has a double meaning.
In English, it stands for the *linking* of both halves of
humanity, rather than, as in androcracy, their ranking.'[2] In
Greek it derives from the Latin verb *lyein* or *lyo*, which in

turn has a double meaning: to solve or resolve (as in ana*l*ysis) and to dissolve or set free (as in cata*l*ysis). She uses the term 'domination hierarchies' to refer to the systems of human ranking based on force, and 'actualization hierarchies' to denote systems within systems: molecules, cells, and organs of the body; a progression towards a higher, more evolved, and more complex level of functioning.

Edward C. Whitmont, on the other hand, favours the terms 'androlatric' and 'gynolatric', while Luisah Teish prefers 'gynandry', all of which make etymological sense. However, as there are so many variations on the same theme, until some standardization is established within the accepted English code of reference I have elected to stay with the traditional 'matrist' and 'patrist' to indicate male or female emphasis or dominance in society, custom or religion.

The innate power possessed by woman has often been symbolized by the serpent, the major religions tending to emphasize the negative serpentine traits as applying to women generally. However, serpent energy, in common with most other natural forces, has many facets. It was not without good reason that the priesthood of one of the most ancient civilizations, ancient Egypt, incorporated the Uraeus in their regalia to denote the gift of sagacity and profound esoteric wisdom. From whom did they, in turn, derive the knowledge of this symbology? Doubtless from one or more of those prehistoric cultures which are still considered by many authorities to be purely fictitious, whose memory sages and scholars of integrity and wisdom have kept alive for us during the dark ages of ignorance, superstition and spiritual blindness.

Both anthropology and arcane tradition confirm the antiquity of the creatrix concept, while scientists studying population genetics have recently stated that all humans are descended on the maternal side from one woman, who probably lived in Africa and has since been called the Black Eve. Since the creative feminine principle would appear to have preceded that of a male creator, how did it become distorted and destroyed? And if it can be equated with serpent power, then surely its energies are in resonance with the esoteric symbology of the Ouroboros, depicted by the Gnostics as a dragon, snake or serpent biting its own tail. The Ouroboros is seen to represent, among other things, self-fertilization and a nature that continually returns within a cyclical pattern to its own beginning, thus forming a circle of completion, from which its energies are then ready to ascend to a higher frequency or more exalted mode of expression.

This symbology appears to be specifically applicable to the Goddess or Creatrix concept in that the Sophia, Wisdom, or first feminine principle whom the Gnostics referred to as the World Soul, having ascended to a given evolutionary level or aeon within the spiritual hierarchy, is required to descend to the sacrificial nadir before reascending to claim her true Divinity, thus completing both the ouroboric circle and bringing a particular evolutionary era to a close. In personal terms, once the creative cycle has been realized at the material level, the spirit is free to incorporate its productive energies to further the process of its own transcendental quest. This may be confirmed in the apocryphal *Gospel of the Egyptians*, in which the following conversation is recorded as having taken place between Christ and one of his women disciples, whose name was Salome:

> When Salome asked how long Death should prevail, the Lord said: So long as ye women bear children, for I am come to destroy the work of the Female. And Salome said to him: Did I therefore well in having no children? The Lord answered and said: Eat every Herb, but eat not that which hath bitterness. When Salome asked when these things about which she questioned should be made known, the Lord said: When ye trample upon the garment of shame; when the Two become One, and Male with Female neither male nor female. [3]

This statement is often taken by metaphysical philosophers and psychologists as meaning that the alternative to the creation of a human child as a way of expressing the divine spark is the assimilation of that creative energy into the individual spirit: the inner marriage of the anima and animus, or male and female elements of the psyche, leading to true transpersonal individuation. This concept is re-echoed in the Hindu saying, 'What need have we of children — we who have the Self?' [4] Primitive myths have always recognized and emphasized the antithesis between immortality and the bearing of children.

Why is it the work of the female that needs to be destroyed before such transcendental heights can be achieved? Why not the work of the male? Perhaps it is necessary for us to follow the trials, tribulations and triumphs of the ouroboric odyssey of the Creatrix — the ascent and descent of the matriarchal age, the symbolic 'fall' of the Sophia, the onset of female subservience with its attendant suffering and denigration — in order to understand what has taken place at *all* levels. I hope that these explorations will serve to throw some light on the nature and *raison d'être* of those subtle energies or external intelligences that appear to exert such a powerful influence on the functioning of the social order at the material, practical, and everyday levels of earthly existence. I have no intention of dogmatizing on these issues, nor do I claim my suggestions to be the one and only answer, but they may illuminate grey or clouded areas in female psychology and experience.

The Silver Age of Cancer

Every two thousand years or so the poles of the Earth's axis complete an entire circle round the path of the ecliptic, this being referred to as an 'astrological age'. Most followers of astrology and New Age philosophy will be familiar with this concept and the influence these ages are believed to exert on our planet as a whole. For example, the twenty-first century is said to be the time when the Age of Pisces gives way to the much heralded Age of Aquarius, during which old, established concepts and beliefs will give way to a new order and way of thinking.

There was a period in the past beginning around 8000 BC that is believed to have exerted a profound influence on womankind: the matriarchal Age of Cancer, designated by the Greeks as the Silver Age and vividly described by Hesiod. He tells us that the people of those times were mainly agriculturalists who did not indulge in war, were vegetarians, and lived to a ripe old age. Their menfolk, however, were subject to their mothers, which failed to meet with Hesiod's approval; he referred to them as disputatious and lacking in manliness. They failed to offer sacrifice to Zeus, which angered the god to the extent that he eventually destroyed them, after which they sank into the depths of the earth to appear in later myths as the subterranean blessed, in which capacity they were accorded some small degree of veneration. Most authorities tend to equate the Silver Age with that period just prior to and directly after the flood when goddess worship predominated throughout Europe and the Middle East.

The zodiacal energies of Cancer have long been associated with motherhood and nurturing in all its manifestations. Cancerians, astrologers tell us, are home-loving people who like to stay within the family influence if possible. If not, they will create a home-like environment for themselves and fill it either with their own offspring, or with stray people, children, or animals whom they judge to be in need of nurturing. The sign of Cancer is traditionally shown as a crab, indicating the protective shell of the creature's home, which shields it from predators and the outside world as a whole, and into which it can retreat when it feels threatened. This it carries on its back, and in similar manner Cancerians tend to make a home wherever they go. Due to the association of this sign with the killer disease which shares its name, there has been a recent plan afoot among American astrologers to have it changed to the Sign of the Cat. Cats have been observed to show strong maternal instincts, and are also associated with the moon — though I would question this, as cats for me are decidedly solar beasts! Both Cancer and the moon are still and have always been associated with femininity.

For some time I have suspected that there is more in the crab-cancer symbology than might be apparent at first glance, especially as far as the feminine experience is concerned. Many healers (and some traditional doctors, too) are of the opinion that cell growth gone haywire assumes an individuality in its own right or in occult terms acquires a resident invading entity, all life forms being dependent upon the influence of intelligence. In other words, cancer is the creative factor in the chaos mode. It is creativity gone haywire, or as one dictionary describes it: 'a pernicious, spreading evil'. Translate all this into the language of astrology at a cosmic level (i.e. as applied to external influences on a planet), and we can start speculating as to where we acquired the particular imbalance that has resulted in women being viewed as second-class citizens in many of the major world cultures and religions.

Sometime during, or just prior to, the Age of Cancer, a pernicious and chaotic influence appears to have invaded our world causing the pendulum to swing first to the matriarchal age and then to its opposite extreme — patrism — from which it is believed it will once again return (ideally to the centre) during the Age of Aquarius. According to the laws of 'Chaos Science' these swings are an inevitable part of evolutionary progression, Chaos and Order being ever in conflict. But is this necessarily the case? Are we really governed by such random factors or is there some intelligent force behind their manifestation?

Although the period of duration of one or other extreme of the swing may seem endless to those who are on the receiving end of the resulting imbalances, in the present case the female sex, it should be borne in mind that in the subtle dimensions of timelessness all is happening simultaneously. Therefore, while that aspect of our soul or psyche is suffering or has suffered during the periods concerned, our higher or more mature self may well be enjoying the fruits of the opposing angle of the pendulum, in a time zone where all is harmonious and well ordered.

I appreciate, however, that all this borders on the metaphysical and is therefore of little consolation to those women who are at present on the receiving end of the psychospiritual cancer that has permeated the minds of so many and blinded them to the real nature, role and destiny of women. But take heart, sisters, there is light at the end of the tunnel, albeit a pinprick, and if we hold together we can make it once again to the sunshine beyond.

Prior to the Age of Cancer there were, of course, the Ages of Leo and Virgo. During the latter, legend and arcane teachings tell us that because the creative force was acknowledged equally in both its feminine and masculine aspects, a true state of balance existed between the sexes. It was therefore understood that the creativity inherent in both women and men could manifest in any of several different ways, a truth which has filtered down to us via the god-forms and mythologies of many lands. The Age of Leo, which directly preceded the Age of Cancer, is sometimes equated with the Golden Age of Greek mythology. The first men of this race, we are told, lived like gods while Cronus (time) reigned. Free from worry and fatigue, old age did not afflict them and they rejoiced in continual festivity. Hesiod emphasizes, however, that these people were not immortal, but died peacefully as in 'sweet slumber'. All the blessings of the world were theirs: the fruitful earth gave forth its treasures freely, and the people ate honey and drank the milk of goats. After their death they became benevolent genii, protectors and tutellary guardians of the living. They bestowed good fortune, were patrons of music and helped people to uphold justice if their spiritual advice was heard and heeded.

This Golden Age of Leo, and the preceding Ages of Virgo and Libra, are often associated with the lost continent of Atlantis, which many researchers now estimate to have sunk during violent seismic upheavals precipitated by a shift in the earth's axis that took place sometime during the Age of Cancer. That the moon played some part in the drama there is little doubt, and as the moon has assumed such an important role in the lives and cycles of women, an examination of the overall role played by that orb in Gaia's evolutionary drama begs for analysis.

Sun, Moon and Myth

It is interesting to observe that the earth as a living entity has now been officially accorded a feminine identity — Gaia. According to ancient Greek sources Gaia (Earth), united with her son Uranus (Heaven, or Sky) to produce the first race, the Titans, a name that derives from the Cretan word for 'King'. The Titans were ultimately honoured as the ancestors of humanity, and to them was attributed the invention of the arts and magic (science). There were, we are told, twelve Titans, six males and six females, which rather indicates that in the very early days of its existence, the human race did not suffer from the pronounced sexual differentiation with which we are at present afflicted. However, all of Gaia's offspring were not as tall, handsome and clever as the Titans, in fact some of them, notably the monsters Cottus, Briareus and Gyges, known as the Hecatoncheires or Centimanes, were so horrific in appearance that as soon as they were born their father shut them in the depths of the earth.

No doubt the myth is simply telling us that in those early experimental days of the emergence of our species from its primitive state there were plenty of oddities and genetic mutations, some of which, like the saurians, eventually died out. However, Gaia, it seems, took great exception to her husband's rejection of his offspring and planned a terrible revenge. Fashioning a sharp sickle of *harpe* for the deed she had in mind, she told her children of her plan, but they were horrified and refused to have any part in it. Only the sly Cronus agreed to help his mother by carrying out the dastardly deed. When night fell, Uranus joined his wife in their bedchamber, and no sooner was he asleep than Cronus, who had been hidden there beforehand, castrated him and cast his testicles into the sea. The Golden Age of Cronus (Time), precipitated by his mother Gaia (Earth), had begun.

The idea that the earth has a feminine identity appears to have persisted down the ages, although not in all cultures. Nor were all the ancient goddesses associated with the moon. There were sun goddesses in the lands of Canaan, Anatolia, Australia, Arabia, and among the Northern European peoples, Eskimos, Japanese, and Khasis of India. Interestingly, somewhere along the line the last three acquired subordinate brothers, who assumed lunar characteristics. This seems to imply that these lunar companions were added later, probably following certain terrestrial events observable in many parts of the globe which either involved the capture of the moon itself or, if it was already established as a satellite of Earth, a shift in the axis of the 'parent' which gave the sky watchers of the time a different view of its orb. Another explanation is that just as each individual carries the propensity for male or female emphasis depending on the state of balance existing between the anima and animus, so also do the planetary bodies. Therefore, the dominating principle behind the nature of a tribe, culture or ethos will be the deciding factor as to which aspect of the spiritual economy of the heavenly body in question is contacted — love god or goddess, warrior queen or king, and so forth.

In ancient Egypt the Goddess Nut symbolized the sky, while her husband Geb represented the earth. As for female creation goddesses, these are to be found in the myths and legends of Sumer, Babylon, Egypt, Africa, Australia, China, and India, to name but a few places. There were also legions of lesser known female tribal deities, a study of which would probably fill several books.

Enter the lunar satellite. The moon has long been associated with both the day-to-day affairs and hidden mysteries of women. Its influence upon female physiology may be seen in the cycles of menstruation and fertility, while the psychological effects of its energies apply to both men and women alike. Besides these, however, women's mysteries are frequently centred around the moon, and to this day the silver orb would appear to play an important role in the acknowledgement and worship of the Goddess principle.

In astrology the moon rules the zodiacal sign of Cancer, and it is interesting to observe how the principle of fertility is emphasized in the lives of women who have this sign prominent in their charts.

But was this always so? I count myself among the few researchers who have seen fit to question the idea that the moon has always exerted its influence over both the zodiacal sign of Cancer and the lives and cycles of women. Sun-moon conflicts can be traced back to before the days of recorded history. Anne Kent Rush, writing in her informative book *Moon, Moon* comments:

> Most myths relating to the moon tell of an original time of total blackness out of which the life force molded a cosmic egg. This world egg split in two; one part remained in the sky to become the moon and the other became earth. These two parts of the mother egg have historically alternating sexes, but most often the earth is thought to be female as well as the moon, and the sun is male. At various times, the moon was thought to be male symbolizing either her independent wholeness or the struggle between the two principles for dominance. The story of the clash between the two world views is most often personified as strife in the relationship between the moon and the sun (thought either to be her husband or rebellious son-lover). The normal pattern of the story is that at one time, long ago, the sun and moon were of equal brilliance and were one planet. They had a fight and split in two. Their spat continues (indicated in the heavens by eclipses, sunspots and moonmarks) but they visit now and then. When the moon is angry with the way the peoples of the

earth are living she sends floods, but they are always followed by rebirth and resurrection.[5]

There is a mountain of evidence which suggests that for a long period in the history of mankind either there was no moon in our skies, or it did not occupy its present position in relation to the earth (see Murry Hope, *Atlantis — Myth or Reality?*). This being the case, what external force was responsible for the fertility cycles of women prior to or during those times? There are tribal and arcane legends which insinuate that female fecundity was at one time under the direct influence of the sun, and that those festivals that were orientated to the solstices and equinoxes were specifically designed to stimulate and accommodate the prevailing fertility energies, so as to ensure the continuation of the tribe or group concerned.

I realize that this concept is out of line with popular (and many traditional) ideas concerning the origin of women's rites and goddess worship generally, but it is certainly deserving of consideration. The Norse and Teutonic peoples for example, regarded the sun as feminine, while the Egyptian goddess Sekhmet was decidedly solar in nature. The ancient Egyptians also conceived of a female sun whom they called Rat, seen by some as the feminine aspect of their god Ra. Although Ra is usually assumed to represent our own star, he also has strong connections with the binary star, Sirius, around which so much of the earlier Egyptian religion was formed.

Although Osiris and Khonsu were also lunar deities, Thoth was the principal Egyptian moon god, and his role in the acquisition of the five epagomenal days that make up our present year must surely have some bearing on the lunar enigma. Prior to the estimated time of 6000 BC (some say earlier and others later) the calendar consisted of only 360 days. The ancient Egyptian deities Geb and Nut (Earth and Sky) offended Ra, who swore that Nut should not be delivered of a child on any of the 360 days of his year. Now this might have caused the goddess considerable difficulty had not Thoth, god of science and mathematics, keeper of the Akashic Records, Divine Advocate and Lord of Time played his famous game of draughts with the moon, from which he won a seventy-second part of her light ($1/72$th of

360 is exactly 5!) which he made into five new days called 'epagomenal'. Nut was then able to give birth to the five children she had been carrying: Osiris, Horus the Elder, Set, Isis, and Nephthys, in that order. This legend is also reiterated in the Greek myth of Cronus swallowing five of his own children and disgorging them after imbibing a potion administered to him by Metis (Justice), while the Sumerian moon god Sîn was also credited with having power over time.

Although various magical and mystical interpretations have been placed on these legends by scholars, mystics and romantics over the years, what they are basically telling us is that the outcome of some celestial drama involving the earth, the moon and the starry night sky, necessitated changes in the calendar system, and it was Thoth, a *lunar* deity who effected the alteration.

I hope the aforegoing will serve to emphasize the role played by the moon in our archaic past, as well as the waxing and waning of the feminine influence, or at least its effect on women ever since Thoth's somewhat questionable board game.

The Lunar Influence on Women

If we are to pursue James Lovelock's Gaia hypothesis to its ultimate conclusion, we must, as I have already suggested, also accept that *all* cosmic bodies are living entities, and therefore the same cosmic laws apply to them as to us in that they also each carry the masculine/feminine or animus/anima potential. Let us assume that a planet, for example, Gaia, is manifesting its material energies in the feminine (anima or yin) mode, but with spiritual masculine (animus or yang) overtones, in the same way that countless women are believed to have done over the centuries, and that the balanced functioning of this polarity is, in turn, dependent upon the equipoise of another, closely related orb — the moon.

If Gaia and her satellite are so closely linked, perhaps the polarities have become confused over the ages. After all, as any astrologer will avow, the moon *reflects* in much the same way as a mirror. Is it therefore, like Dorian Gray's famous picture, reflecting some imbalance in Gaia or her progeny? Or is it, perhaps, the lunar polarities that have deviated and 'she' is now 'he', or vice versa as the stories of Thoth and Sîn might connote? Should the latter be the case, then the moon might well prove to be the bogey of our piece. Let us consider those aspects of our daily lives that come under her influence, menstruation for a start, referred to by women over the ages as 'the curse'.

Now surely, a curse, as such, implies the intrusion of an external agency or alien mind. In fact, one dictionary defines it as 'an appeal to a supernatural power for harm to come to a specific person, group, etc'. Ancient records show that women have been subjected to this form of suffering and inconvenience since historical records began (and probably before that). Clement of Alexandria (AD 150-220) referred to the gods Hermes, Ptah and Imhotep as being strangers from a land across the seas that existed before the Flood, who brought with them certain books of a medical nature that were indispensable. These numbered 42 in all, the last six referring to medical matters. Number 42 was entitled *The Maladies of Women*. Whether these maladies included menstrual pains Clement failed to tell us, but then he probably would not have known. These sacred books, and others of their kind, were no doubt among those destroyed by Christian and Islamic zealots in later years, and it has taken many centuries of needless suffering and experiment to close the gap of medical ignorance.

If, therefore, women are ruled by the lunar influence, it does not seem to have done them much good. Female characteristics, if used wisely and in the right context, have an enormous amount to contribute to the welfare and well-being of this planet. But when they are subjugated — often by force — their energies spiral inwards, effecting the kind of somatizations which have caused some of us to consider that whoever designed the female body must have had a twisted mind!

Was it not Hermes who visited upon the android Pandora, she of the mythical box of ills, the curse of a warped mind? Jung had much to say concerning the alchemy of chaos, highlighting the close and mysterious relationship that exists between the Mercurius, the planetary genius of Mercury, and Saturn, the Grim Reaper (time). Mercurius in his many names has always been associated with the healing process, but according to Jung his functions are also closely related to those of Saturn. In Gnosticism, Saturn is Ildabaoth, meaning 'child of chaos', the highest archon, corresponding to the Egyptian Set, but in alchemy the child of chaos is Mercury.

Thus the symbol of Mercury, which is the insignia of many branches of the healing profession to this day, features two serpents entwining the central winged rod, believed by many to be emblematic of Chaos and Order. Healing, therefore, involves the balancing of these two forces which, the symbol tells us, may be achieved by the mind or higher self, as represented by the surmounting orb or wings. Since the Egyptian Thoth is often equated with the Greek Hermes or Mercury, time would appear to be the significant factor in this whole cosmic drama, and what we are therefore up against are the effects of polarity swings between the chaotic and stable modes, which affect intelligent life at all of its levels.

The present gender or polarity imbalances that are manifest in the human race were precipitated by the cosmic drama that took place at the time of the arrival of the five epagomenal days, when the earth-moon polarity was in some way changed. This disturbance was also responsible for both the ensuing Cancerian (matriarchal) age and the subsequent swing to patrism. I do not see this as representing the beginning of the 'Fall' in the generally accepted meaning of the term — that occurred many aeons earlier — but simply as another manifestation of the succumbing of mankind to the subjection of that external 'testing influence', which is the refining fire of the spirit through which we must eventually pass on our homeward road to our creative source. As it is the Sophia or World Soul that has elected to descend and suffer with us, so are her sufferings on earth reflected most strongly in her feeling and intuitive daughters.

Those traditions, past and present, which subscribe to the idea that the sun is feminine rather than masculine, seem more disposed to accommodate the idea of equality between the sexes. A feminine sun, masculine moon and feminine earth might make sounder sense for women, but whatever the truth of the matter, it is my contention that the 'woman problem' is somehow tied up with this confusion of celestial polarities and identities. After all, as above, so below!

In a just world the quota of suffering would surely be equally divided between the sexes. The male myth of woman as the Evil One, the serpent in the Tree of Knowledge, is nothing more than a convenient scapegoat through which some external programming agency plays its game of celestial draughts with the psyches of both men and women, convincing the former that they are superior and the latter that they are second-class human beings, fit only for breeding and serving. No doubt it would hurt the male ego to know it was being manipulated to destroy and dominate, just as it pains many women who have become sufficiently alerted to its subtleties to know that it is demanding that they should adopt the role of submission.

A strong feminine spiritual influence is needed on earth to counterbalance the tendency towards male competitive dominance and its accompanying mode of left-brain, mechanistic thinking. On the other hand, care must be taken to avoid going to the other extreme, where logic flies the coop and emotions hold sway. Sexual extremes are for the young in body and soul. Spiritual maturity, like individuation, balances the masculine and feminine, the yang and the yin, the animus and anima in both sexes, which makes for an end to strife and a greater understanding each of the other.

But the end is mercifully in sight. During the Aquarian Age both men and women will be afforded the opportunity to cast off the shackles of mental slavery and enter a period of time in which each will think for him or herself. Woman has passed her ouroboric nadir and is now ready to reascend and complete the evolutionary circle that is her gateway to more exalted dimensions. It will not be long before humanity on this planet is once again reunited in understanding with the other life forms to which Gaia gives nourishment and shelter.

Chapter 2
The Silver Years

A N analysis of the growth, flowering, and subsequent
decline of goddess worship, and the matrism that
accompanied it in many early tribal societies and those
cultures that later gave birth to civilization as we know it,
demands that prior to an examination of the psychological
or metaphysical considerations involved, due deference
should be paid to the evidence available from mythological,
archaeological, anthropological and other established
scholarly sources.

Prominent among the researchers in this field is the
archaeologist Marija Gimbutas, referred to in a recent
article by the American shaman Vicki Noble as: 'the
archaeological grandmother of feminist scholarship, having
provided us with a scientifically-grounded documentation
of ancient "matristic" (female-centered) civilization in old
Europe.' Gimbutas's initial enquiry appeared in 1982 in
Goddesses and Gods of Old Europe, which concentrated
on the period from 7000 to 3500 BC, and led into her latest
literary venture *The Language of the Goddess* in which 'she
maintains through "hard evidence" that the Goddess tradition can be traced from the Palaeolithic period (as much
as 30,000 years ago), through the Neolithic agricultural
civilizations (around 9,000 years ago), through the "Patriarchal transition" (5,000 years ago), and even into the
present time. Gimbutas, a Lithuanian by birth, says this
ancient tradition has not died out in Europe, especially
Eastern Europe.'[1] Not all scholars are in agreement with her,
however. An article in the *Los Angeles Times Magazine*
(June 11 1989) quotes fellow archaeologists describing her as
'romantic' and suggesting that she 'habitually presents

debatable assertions as fact.' Whether or not we agree with
Gimbutas, the following table of periods and dates in the
earth's early history will prove helpful.

Palaeolithic or Old Stone Age: the cultural period beginning
with the earliest chipped stone tools about 2.5 to 3 million
years ago until the beginning of the **Mesolithic**, or Middle
Stone Age, c.12,000 years ago.

Neolithic or New Stone Age: the cultural period between
10,000 and 7,000 BC in the Middle East and later elsewhere,
characterized by the development of farming and the making of technically advanced, polished stone implements.

Bronze Age: the period that brought the Stone Age to an
end, distinguished by the invention of bronze, which is
believed to have been c. 3,000 BC.

Iron Age: period that followed the Bronze Age, typified by
the spread of iron tools and weapons, beginning in the
Middle East around the 12th century BC and in Europe
around the 8th century BC.

Of the earliest Age mentioned by the Greeks, the Golden
Age, we have little empirical evidence although Barbara
Walker has shown that, according to myth and legend, it
represented a time when there was 'no wildness nor eating
of each other, nor any war, nor revolt against them . . . There
were no government nor separate possessions of women and
children. For all men rose again from the earth remem-
bering nothing of their past. And such things as private
property and families did not exist.' She continues: 'This
was regarded as a figment of Plato's imagination until
research discovered the pre-urban community of the
Neolithic cultivator.'[2] It has been suggested that the matriarchal society came into existence at the end of the last Ice
Age, if not before, when 'the long process of domestication
had come to a head in the establishment of small, stable
communities with an abundant and varied food supply:
communities whose capacities to produce a surplus of
storable grain gave security and adequate nurture to the
young. The rise in vitality was enhanced by vivid biological
insight.'[3]

From the above chronology we may observe that the

matriarchal society under which the virtues of equality, social caring and peace, referred to by Plato and others, flourished *after* 10,000 BC. In other words, it came into existence with or during the Cancerian Age, when goddess worship was the predominant religious influence.

Jacquetta Hawkes, James Frazer, Margaret Mead and other recognized authorities generally agree that the origin of the Mother Goddess, or Creatrix, arose from the fact that in primitive societies the function of impregnation had not been understood. Therefore, before coitus became associated with childbirth, only the female was seen as the giver of life. This naturally accounted for the matrilineal systems that existed for many centuries and that were carried on long after the role played by the male in the reproductive process was fully understood. The belief that ignorance of the male-female creative processes was present in every single pocket of culture that existed in the prehistoric world does tend to strain credulity, however, since according to Gimbutas and other feminine-orientated researchers in this field, the total significance of serpent energy was probably understood by certain women, if not all, from very ancient times.

Experts also opine that the Venus figurines, some of which date back as far as 25,000 BC, and other female figures, which have been found in areas as far apart as Spain, France, Germany, Austria, Czechoslovakia, and Russia, and appear to cover a span of some 10,000 years, were probably clan mothers or ancestral spirits rather than goddesses, idols, or mothers of a god.

The Aurignacian peoples, so-called after Aurignac in the French Pyrenees and related to the Upper Palaeolithic culture between Mousteria and Solutrean, are believed to have been directly descended from the early form of modern man known as Cro-Magnon, characterized by a stature of six feet and over and identified in skeletal parts found in the Cro-Magnon cave in southern France. Cro-Magnon man made his appearance in Europe during the late Palaeolithic era. The fact that these people also acknowledged the sacrality of the feminine may be evidenced in the famous Gravettian--Aurignacian Venus of Willendorf, which has served as a model for the numerous figurines of Gaia that are currently in circulation among New Age goddess worshippers

The carved limestone figure of the Earth Mother holding the horn of plenty, which now resides in the Bordeaux Museum where it is known as the Venus of Laussel, has been dated back more than 20,000 years, while a similar Cro-Magnon carving, equally ancient, is in the Musée de l'Homme in Paris, known as the 'Venus of Lespouge'.[4]

In the seventh millennium BC, at Catal Huyuk, in what is now southern Turkey, traces of a matriarchal community have been found which indicate that although the rulership was obviously of a sacerdotal nature, as evidenced in the number of priestesses, the kind of chieftainship and rivalry normally encountered in a patrist-orientated society did not appear to exist. Children were buried in the tombs of their mothers. The standard of art and handicrafts was anything but primitive: obsidian mirrors, copper and lead jewellery and tools, woollen textiles, and artistically carved wooden vessels evidence a stable, well organized society that offered personal fulfilment to its members. This community survived for 1,500 years free of massacre and war, and although many hundreds of skeletons have been found, none displayed the marks of a violent death. No less than 40 shrines were discovered, dating from 6500 BC onwards, all of which were devoted to a three-aspected goddess: maiden, mother giving birth, and old woman or crone.

Merlin Stone cites the work of James Mellaart, formerly the assistant director of the British Institute of Archaeology in London (who was also involved in the Catal Huyuk discoveries) as describing the proto-Neolithic cultures of the Near East, which he dates around 9000–7000 BC. He states that during that time 'Art makes its appearance in the form of animal carvings and statuettes of the supreme deity, the Mother Goddess.'[5]

The 3,000 years of the matriarchal Sumerian society, considered for many years to have been the cradle of civilization, reveal no evidence of warfare and strife. Archaeological discoveries in the Neolithic foundations at Hassuna, Tell Halaf, Samarra and Ubaid confirm the absence of male deities and the sanctity of the Great Mother as depicted in the many holy ikons of women nursing infants, a theme which is just as popular in certain branches of Christianity to this day.

Science is, however, slowly nudging back those dates even

further. Tim Radford, reporting for the *Guardian* on the 1989 American Conference for the Advancement of Science in San Francisco, cites the work of Professor Allan Wilson, a biochemist at the University of California at Berkeley, who has produced genetic evidence, gathered over a two-year period, that all present-day human beings are related to an African woman who lived 200,000 years ago. By measuring the diversity of maternally inherited genes in modern racial groups, Wilson and other Berkeley scientists concluded that the oldest lineage was African, dating back 140,000 to 290,000 years, which is partly supported by fossil evidence. Because population genetics dictates that all maternal lineages ultimately stem from one mother, the scientists argued that all people must be descended on the maternal side from one woman. The Berkeley research was based on tissue studies of 147 people in the USA, New Guinea, Australia and South Africa. Since 1987 the results have been confirmed by more than 2,000 gene samples worldwide.

According to Professor Wilson, if *Homo sapiens* had emerged in Asia, or if Africans had mixed with Asian forerunners of modern man, the genes of present-day Asians would be more varied. He believes that mixing probably took place between invading men and resident women during periods of usurpation. No doubt when the genome project gets off the ground, assuming that it will in the fullness of time, we will be afforded a much clearer picture of the family of *Homo sapiens* and the major role played by women in its birth, growth and subsequent development.

Most books that deal with the fall of goddess worship and matriarchy refer to invasions from 'the north' by patrist-orientated, warlike tribes who brought their gods with them and subsequently subjugated the women of the settlements they conquered by force. Merlin Stone mentions the Maglemosian and Kunda people of Mesolithic times (c.15,000–8000 BC) who were generally located in the forest and coastal areas of northern Europe, especially Denmark. Their journeys southwards to the lands of the goddess worshippers do not appear to have taken place suddenly, but over a period of some three thousand years. The invasions that took place during the historical period have been verified by most historians and archaeologists, but those prior to the third millennium BC are purely speculative, based on etymological connectives plus a degree of conjecture.

These northern peoples, described by Jacquetta Hawkes as 'dominantly pastoral, patriarchal, warlike and expansive' are usually lumped together under the title Indo-European, Indo-Aryan, or simply Aryan. Male deities predominated in their pantheons and their cultures were primarily patrist. According to some authorities, they were established on the Iranian Plateau by the fourth millennium, while most scholarly sources agree that they made their appearance in Anatolia not later than the early third millennium. Their descendants were the Hittites, the Mitannian kings and gods often bearing Indo-European names.

Not all of those enigmatic 'people from the north' were patrist-orientated, however. In the *Oera Linda Book*, which contains the sacred writings and history of the Frisian peoples, we read of a matrist society in which the women fought side by side with their men, enjoying equal status in all things. No decision of state was made without the advice of the 'Mother', a woman specially chosen for the role of psychic adviser in all military matters and decisions of state. The *Oera Linda Book* was first brought to the public eye in the latter part of the nineteenth century, having previously been resident in the private archives of the Over de Linden family, in Holland. Although it provoked the usual hoots of derision from the 'establishment', its confirmation of the stories of Homer, Hesiod and other classical historians, previously dismissed as purely mythical, threw a new light on prehistory. Thus, it supported the views held by those researchers who are less hidebound by the straitjacket of academe that old legends contain more than a grain of historic fact.

As far as women are concerned, the Frisian creation myth provides some waters to douse the classical fires that have burned so brightly and for so long among the bastions of learning. Although their creator god, Wr-alda, appeared to have originally enjoyed a masculine identity, their main spiritual allegiance was to Frya, the progenitor of their race, who, according to their theology, was one of the first three humans to be brought forth from the planet Earth, each of whom was a female. Their names were Lyda, who was 'black, with hair curled like a lamb's'; Finda, who was 'yellow, and her hair was like the mane of a horse. She could not bend a tree, but where Lyda killed one lion she killed ten'; and Frya, who was 'white like the snow at sunrise, and the blue of her eyes vied with the rainbow. . . . Like the rays of the sun shone the locks of her hair, which were as fine as spider's webs.'[6]

The ancient Frisians claimed to have originally lived in a land they called 'Atland', which was attached to Scandinavia and stretched out towards Iceland in the west and as far south as southern Scotland in the North Sea. Although we tend to associate those northern parts with cooler climes, the *Oera Linda Book* hastens to assure us that it was not so in ancient times, when their country enjoyed a warm temperate climate, totally unlike the snow-covered lands we see today.

According to Frisian records, their original land was destroyed by a major catastrophe which took place around 2193 BC. However, samples from bore holes taken from the North Sea in that area as recently as 1989 indicate that the offending cataclysm might have occurred nearer to 5000 BC, which would render the ancient Frisian people one of the earliest known matriarchal societies. These ancient people were, we are told, seven feet tall or more. Their women enjoyed complete equality in all areas of life, having been taught the true nature of the sexes by Frya, who founded their race. Frya was a great prophetess who was well schooled in history as well as possessing the gift of being able to foretell the future. Her prophecies, which gave birth to the Frisian dating system, were based on 'Juulfeests', each of which represented a solar year, so that according to their particularly chronology the ancient root races originated around 310,416 BC! Following the sinking of their land beneath the sea, the Atlanders moved south and slowly became absorbed into the tribes they encountered on their journeys. Being expert mariners, their vessels sought the safe harbour of other ports while their exploits earned them the title 'the sea people' or Hyperboreans, who feature in the myth and legend of many other ancient nations.

The origin of their founder, Frya, is open to conjecture. Some see her as being of late Cro-Magnon origin, others assign her a Cretan or Minoan identity, while the more imaginative among us may see her as one of those tall, fair strangers who were the missionaries of culture, science and learning in a prehistoric and often barbaric world that existed prior to the onset of the Cancerian Age. Frisian legends tell us that the Roman goddess Minerva was originally a real person: a Frisian warrior princess who founded the Athenian state. Like her sisters she wore the same armour as her menfolk and, like her later Celtic counterparts, personally led her armies into battle. Her effigy was later deified as the goddess Athene. Needless to say the Frisian accounts of a matriarchal society, which commenced its evolutionary cycle in a gentle, struggle-free way, but was later forced to defend itself against the oncoming forces of patriarchy, are well borne out in the writings of Plato and other scholars of integrity.

In keeping with other Northern goddesses, Frya, who no doubt later became Freya of the Scandinavians and Teutons, exhibited feminine qualities which, unlike many of the Mediterranean goddesses, were not confined to or centred around the maternal function. While motherhood is undoubtedly essential to both the social structure of the community and well-being of the individual in many phases of life, there are also other female roles that call for enaction in some women, whose self-esteem has been badly bruised by a combination of Christian devaluation of the feminine psyche and Freudian phallocentrism. The suppression of such callings can produce traumas every bit as intense as those experienced by the maternally inclined woman who finds herself barren.

As we enter the realms of history the patriarchal takeover becomes more clearly defined. Gods who ruled by force, like the cult-heroes of battle so beloved of fighting men, were seen as the essential allies of the conquering clans. For a while they ruled side by side with the Goddess, both enjoying equal status, but the pendulum slowly started to swing towards the male end. The Indo-European male deity, unlike the son-lover of the goddess religion, rode high in mountain-top and sky, bearing aloft the emblems of his power: Zeus, his lightning bolt, Thor, his hammer, and Hercules, his club. The nature of the myths slowly changed, with the feminine principle taking on a different meaning. Sometimes it was seen as a Serpent or Dragon, both apt, since the Dragon symbolizes woman in her outgoing mode, or animus, and the Serpent her feminine energies, or anima.

Enter the myths of heroes slaying dragons and serpents or, as some feminists would prefer to put it, man quelling woman by sheer brute force. However, I cannot accept that every dragon-slayer in mythology was a woman-hater. Mythical beasts whose appearance could not be related to any known animals were often regarded as associated with the forces of chaos — Typhon, for example. After all, it was Bast, daughter of Ra (or twin sister of Horus and therefore daughter of Isis and Osiris, according to Herodotus) who slayed the serpent Apep in the Egyptian legend, while Ra also has his anima or alter-ego in the feminine persona of Rat.[7]

India presents us with some of the clearest evidence of the Indo-Aryan invasions when the original goddess-worshipping people of those parts, the Dravidians, were conquered. Their Northern oppressors, we are told, did not possess a method of writing, but later adopted two alphabets, possibly from the Akkadians, which eventually developed into what we know today as Sanskrit. The Indo-Aryan culture was decidedly patrist, evidence of ancestor-worship of the father occurring in several hymns of the Rig Veda, while the Indo-Aryans daily recited the Pitriyajna, the worship of the ancestral fathers, in which ritual the father of the family acted as high priest, later passing these rites on to his eldest son.[8]

Archaeological evidence suggests that the earliest cultures of the Indus valley were in touch with Sumer and Elam around 3000 BC, and that they shared a common belief in a female divinity. Following the imposition of the male pantheon by the Indo-European conquerors, the goddess-worshippers took their religion underground, although it emerged on certain 'safe' occasions, notably around AD 600 when the female deity appeared in the Pranas and Tantras under many nomenclatures combined in the name *Devi*, which simply meant 'goddess'. Devi, however, came from the Sanskrit *Dev*, her original name of *Danu* or *Diti* having been long forgotten.

Dualistic religions — those which embraced the belief that there is a continual battle taking place between the forces of darkness and the forces of light — were much favoured in early times. Many of them found their way into

Egyptian mysticism and the classical religions of Greece via the Oriental Mysteries, which served to shape much of what was later known as Gnosticism. These dualities occasionally involved female personalities, Indra's murder of Danu, the 'Cow Goddess', which no doubt symbolized the imposition of the Indo-Aryan male pantheon over the goddess-worshipping Dravidians, being one example.

It is interesting to observe how even in our so-called 'enlightened' times the term 'goddess' is evocative of fear and prejudice in both women and men. Barbara G. Walker comments: 'Few words are so revealing of sexual prejudice as the word Goddess, in contrast to the word God.'[9] This was not the case, however, in the ancient world, when the many names accorded the Great Goddess were readily acknowledged as aspects of a single divinity fashioned by the prevailing ethos, and could operate independently according to the devotional needs, sacrifices and, prayers of the supplicants. Male writers down the centuries have been quick to seize upon the polytheistic nature of goddess worship but, as Walker points out, had such a system of criticism been applied to the usual concept of God, 'there would now be a multitude of separate gods with names like "Almighty", "Yahweh", "Lord", "Holy Ghost", "Sun of Righteousness", "Christ", "Creator", "Lawgiver", "Jehovah", "Providence", "Allah", "Saviour", "Redeemer", "Paraclete", "Heavenly Father", and so on *ad infinitum*, each one assigned a particular function in the world pantheon.'[10]

In primitive times both gods and goddesses were seen to manifest their energies throughout the whole of creation. Thus, the spirit of a river such as the Nile was accorded divine status, as were trees, stones, groves, caves and other sacred locations that emitted frequencies of a specialized nature. So it was that the ancients, and those later followers in their footsteps who saw fit to blend with the natural laws of both this planet and the cosmos, would construct a healing temple at one site, and a place of worship or an institute of learning at another, according to the specific quality of the telluric energies.

All sentient life (which in shamanic terms includes everything) exhibits either an active or passive emphasis in accordance with the Law of Polarity. It therefore seems logical that the creative principle must, by its very nature and in order to fulfil its role of completion, combine both masculine and feminine elements in equal proportions. If, as certain religions and esoteric schools opine, we are all destined to rejoin the Source on the completion of our evolutionary journey, what happens to men and women at that point? Assuming reincarnation to be a reality, which of the sexes we have negotiated over many lives will we assume when we get there — wherever 'there' may be?

It would seem that at certain times in the evolution of a planet — and the same applies to the lives of individuals as well — there may be a need to emphasize one aspect more than the other. But we should be free to effect our choice according to those needs, without fear of ridicule, persecution or cries of heresy. From a psychological point of view, the over-emphasis of either the masculine or feminine principle is indicative of a basic imbalance at either or any of the transpersonal, psychological or physical levels, which should be taken into account and allowed for both religiously and sociologically.

Another interesting manifestation of the Law of Polarity is that it is not always determined by the sex of the body. The Greeks were obviously aware of this as, no doubt, were many other earlier cultures. How they chose to display this knowledge to both the erudite and the uneducated will be coming under scrutiny in Chapter 4.

Goddesses such as the Egyptian Sekhmet, although designated the wife of the Artisan god Ptah and mother of the gentle Nefertum (or Imhotep, god of healing, according to some authorities), was anything but an 'airy-fairy' female. Her power and strength were personified in her portrayal as a lioness with a woman's body. Her husband, on the other hand, was a gentle soul much loved by the ordinary people, who could relate his talents to the skills and crafts they themselves used in their everyday lives. One could therefore say that Sekhmet manifested a strong animus, whereas her gentle husband's caring attitude towards the everyday affairs of ordinary people demonstrated an evolved anima. When viewed metaphysically, Sekhmet, as a goddess of destruction and regeneration, in partnership with Ptah, a god of construction, are seen to produce a third or healing principle as personified by Nefertum (Imhotep). What the ancient sages were probably trying to demonstrate was that the principle of death and rebirth, as represented by the Goddess, when coupled with the principle of construction into which Ptah, the universal mason, has built the virtues of caring and understanding, produces a healing or balancing effect on all who are able to absorb those energies and comprehend their message. This is how it should be, and yet it is not so. As to the whys and wherefores — we still have much ground to cover.

A comment frequently proferred by feminist writers is that historical evidence suggests that the early matriarchal societies were free of war, torture and similar male-associated perversions. Given the circumstances, however, women can be as ambitious, competitive, and cruel as men, and it is only when their nurturing instincts are roused that they display the warmer, more caring side of their nature.

Chapter 3
Stella Mater

ONE of the earliest known manifestations of the Great Goddess was the Chaldean Tiamat (Tiamut), usually depicted as a dragon and described in the Babylonian Creation Narrative as being present 'in the time when nothing which was called heaven existed above and when nothing below had yet received the name of Earth.'[1]

Larousse refers to Tiamat as a personification of the sea, representing the feminine element that gave birth to the world. From these and similar statements from Professor Gaston Maspero, and other experts in that field, one may assume the feminine principle to be a permanent force in the universe which, when fecundated, produces a stratum of creation in keeping with the nature of the implanted seed.

We have already established in Chapter 2 that Goddess religions dominated the Middle East and Mediterranean area in the Mesolithic, Neolithic and Bronze Ages. We now need to ask if there were any other influences aside from those warlike invaders from the north that left their imprint upon the religion and social life of earlier times. For the answer we need to take a journey to early dynastic Egypt, whose origins are certainly open to conjecture.

Much of the knowledge available regarding ancient Egyptian religious beliefs has been culled from *The Book of the Dead*, which was sometimes taken too literally in later times. The very title is a misnomer, its literal translation being 'Chapters of the Coming Forth by Day'. The sole reason for referring to it as the *Book of the Dead* would appear to be the preoccupation of its contents with death and the life hereafter. Whole sections are devoted to the state of the departed soul and its trials and existences in other dimensions. Several scholars, notably A. E. Wallis Budge, are of the opinion that the work is *not* of Egyptian origin.

The Heliopolitan or First Recension, which was in use during the fourth and fifth dynasties, can be dated back to before 3500 BC, and there is evidence from the copying that the scribes of the time were dealing with texts so remote as to make their job extremely difficult, if not impossible. Thus many original meanings were lost, and inaccuracies crept in. Gods and goddesses appear to have received equal veneration in the old Egyptian religion, although many authorities accord Neith (Net, Nuit) special status as one of the earliest forms of the Creatrix acknowledged in pre-dynastic Egypt; as James Bonwick writes: 'Neith or Nout is neither more nor less than the *Great Mother*, and yet the *Immaculate Virgin*, or female god, from whose bosom all things proceeded.'[2]

Mariette Bey was also satisfied regarding the extreme antiquity of this goddess, believing her worship to have been all of 7,000 years old.[3] Larousse cites her epithet 'Tehenut, the Libyan' as suggesting that she originated in the west, which could mean she was either an Atlantean goddess or a divinity of the sea people, or Atlanders from the north. The latter is probably more likely since her fetish was two crossed arrows on an animal skin and this, plus her weaver's shuttle, would appear to afford her many points in common with the Greek Athene or the Frisian warrior queen who, according to the ancient annals of that race, was the founder of Athens. Another similarly named early Egyptian goddess was Nut, goddess of the sky, whom the Greeks identified with their Rhea, and whose role in the acquisition of the epagomenal days we have already discussed. There are also other goddesses of great antiquity in the ancient Egyptian pantheon, but there is a point at which the totem deities of the various Nomes gave way to the more sublime, exalted concept of the Creatrix which also embraced a complete cosmology combined with an understanding of scientific principles only recently rediscovered in our own age.

As regards the beliefs held by the peoples of pre-dynastic Egypt, Cyril Aldred has this to say:

The spiritual life of these early inhabitants of the Nile Valley can never been known to us. They evidently believed in a hereafter, since in the burials of the period the body is usually crouched on its side as though awaiting rebirth, and is accompanied by pots, weapons, cosmetic palettes and sometimes rudimentary figures of women, which suggest that this after-life, for the male at least, was expected to make the same demands upon him as he had known on earth.[4]

The female figurines mentioned would surely indicate both goddess worship and the belief that people could be born again through the womb of the mother, or reincarnated, in which case the impedimenta of life would again be of use to them. Although the First Dynasty is officially seen as commencing with the unification of Egypt under Menes around 3200 BC, the evidence suggests that there were thriving communities in those parts well before that time.

Aldred's views are in keeping with standard textbooks on the subject, but other scholars and researchers, notably the late R. A. Schwaller de Lubicz, present us with a vastly different picture, ascribing to the ancient Egyptians a knowledge of science, mathematics, architecture and medicine in keeping with and in many ways ahead of our own. Their knowledge of atomic structure, for example, he saw as evidenced in their familiarity with the nature and cosmic purpose of the large blue-white star in the binary system of Sirius (Sothis). Sacred to the goddess Isis, this star was also seen as a manifestation of her energies and referred to in the ancient Pyramid Texts as the 'Great Provider'. The Egyptian priests were well aware that Sirius was the nucleus or propagating point for the particular section of the galaxy that houses our solar system, which confirms the stellar nature of the goddess.

The name Isis, or Aset to be correct, simply means 'a throne', which is the symbol portrayed on the head of the earlier representations of this goddess. Like her husband Osiris, Isis was a highly civilized and fully integrated personality and a ruler in her own right. She taught men to grow corn (a grain sacred to her), spin cloth and make garments for themselves. She instituted marriage, instructed the people in the art of healing, and brought civilization to a primitive society. (For those interested, the story of Isis, Osiris and Set receives detailed coverage in my book, *Ancient Egypt: The Sirius Connection.*)

Some students of the esoteric are of the opinion that the Isis/Osiris saga is both factual and prophetic. The Set factor symbolizes Chaos which inevitably topples the reign of Order as represented by the stable rulership of Osiris. Caught in the centre of this affray is Isis, whose love for her husband prompts her to search for the 14 pieces of his body, which has been dismembered by the evil Set. It is therefore to Woman that the task of redeeming Order from Chaos falls. The lamenting and tearful Queen Isis surely represents all womankind who have suffered the Settian slings and arrows of Chaos since the Golden Years when the anima and animus (as represented by Isis and Osiris) were in a reasonable state of balance, at least in some areas of our planet. And so we weep with Isis and seek those lost aspects of ourselves that will eventually free us from the sacrificial burden we have carried for so long, while Set manipulates his male henchmen and minions to ensure that our lives, like hers, are made as difficult as possible.

However, the Egyptians have done us one great favour in telling us how the story ends: the finding of 13 of the pieces, the disappearance of the fourteenth piece (the original phallus, representing male domination), and the Goddess being able to procure a conception through her own mystical powers, the magic of Thoth (Time), and the influence of Osiris *from heaven* (the coming together of the anima and animus via the transpersonal or higher Self). In other words, a time *will* come in the future when women will be able to effect a control over their own sexuality, fecundity and personal fulfilment *by the power of their minds*. Until then we would appear to be very much in the hands of a male-dominated world. Fortunately, the waves of evolution are never static for very long, and the pendulum, having reached its farthest point in Chaos is now quivering ready for its return swing to an Order in which the feminine will once again be accorded its rightful status in human affairs.

But let us return once more to those clues, so generously supplied by the ancient Egyptians, which tend to indicate that our problems are in some subtle way tethered to the Sirius factor and therefore constitute part of a much wider, even cosmic picture. The dismemberment of Osiris, for example, when viewed in the anthropological context

accords with both certain ancient tribal rites and the
shamanic initiatory process in which the etheric or astral
body is cut into pieces and reassembled in a form suitable
to the aspirant's calling.

Many students of Atlantology, notably Ignatius Donnelly
and more recently Otto Muck and Colonel Braghine, view
the gods of Egypt and Greece as Atlantean colonists or
missionaries who took their religion, scientific skills, and
culture to what had hitherto been primitive societies. Even
a little knowledge of science must have appeared as miracu-
lous to peoples unused to any form of technology, and
although these tall, fair strangers (sons of god?) saw fit to
take the local women to wife (daughters of men?), as the
technological impendimenta which aided their skills soon
wore out, tales of its past functioning slowly assumed an air
of magic and mystery to ensuing generations who could not
conceive of such things within their limited field of
resources.

It is time that physics and metaphysics reunited with
psychology, parapsychology and transpersonal psychology.
Quantum physics may well provide just the key to open that
very door. Over the past few centuries the closed portals of
scholarship have been mainly controlled by men, and in
later chapters I shall be giving some amusing, albeit
pathetic anecdotes I have collected from major seats of
learning which emphasize this sad state of things.

Chapter 4
Ancient Feminine Archetypes

THERE is a general tendency to acknowledge certain traditional basic differences between men and women which are deemed acceptable to society generally. Given roles and behaviour patterns have become associated with each sex. Men, for example, are believed to be predominantly left-brain orientated and therefore more suited to pursuits concerned with linear time, demanding the faculties of logic, language, and analysis. Women on the other hand, are viewed as right-brain orientated and emotionally motivated. Therefore their activities should be confined to the raising of children, service to the community or within the home, or to other right-brain activities such as those associated with spatial perception, musical and visual appreciation, abstract thought and the intuitive states usually associated with timelessness. However, since these basic categorizations frequently fail to accommodate the complex anima/animus combinations that are likely to manifest within the human psyche, they constitute possible areas of psychological disturbance for those who, through no fault of their own, are unable to conform.

The French philosopher Dr Elisabeth Badinter, comments on an observation highlighted by ethnologists and psychoanalysts: that confusion or lack of sexual differentiation seems to pose a dangerous threat to people's sense of identity. Boys in particular find it much more difficult to acquire this sense than do girls. Margaret Mead confirms that girls are often sure of their maternal role in life from an early age, and are therefore faced with few if any problems in accepting it. [1]

Society likewise unquestioningly accepts the feminine

role of motherhood. If a woman has not herself produced progeny, she is at least expected to be at ease with and approving of the offspring of others. Sadly for some women, this is not always the case, and much personal suffering can arise from judgmental attitudes of this kind. It would make for much less personal anguish and self-doubt if both women and men could be educated into the idea that the feminine archetype (and the masculine archetype, for that matter) has many faces. This is so well illustrated in the mythologies of many cultures.

An in-depth study of archetypes will demonstrate that they remain constant in essence throughout the ages, any surface differences being purely due to the distinctive imprint of each culture. For example, in the Greek pantheon the Love Goddess, Aphrodite, appears in the feminine mode whereas the Love Principle in the Irish Celtic pantheon is portrayed in the masculine form of Angus Og. Here we have two typical examples of how a people or culture will tend to fashion its gods and goddesses in its own image and likeness: the reign of Zeus being predominantly patri-archal, and therefore favouring a feminine figure epitom-izing the object of male desire. The Celtic ethos was more matriarchal; women enjoyed warrior and queenly status equal to that of their men, and doubtless saw fit to relax into the gentle arms of their musically and artistically orien-tated males. Let us therefore see what lessons we can learn from the sages of the past concerning the many fulfilling roles open to women which fall within the framework of what would pass muster as 'normal' or 'natural' for a woman according to the standards set by current collectives (see pages 159-60).

There is, however, a dark side of the moon in more ways than the obvious, which did not escape the notice of the ancients. The Egyptian goddess Nephthys, sister of Isis and sometimes seen as her alter-ego, is a typical example of this. Nephthys, goddess of sleep, whose symbol is a chalice or receptacle that she wears on her head, was designated both the 'Revealer' and the 'Hidden One' or 'Concealer'. This is because she reveals her secrets to the true mystic, genuine psychic and dedicated seeker after truth, but hides them from the devious, deceitful and ego-ridden to whom she reveals only their personal shadow or id. The dark side of the moon can also represent a perversion of the light, so as far as lunar energies and the feminine psyche are concerned one can only adopt the old axiom that 'like attracts like'.

In Judaic legends, Lilith, first wife of Adam, and depicted as a fiery demon who rode upon a unicorn, was often seen as representing the dark side of the moon. The story goes that she refused to lie beneath her husband (be subjected to the laws of patrism). Her later consort was Samael or Lucifer and these two together formed the Leviathan, or serpent power that ascends the Tree of Life in much the same way that the Kundalini Serpent is believed to ascend the seven chakras. Jungian psychology recognizes the importance of Lilith's integration into the female anima as the instinctive female nature that rebels against the traditional roles played by women in patriarchal society. Perhaps what we are dealing with here is the Lunar animus; it certainly bears consideration. Barbara Walker, in referring to Aradia, Queen of the Witches, whom she designates as the daughter of Diana (Artemis?) states: 'She represented the Moon and her brother Lucifer the Light-bringer represented the sun.[2] However, I have, over the years, read more references to Lucifer as being associated with the moon, and on occasions the planet Venus.'

According to another source, Lilith was the sister of Eve, just as Nephthys was the sister of Isis. This 'sister', or 'bipolar' relationship may be seen among many of the goddesses of the earlier pantheons and has strong psychological connotations. Nephthys represents the darkness or that which is concealed, the deep unconscious in which is stored those innermost feelings, joys and conflicts that form the sum total of our experience in *gestalt*. Hence, her marriage to Set (Chaos), the Egyptian Lucifer, and her association with all things both chthonic and watery, like the ocean depths, the *Ka* or Double, the positive virtues of mysticism, receptivity, tranquillity and reservedness, and the negative traits of diffusion, psychosis, deviousness, tension and illusion. What the ancient psychologists were doubtless trying to tell us was that unless we can come to terms with our shadows, we cannot ascend from the chthonic realms of unconscious acceptance (the rising Kundalini serpent?) to the exalted frequencies of self-realization and spiritual fulfilment.

Isis, on the other hand, represented all things 'natural', to which most women could relate. She was the archetypal mother, queen, and devoted wife all rolled into one — the light side of the moon according to some authorities, while others see her as having either solar or stellar connotations on account of her mastery over Ra on the one hand, and her association with Sothis/Sirius on the other. However, it should be remembered that there are negative aspects of each of these archetypal manifestations — the over-possessive mother, the heartless ruler, and the jealous wife. Isis was also Mistress of Magic, the magician or occultist *par excellence*. As such she could be seen to represent the inner power of the feminine psyche, the use of which, we are told, has been forgotten by women since the mythical Fall. In telling us of the sufferings she underwent while wandering the earth in search of the pieces of her husband, and then hiding and nurturing the infant Horus in 'the wilderness', surely the myth is implying that over the past centuries, woman has been less powerful at the earthly level and therefore subject to persecution by the forces of Set (Chaos): male egotism, the over-accentuated animus, and those hormonal or chemical imbalances that are calculated to engender aggression providing excellent channels for the manifestation of the chaotic principle at the expense of women generally.

Viewed psychologically, it would seem that we all have the propensity for Isian or Nepthian qualities, and whether we choose to manifest these in their positive or negative modes will, to an extent, depend on our strength of mind and spiritual maturity.

There were, of course, many other goddesses in the Egyptian pantheon, but as the Egyptian Empire spanned so many centuries, most of these can be condensed into a few highly important archetypes, one of which is undoubtedly Hathor/Sekhmet. The Egyptian Hathor was essentially a goddess of beauty, love, and strength, that element of the spiritual economy known as the *sekhem* (power) being symbolically allocated to her. She was also designated patroness of women and her main attribute, the Mirror, caused her to become associated with all aspects of female adornment. The Mirror, however, has other, more esoteric and psychological implications. The gods of yesterday and today, for example, can be seen to mirror their invocators (or evocators as the case may be), and those personal failings that people see mirrored in others are usually calculated to give them the most offence. There is a Medusa-like quality about mirror complexes in that the Gorgon could be seen to mirror the real self that cannot be faced, much like Dorian Gray's famous picture.

Hathor, or Athyr as the Egyptians called her, was said to be the daughter of Ra and custodian of his Divine Eye. The Egyptians called her Het Heru, which means 'House of Horus', since she was the wife of Horus. Her femininity, however, was of a different quality from that of either Isis or Nephthys, the virtues of fortitude, nourishment, organization and confidence being ascribed to her, while her negative traits were seen as intimidation, vanity, bossiness and over-indulgence in food. As the gentle celestial cow she nourished the gods, protected women, patronized the art of astrology and conferred the creature comforts of life. She was 'The Lady of the Sycamore', the Egyptian Aphrodite, in which role she presided over all aspects of women's beauty such as make-up, adornment, jewellery and clothing. But, like many other goddesses, Hathor had another aspect: Sekhmet, the lion-headed goddess of retribution, destruction and renewal, who was both loved and feared in ancient times, and whose relationship with her syzygy (polarity), Ptah, and their allotted son Imhotep, we have already discussed.

Sekhmet was essentially a solar goddess, a being of fire and of the searing heat of the sun in both its destructive and constructive aspects. She has much in common with the Norse sun goddesses in that she is as powerful, if not more so, than her father/creator, Ra. Seldom has a figure from mythology evoked such interest among male students of the human mind. Psychologist/sexologist Robert Masters, for example, claims a direct encounter with the goddess in a series of telepathic trance states in which he was given the teachings of the sacred books of Sekhmet that were lost, pillaged in temples or destroyed by unbelievers, all of which has been published in a book dedicated to her acknowledgment and worship.[3]

Sekhmet represents the archetypal woman who appears when she is needed, has the strength to make her mark in

a male-dominated society, do a good job of 'polishing off'
that which has outlived its usefulness during which process
she naturally makes numerous enemies and can, on occasions, overstep her mark in which case she needs to be, like
Sekhmet, 'recalled' by Ra (those who perceive that she has
gone a little too far).

The myth tells how the old god Ra reigned peacefully over
all creation before the other gods were born. While he was
still young and strong all paid obeisance to him, but in his
declining years a group of dissenters moved to take advantage of his waning strength. We are not told who these beings
are or where they came from. However, the inference drawn
is that they were not necessarily connected with this Earth
as we know it, but were probably players in some grand,
cosmological drama. Ra was so enraged by this uprising that
he hurled his Divine Eye at the revolutionaries in the form
of his daughter, the great and powerful Lion-headed
Goddess Sekhmet, who went among the evil ones dis-
pensing havoc and bloodshed until Ra finally called her off,
fearing that she might overdo things and polish off his
handiwork completely.

The Hindu goddess Kali is often equated with Sekhmet,
as are also the Scottish Cailleach and the Irish Morrigan,
which implies that most of the peoples of the ancient world
were aware of this particular archetype and the many forms
through which it could manifest. The basic message is that
Chaos eventually turns on itself, and in so doing provides
the impetus for the reverse swing back to Order. It is also
interesting to observe how the exacting of divine or cosmic
retribution inevitably falls to a feminine archetype (the
Greek Nemesis?), which suggests that the power to effect
the ultimate rebalancing process lies in the hands of
women.

In her book *Descent of the Goddess*, Jungian analyst
Sylvia Brinton Perera draws her reader's attention to the
symbolic significance of the many myths and tales of the
descent of and to the goddess. The Japanese Izanami, the
Greek Kore-Persephone, the Roman Psyche, and those fairy
tale heroines who inevitably end up in the house of the
witch which is buried deep in the heart of the forest. She
cites the oldest known myth to state this motif as being
written on clay tablets in the third millennium BC,

although it was doubtless much older, which is usually referred to as 'the Descent of Inanna', (the Sumerian queen of heaven and earth). There are, she tells us, 'two later Akkadian versions based on this source, but with variations that we know as 'Ishtar's Descent'.[4]

Sîn, the Babylonian god of the Moon, and his wife Ningal had three children: the Sumerian goddess Inanna, known in Assyrian/Babylonian mythology as Ishtar (the planet Venus); the god Shamash, who represented the sun; and Nusku, the god of fire. Sîn had many functions not the least of which was the measuring of time, which serves to connect him with that other male lunar deity, the Egyptian Thoth, who was also a 'Time Lord'. In the Sumerian version of the story, Inanna, the Queen of Heaven, seeks to visit the Underworld from which there is normally no return. The Queen of the infernal regions, referred to as the 'Great Below' is Ereshkigal, and it is the funeral of Ereshkigal's husband, Gugalamma, that Inanna wishes to attend.

In keeping with tradition, the gatekeeper removes one piece of Inanna's magnificent garments at each of the seven gates so that she is eventually stripped bare, as was the custom in all Sumerian burials. Inanna is then judged by seven judges, after which Ereshkigal kills her and hangs her corpse on a peg until it has decayed. After three days, when Inanna fails to return, her assistant Ninshubur assumes she is dead and makes the necessary arrangements for a public ritual mourning. Ninshubur then seeks the aid of Unlil, the highest god of sky and earth, and the moon god, Inanna's father, neither of whom wish to become involved in matters concerned with the Underworld. Ninshubur's plea is finally heard by Enki, the god of waters and wisdom, who proceeds about the business of rescuing the goddess from the clutches of the Infernal queen, which he successfully accomplishes with the use of various magical and psychological ploys. Inanna knows, however, that she must pass the seven gates through which she has entered in order to regain her queenly robes, while she is also aware of the law which decrees that a substitute must be found to take her place, as Ereshkigal may not be cheated of a soul in this way.

The final passages of the myth are concerned with Inanna's search for a substitute, and she is careful not to hand over anyone who had mourned for her during her absence. Finally she chooses her primary consort, Dumuzi, later known as Tammuz. Tammuz first seeks the help of the sun god, Inanna's brother, who transforms him into a snake to help his escape. But in another version it is to his sister Geshtinanna that he turns, following a strange dream which he begs her to interpret for him. Anticipating the inherent danger outlined in the meaning of the dream, Geshtinanna initially shelters him, and then offers to sacrifice herself in his stead. Inanna decrees that they shall divide this fate, each spending half a year in the Underworld.

In the later Babylonian/Assyrian version of this myth, Ishtar appears in a rather different light, probably because Nineveh was less matrist than Sumeria. The Babylonian Ishtar was a warrior queen, the 'Lady of Battles, valiant among goddesses'.[5] She is represented standing on a chariot drawn by seven lions, with a bow in her hands. Her main places of worship were Nineveh and Arbela (Erbil). In this version of the myth Ereshkigal appears as her sister, whose regions Ishtar has helped to populate in the course of her victorious battles. In spite of her military associations Ishtar was also revered as a goddess of love, but this possibly reflects her image as created by people who worshipped at the shrines of battle and sex, rather than an accurate representation of the archetype. In other words we are seeing a perfect example of how the prevailing ethos imprints itself on the god-form and, no doubt, the feminine principle as manifested in the women of the time — only aristocratic warriors or prostitutes being seen as useful to the state and social life of the male community generally.

Aside from the obvious shamanic connotations, there are many ways in which this myth can be interpreted and applied to the feminine psychology. Sylvia Brinton Perera explains it thus:

> It is precisely the woman who has a poor relation to the mother, the one through whom the Self archetype first constellates, who tends to find her fulfillment through the father or the male beloved. She may be a woman who can find no relation to the Demeter-Kore myth because she 'cannot believe' as one put it, that 'any mother would be there to mourn and to receive' her again if she vanished into a crevasse. She may have an intense experience in the contransexual

sphere, but she lacks the ballast of a solid ego–Self connection. One patient expressed this early in her analysis, almost as a manifesto:

'I insist on caring coming from a man. A female source enrages me. A male is in charge of the universe. Females are second best. I hate tunnels and Kali and my mother and this female body. A man is what I want.'[6]

Personally, I do not share Ms Perera's views regarding these feminine descents to the chthonic regions. In the case of that particular patient, women often tend to espouse the male principle and assume a subordinate role either because they have received a rough deal in our male-orientated society or because they are secretly jealous of the privileges accorded to men, which they feel they can never have. They therefore see male associations, and any caring attitudes shown by members of the opposite sex, as being the only way to gratify these needs. In other words, they are using men as a means of expressing their personal animus, just as many men use women to express their animas rather than developing them for themselves.

For me, however, the Olympian archetypes are the most exciting, probably because they present so many variations on the feminine theme. This is particularly interesting since the Olympian pantheon was, at face value, predominantly patriarchal. Or was it? Perhaps not, for reasons we shall shortly see.

Among the major divinities of Olympus there were six gods and six goddesses: Zeus, Ares, Hephaestus, Apollo, Hermes and Poseidon; and Athene, Artemis, Aphrodite, Hera, Hestia and Demeter. Since it is the feminine archetypes we are concentrating upon at present we will begin with Athene, although the psychological personality variations among the gods are just as cleverly expressed and analysed.

Athene

Athene was the daughter of Zeus, and the story of her birth runs thus: prior to marrying Hera, Zeus contracted several other unions, the most significant being with Metis (Wisdom) who, according to Hesiod, 'knew more things than all the gods and men put together.' Gaea and Uranus,

however, warned Zeus that were he to have children with
Metis they would exceed him in power, which would result
in his ultimate dethronement. So, when Metis was about to
give birth to Athene, in order to forestall the danger Zeus
swallowed Metis and her unborn child, thus avoiding the
risk of embarrassing posterity and at the same time em-
bodying Wisdom.

Shortly after this questionable repast Zeus was afflicted
with a dreadful headache and sought the aid of Hephaestus
(or Prometheus, according to some authorities), who split
his skull with a bronze axe to relieve the pain. As the wound
opened, out sprang Athene shouting a triumphant cry of
victory, fully armed and brandishing a sharp spear. Both
Heaven and Earth were struck by the miracle and the
'bright-eyed goddess' assumed a special place in all hearts.

Being 'head-born' places Athene in the intellectual rather
than the emotional category. As a warrior goddess, so
flawless was her strategy that not even the god of war could
match her in battle. She wore a golden helmet and over her
shoulder was slung the aegis that no arrow could pierce,
fashioned from the skin of Zeus' famous nurse, Goat
Amaltheia, whose image the Father of the Gods had placed
in the sky as the constellation of Capricorn. In the Trojan
Wars she was said to favour the Greeks, eventually entering
personally into the fray and felling the mighty Ares with a
single blow from her magical spear. She favoured heroes and
protected the brave and valiant.

Athene was a virgin goddess by choice, although she had
received romantic proposals on more than one occasion.
Weaving and embroidery were the two domestic crafts in
which she excelled, and she generously gave of the fruits of
her labours to those mortals and immortals who pleased
her. Another area in which she could bestow benefits was
health and healing. Self-healing, or the use of one's own
mental powers to control one's mind and body, is believed
to emanate from the Athenian archetype. She is also
credited with the invention of the flute.

Here we have an extraverted archetype, with a well
developed animus, who was able to defeat the strongest man
and yet retain her beauty and femininity, as evidenced in her
many suitors and those domestic skills she chose to employ
in her quieter moments. She did not need to be a *femme*

fatale, housewife or mother — she had found her strength in the intellectual mode. Her helmet and aegis (higher self and animal nature) had been transformed into a form of protective clothing. In other words, they had ceased to be her enemy — the unknown and unconquered aspects of herself — and had become her defence.

Artemis

Although equally powerful in her own right and in her own territory, the goddess Artemis presents quite a different aspect of the feminine principle. She was the twin sister of Apollo and, according to the myths, was one day older than her brother. The Greek Artemis was essentially a rural deity who enjoyed hunting, and bore no resemblance to her namesake of the many breasts at Ephesus. Because the bear is one of her symbols, she is often confused with Callisto, although Professor Carl Kerenyi, one of the leading experts on Greek history and mythology, asserts that she was originally depicted as a lioness. Whereas her brother is always seen in the solar context, his sister became associated with the Moon. She was, however, frequently portrayed carrying a torch, which is more a solar than lunar emblem, and suggests the superimposition of another archetype.

The story of the birth of Artemis and her twin brother Apollo holds both a historical and psychological significance. Leto, daughter of Coeus and Phoebe, was pursued by Zeus by whom she became pregnant. Upon hearing of her husband's indiscretion, Hera was so enraged that she decreed that Leto could only give birth at a place where the sun's rays never penetrated. In order that this command should not be disobeyed, Poseidon raised the waves like a dome over the island of Ortygia, at the same time anchoring it to the depths of the sea with four pillars. In order to delay the birth as long as she could, Hera deliberately kept Ilythia, goddess of childbirth, engaged elsewhere so that for nine days and nine nights poor Leto underwent dreadful suffering. Finally, Iris was sent to Olympus to fetch Ilythia, and Leto was able to give birth first to Artemis and then to Apollo.

Owing to the difficulties her mother experienced over the

birth, Artemis was designated patroness of childbirth. This might seem an odd assignment for a rural, athletic virgin goddess, but it should be remembered that not all women who are devoted to the service of others as midwives or nurses are themselves married with families. The midwife was often the only medical aid available in outlying agricultural communities in those days (and even in our own times before the arrival of modern forms of communication and transportation).

Shortly after her birth Artemis approached her father with requests for eternal virginity, a bow and arrow like Apollo's, the office of bringing light, and a saffron hunting tunic, all of which Zeus was happy to grant. Animals were sacred to her, but she had little time for people and she severely punished those who made a nuisance of themselves or refused to abide by the laws of her domains. Her saffron hunting tunic is another clue to her solar origin, and the fact that she was born before her brother suggests that her worship preceded his. One of the translations of her name is said to mean 'safe and sound', or 'she who heals sickness'. She was also accredited with a beautiful singing voice.

Her expert markmanship tells us of yet another feminine skill that is, perhaps, neglected in the present age. The esoteric significance of the hunter archetype is suggestive of the hunting for souls or the Self rather than the slaughter of animals — the 'prey' representing a spiritual goal. The bow and arrow therefore carry a profound metaphysical significance, being representative of the yin/yang or anima/animus polarity, both of which need to be stretched to their finest tension before the 'target' of individuation can be achieved.

Artemis exemplifies the animus introvertedly expressed through the athletic feminine mode, although the archetype can be seen to have even wider connotations in that it is easily recognizable in our present age as manifest in those female personalities from the physically active worlds of sport, athletics and other spartan pursuits, as well as those who place the love and care of animals above their own personal needs or wants. Artemis-type women brook no nonsense from their menfolk, as may be evidenced in the story of Actaeon who dared to intrude upon the goddess

while she was bathing, for which blasphemy he paid with
his life.

Aphrodite

In the beautiful Aphrodite we have something a little nearer
to what many people see as the ultimate expression of
femininity: the classic beautiful woman — fair of hair, blue
of eye, and voluptuous. This is Jung's 'Eve', the temptress and
archetypal sex symbol. In the context of the myths
Aphrodite was capable of arousing desire in anyone in
whom it pleased or amused her to so do. With the exception
of Athene, Artemis, and Hestia, all gods, heroes, and
mortals yielded to her power. However, on occasions she
received a dose of her own medicine, as with the Anchises
episode. As a punishment for distracting his divine mind,
Zeus caused the goddess to fall blindly in love with a
mortal, the shepherd Anchises. After a blissful night
together, Aphrodite appeared to Anchises in all her divine
splendour. Being fully aware that any man who has lain
with an immortal goddess would be stricken with pre-
mature old age, the shepherd was filled with terror, but
Aphrodite reassured him and promised him a god-like son,
asking him only that the name of the child's mother should
never be revealed.

Aphrodite also possessed many domestic skills, but it
was decreed on Olympus that she should not make use of
them as her talents were better employed in the arts of love.
One of Aphrodite's most interesting attributes is her Girdle,
or Zona, which was so powerful that it could deflect even
the thunderbolts of Zeus. Only the virgin goddesses were
not affected by it but as far as everyone else was concerned,
both immortal and mortal, Love was all-powerful.

The Aphrodite/Venus archetype, which is mostly acknowledged in its courtesan or *hetaira* mode, represents the
extraverted expression of the anima. Like the Egyptian ankh
or *crux ansata* (which is also seen erroneously as the
emblem of carnal love, although it symbolizes the blending
of the masculine and feminine elements within the Self,
which provide the Key to Eternity), the Aphrodite archetype
also has far deeper and more sublime connations. The
message is that if physical gratification is one's only concept

of love, then one cannot hope to attain to the higher frequencies of this profound feminine archetype or partake of its transpersonal energies.

Hera

Hera was the wife of Zeus, and consequently often referred to as the Mother of the Gods. The story of how she came to be married to Zeus tells us a lot about the archetype. Zeus, having become enamoured with the goddess, visited her in the form of a cuckoo in distress, upon which the kindly Hera took pity. Renowned for obtaining the gratification of his desires, Zeus promptly changed back into his Olympian form to claim his prize (the Greek gods, in true shamanic tradition, being adept at shape-shifting). Hera, however, resisted, and refused to succumb to his advances until he promised to marry her. Although the wedding was solemnly celebrated on Olympus it failed to put an end to Zeus' romantic inclinations. Hera's resulting jealousy and constant efforts to thwart her husband's affairs are well recorded in the classics.

Hera represents womanly stability in a male-dominated society, her only advantage being her marital status. She typifies the many women down the ages who have trapped men into marriage by subterfuge. Hera is the faithful wife and mother forever hovering in the background, angered by her husband's infidelities, which she seems powerless to prevent, in spite of her own divine power. She is the Queen of whom propriety demands that she must not rock the stability of the throne.

The Hera archetype is the anima introvertedly expressed through the possessive feminine mode, while the myth summarizes succinctly the position of the married woman in a male-dominated society. As regards her husband's infidelities, and decisions generally, she has no comeback if she is to retain her home and status and hold the family together. She may well employ any devious means known to her to achieve these ends, but short of breaking up the marriage she is left with little or no options. Hera types, in true queenly fashion, will always fight to maintain the outer status quo.

Hestia

The goddess of the hearth and home seems an unlikely candidate for eternal virginity. Yet there is the wisdom of observation behind this archetype which is as easy to understand in modern times as it was in the classical past. Hestia was one of the older goddesses, being the sister of Zeus, Demeter, Poseidon, and Hera. Her name means 'hearth', or the place in the house where the food was cooked, and from which warmth and comfort were derived. Fire was very important to primitive people, as it provided a dialogue between men and the gods via the sacrificial flame.

Hestia's origins are obscure and classical literature provides us with little information concerning her nature and deeds. She was essentially a virgin goddess who chose a modest existence and eschewed the splendours of Olympus. Her character was one of reserved dignity and repose that served to contrast her with the more flamboyant Olympian females. Although unmarried herself, as protectress of the hearth and home she ensured their stability and continuity.

Hestia epitomizes the animus introvertedly expressed through the self-effacing feminine mode: the strong, silent woman who seldom argues and gets on with the job on hand. In depicting the maiden lady within the home and family situation, the Greeks were surely suggesting that it is not necessary for the dedicated student of humanity to withdraw from the social scene in order to effect his or her good deeds. In fact, the person who can mix easily in these circumstances but still retain their objectivity, is better able to help in the mêlée that constitutes the ups and downs of much of family life. Aside from those dedicated nuns, social workers, hospital sisters, doctors, and reformers who put the welfare of others before their own personal needs or desires, this archetype could be seen as manifesting through the ever-popular 'agony aunt', the contents of whose columns appear to provide interesting reading for men and women alike.

Demeter

The story of Demeter, and Kore her beloved daughter (later renamed Persephone) constituted the basis for the goddess-orientated Eleusinian Mysteries, which held sway in the empire of classical Greece for over a thousand years. According to the myth, Kore was out one day gathering flowers when she noticed a narcissus of great beauty. As she bent down to pick it, the earth gaped open and Hades, Lord of the Underworld appeared to claim her as his bride — Zeus having apparently given his permission for this deed. Demeter heard the child's cry for help upon which, Homer tells us, 'bitter sorrow seized her heart ... Over her shoulders she threw a sombre veil and flew like a bird over land and sea, seeking here, seeking there.'

For nine days the goddess, bearing a flaming torch, searched the world for her daughter, but to no avail. On Hecate's advice she finally consulted Helios, who revealed to her the name of Kore's abductor and Zeus' compliance in the scheme. In a rage, the despairing goddess withdrew from Olympus in the guise of an old woman seeking refuge among the cities of men. Many were the trials of poor Demeter while she strove to regain her daughter and, because of her distress, she withdrew her energies from the earth so that nothing grew. Both gods and men pleaded with her to restore her bounty, but Demeter was adamant — she would not permit the earth to bear fruit until she was reunited with her daughter.

Zeus finally sent Hermes to Hades with a request to return the maiden. Hades grudgingly complied, but managed to persuade Persephone to eat a few pomegranate seeds, the symbols of marriage, before she left, thus sealing the union. Demeter questioned her daughter as to whether she had partaken of any food while in Hades' domains because, 'If thou hast not eaten thou shalt live with me on Olympus. But if thou hast, then thou must return to the depths of the Earth.'[7]

Much to Demeter's chagrin, Persephone admitted to eating the pomegranate seeds, but as a compromise Zeus decided that Persephone should dwell one-third of the year with her husband and the remaining two-thirds with her mother. Demeter settled for this arrangement, and once again the Earth produced fruit in abundance and all things flourished.

This myth is often given a seasonal interpretation, the comings and goings of gods and goddesses being associated with the equinoxes, solstices and other related phenomena. However, this theme appears with some regularity in the legends of most pantheons, and although many of the myths can be seen to contain records of actual events they would also appear to embody certain basic truths. This applies particularly to the stories that have come down to us from ancient Greece.

In my own studies of personality types, I have employed the term 'Persephone Syndrome' to describe that stage in the development of the psyche at which it is poised in a seesaw-like manner between childhood and maturity, causing the Self to fluctuate precariously between its transpersonal frequencies and those depressing depths of the unconscious that are not fully understood. 'Persephone people' are among the few who can literally live in two worlds without suffering personality fragmentation, but since I have covered this subject in some detail in my self-analysis aid *Olympus*, I will refer my readers to this publication, which is not specifically involved with the subject matter of this book. The zodiacal sign of Gemini would also appear to connect with the Persephone myth, and may be understood esoterically as providing the psyche with the opportunity to make that vital step from childhood to maturity.

Demeter embodies the introverted expression of the anima via the maternal mode — the mother in all her aspects and implications. There is a psychological theory that women fall into two categories as far as men and children are concerned: those who always put their men first, and those for whom their children take top priority regardless of the consequences. The Greek archetypes confirm this observation in the characters of Aphrodite and Demeter. Both were mothers, but Demeter's attachment to her daughter was so strong that she saw fit to withdraw her energies (her fertility and sexuality) during her period of separation from her beloved Persephone. Aphrodite's son, Eros, on the other hand, played havoc with the emotions of mortals and immortals alike while his mother entertained her paramours. A third approach to the maternal principle is symbolized by Hera, who represents the woman of social status whose family are required to conform outwardly to her standards so as not to let the side down.

The unmarried or 'virgin' status in the context of the Greek archetypes does not necessarily imply sexual abstinence, but rather suggests an autonomous state in which energies are channelled into, for example, executive, academic, agrarian, animal welfare or religious avenues of expression, rather than the maternal function. This is understandable within the context of the culture in which these archetypal figures found form, in which women of learning, and those wishing to escape the domestic scene, frequently entered religion. Thus, depending on the nature of the deity at whose temple they served, they could express their priestly role as philosopher, teacher, oracle, or sacred prostitute. Strict chastity was required of the priestesses of Artemis, whereas those who served Dionysus or Aphrodite discharged their calling in more corporeal ways.

The six Olympian goddesses which represent different expressions of the feminine principle may therefore be assessed as follows:[8]

Animus-orientated	Anima-orientated
Athene (extravert)	Aphrodite (extravert)
Artemis (introvert)	Hera (introvert)
Hestia (introvert)	Demeter (introvert)

Interestingly enough, the six male gods complement this pattern having four extraverts to two introverts between them.

From the above model it is made quite clear that even within the confines of a male-dominated pantheon the women of the Olympian court, with the possible exception of Hera, held several trump cards. After all, it was a woman, Athene — who chose not to enter battle for its own sake but only in the cause of protection or defence — who was able to defeat Ares, the surly old god of war, at his own game. Aphrodite's girdle was invincible, even against the thunderbolts of the Father of the Gods himself, while any male who dared to attempt to violate Artemis was torn to pieces by her hounds. Demeter brought both gods and mortals to their knees when she withdrew her creative and reproductive energies. However, there is no record of the gentle Hestia ever falling foul of the divine wrath of Zeus or any of his

Olympian male colleagues. Hera, in spite of her marital problems, still retained her queenship, her stability proving more important to her husband than the sexual gratification offered to him by a younger generation of nymphs and mortals.

Chapter 5
Her Mysteries

THE pagan religions that preceded Christianity were
served by both priests *and* priestesses which attests to
the liberality of thought in those times. It is to Plutarch
(c.AD 46-120), himself a priest of Apollo and Dionysus, that
we owe the clear and concise account of the nature and
requirements of the priesthood in the second half of the first
century AD. This takes the form of an essay addressed to
the Lady Klea, who held a distinguished position among the
Delphic priestesses, and who had been initiated into the
Osiriac mysteries. As 'Klea' was, no doubt, her mystery
name, she was probably able to read more into Plutarch's
words than might appear on the surface. Referring to this
work, the Theosophical scholar, G.R.S. Mead comments:

> It is, moreover, of interest to find that Plutarch addresses his
> treatise to a lady. For though we have extant several moral
> tractates addressed to wives — such as Porphyry's *Letter* to
> Marcella, and Plutarch's *Consolation* to his own wife,
> Timoxena — it is rare to find philosophical treatises addressed
> to women. [1]

It has been speculated that Plutarch probably based much
of his metaphysical information on a now-lost treatise of
Manetho on the old Egyptian religion because, like
Manetho, he writes as a commentator rather than a dog-
matist, covering many aspects of the mythology and symbology. For those interested, the treatise is reproduced in
full in Mead's translation of the *Hermes Trismegistus* or
Thrice Greatest Hermes. However, a few salient points
relevant to the role and requirements of a priestess in those
times (and earlier) are worthy of mention.

The robes of an Initiate of Isis were white, ornamented with blue and gold. Members of the priesthood refrained from wearing woollen garments to prevent any impure associations from the sheep, their apparel being instead made of flax. Meat did not form part of their diet and they eschewed strong brews, although a small quantity of diluted wine was occasionally permitted, though never before undertaking any magical or religious work. Cleanliness at all times was of paramount importance, which was one of the reasons why the males shaved not only their heads, but all other body hair. From descriptions of ceremonies involving priestesses, however, it would seem that the ladies were not obliged to part with their crowning glory.

Water was considered impure on account of the living organisms within it that caused pollution, a fact of which the priests and priestesses were apparently well aware, even in those distant times. Lesser ranks were permitted to eat fish, but not those of the higher orders. They must also have been familiar with the dangers of a high salt intake since Plutarch emphasizes:

> And the priests handle so hardly the nature of superfluities, that they not only deprecate the many kinds of pulse, and of meats the sheep-flesh kinds and swine-flesh kinds, as making much superfluity, but also at their times of purification they remove the salts from the grains, having other further reasons as well as the fact that it makes the more thirsty and more hungry sharpen their desire the more. For to argue that salts are not pure owing to the multitude of small lives that are caught and die in them when they solidify themselves, as Aristagoras said, is naive. [2]

From information gleaned from the above, as well as many other authenticated sources, it would appear that the disciplines of diet, personal hygiene and chastity imposed on both the priests and priestesses of Isis were nothing if not exacting. Although there were other cults whose priestesses were little more than sacred prostitutes, this was not the case in the Iseums where such behaviour was frowned upon by the state. Josephus tells us of a scandal centred around a temple of Isis, where a noble lady, Paulina, who was a devout worshipper of Isis, sought spiritual aid from her temple and was induced by the oldest priest of the temple to spend a night there to be favoured, perhaps, with a visit from one of the tutelary deities. In his informative book *Isis in the Graeco-Roman World*, Dr R. E. Witt continues the tale:

> Bribed by her lover Mundus, the priest adopted this ruse so that Mundus himself might play the role of Anubis, said to have been good enough to fall in love with the lady, who was to sup and lie with him. When darkness came and all the lights were put out, Mundus hidden in the inmost part of the shrine was able to enjoy his illicit 'wedding night' because Paulina, a lady whose chastity was unimpeachable and whose husband had consented, believed like some character out of Boccaccio that sexual intercourse could take place between a human and a divine partner.[3]

When the news of the dastardly deed reached the Emperor Tiberius, it so enraged him that he shut the temple, smashed the statue of the goddess into smithereens and crucified the priests *en masse*.

Witt gives some interesting accounts of the rites, both public and private, that were undertaken by the Isian clergy of both sexes, the best known of which is probably that of *The Procession of the Ship*. Herodotus states that the first people to institute festivals, processions and religious presentations were the Egyptians: 'and the Greeks have got their knowledge from them.'[4] Witt sees this as a clear recognition of the great antiquity of the pageants of the Nile. He tells us:

> The launching of Isis' ship was a natural development in a religion that was never land-locked. It drew its warrant from the processions in honour of Isis at such centres as Philae and Busiris. Isis 'of the sea', Isis *Pelagia*, was essentially the goddess whose tears yearly filled the Nile, the Isis who in a *Pyramid Text* held the forward cable of the Sacred Bark; the Isis, moreover, who on discovering that the Ark of Osiris had been cast up by the Mediterranean in the region of Phoenician Byblos went across the sea to find it, and then shipped it back with her to Egypt.[5]

His vivid description of the procession, its priests, fancy dress characters and other *dramatis personae* conjures up the picture of an age and a religion whose music and pageantry express the joy and happiness associated with the worship of the feminine principle in the form of a much loved and venerated Mother, Queen, and Mistress of Heaven. His book is well worth reading for this account alone, although it is also packed with information about the goddess in her many names and forms, well researched and lovingly written. It is little wonder that Bishop Cecil Northcott chose to conclude his review in the *Daily Telegraph* (6 May 1971) with the following sentence: 'In a day when the cults are on the way up and the most weird beliefs pass as religion a few doses of Isis might be worth having.'

The role of Isis as Mistress of the Sea (*Stella Maris*) later passed to the Virgin Mary. In the words of the hymn:

Ave maris stella
Dei Mater alma,
Atque semper Virgo
Felix caeli porta.

Other manifestations of the Goddess were later incorporated into Christian beliefs, some of which we will be examining in Chapter 6.

The role played by women in the sacred rites of ancient Greece has been well documented by the great classical scholars of the past. Some writers have tended, however, to place what I feel to be excessive emphasis on the element of frenzy in the ancient rites of divine possession. Certain rituals were known particularly for their orgiastic content. These formed part of the cults and attendant mysteries of Dionysus, Sabazios, Zagreus the Phrygian, or Thracian Bacchus, Cybele and Ida's Zeus, which were subsequently appropriated by the Orphics. Towards the end of the sixth century BC Dionysus had become the symbol of universal life in that he grew up, suffered, died and was reborn in new circumstances. With the advent of philosophers, the violent elements of Greek ritual slowly receded, giving way to a more spiritual approach to the gods.

In Euripides' *Cretans*, the chorus of Bacchants are credited with the following song:

Purity has been the law of my life from the day when I was initiated into the Mysteries of Ida's Zeus; when I took part in the sacrifices according to the rule of Zagreus, the lover of nocturnal journeys, lit torches in honour of the Great Mother and received the double name of Curetes and Bacchant. Clothed in pure white garments, I flee from the birth of mortals; I do not approach graves, and I do not tolerate in my food anything which has lived.[6]

The cult of Bacchus, although frequently associated with drunken satyrs and nymphs, claimed women among both its sacerdotal hierarchy and followers. Although originally believed to have been brought to Greece by Melampus, general opinion tends to credit it with oriental or northern origins, possibly Indo-European.

The Mysteries constituted one of the most important features in Greek religious life, the best known being the Samothracian, Bacchic, Eleusinian and Orphic. According to Lewis Spence, the Samothracian Mysteries centred around four mysterious deities: Axieros, the Mother, her son Axiocersos and her daughter Axiocersa, from whom sprang Casindos, the originator of the universe. Closely connected with these rites was the worship of Cybele, goddess of the earth, both cities and fields, whose priests were the Corybantes, noted for their blood-letting, orgiastic rites. Mead, however, asserts that the initiation temple of the Samothracians contained two statues of naked men with both arms raised to heaven and ithyphallic, like the statue of Hermes in Cyllene, which are believed to represent Adamic Man. No doubt the original goddess cult gave way to the advancing patrist elements during the Geminian years that followed the Age of Cancer.

The greatest of the ancient mystery religions was undoubtedly the goddess-orientated Eleusinia, originally based on the Demeter–Persephone drama, and later incorporating the characters of Asclepius and Dionysus. Homer's celebrated *Hymn to Demeter*, however, makes no mention of Dionysus among the resident deities of the Rites and it is generally believed that both he and Asclepius were later admitted because they, like Demeter and Persephone, had also visited the dark regions of Hades.

Unlike other pagan religious rites, the cult of Demeter was not open to the general public in the manner of a normal state religion. Its admittance was limited to those who had, by prescribed ritual and tradition, sworn not to divulge its innermost secrets. So closely was its arcanum guarded that Athenian law punished by death anyone who tried to probe it, whether out of sheer curiosity, rebelliousness or egotism. It acquired the name the 'Mysteries of Demeter', and, since it was held at Eleusis, the Eleusinian Mysteries. George E. Mylonas tells us:

The Panhellenic character of the cult is indicated by the establishment, perhaps in the fifth Olympiad (760 BC) of a festival and sacrifice at Eleusis known as the *Proerosia*. About the time of that Olympiad a great famine desolated Greece. The Oracle at Delphi ordered the Athenians to offer a sacrifice to Demeter in the name of all the Greeks before the beginning of the ploughing season. The sacrifice was held at Eleusis and the famine came to an end. Under the leadership of the Athenians, the Greek states voluntarily sent to Eleusis annual offerings of the first fruits, known as $\alpha\pi\alpha\varrho\chi\rho\,i$, as a token of gratitude. [7]

As time progressed, the ever-increasing popularity of the Eleusinian cult involved a continuous expansion of the precinct area and the facilities for the initiation of the many pilgrims who came from far and wide to pay homage to the goddess or to become initiated into her mysteries. When the Mysteries were at their height, three grades were involved: the Small Mysteries, the Great Mysteries and Epoptism. Every respectable citizen of Athens endeavoured to become initiated at the higher or more esoteric levels, but there was also a public side in which glorious pageantry and outward display served to keep the man in the street happy. The priestly or inner ceremonies were administered by two families: the Eumolpides and the Kerykes, whose offices extended throughout the whole period of early paganism until the eventual triumph of Christianity.

Clement of Alexandria (c.AD 150-221) commented freely on what he saw as certain undesirable aspects of the Mysteries of Deo — 'Deo' being the poetic form of the name Demeter, although the learned Bishop does not state specifically that the said mysteries were synonymous with those of Eleusis. Mylonas believes that the orgiastic content referred to by Clement was more in keeping with the Phrygian rites of Rhea-Cybele-Attis, although Clement's second statement, which concerns the story of Baubo, would appear to confirm Mylonas's suspicions that Clement did have the Eleusinia in mind when he wrote it. It tells of Baubo, an aborigine of Eleusis, with whom Demeter sought shelter during the period of her wanderings in search of her daughter, the others being Dysaulus, Triptolemus, Eumolpos and Eubouleus.

The last three named were herdsmen, progenitors of the

Eumolpides and Kerykes, who later formed part of the priestly cast of Athens. Baubo, it seems, offered the goddess food and drink, which she declined, causing Baubo to believe that she had in some way offended the divinity. She therefore displayed her pudenda to the goddess, which seemed to please her so that she then partook of the refreshments offered. The Baubo legend is obviously founded on some ancient matrist rite which involved a form of sacred exhibitionism similar to that expressed in the Sheela-na-gigs of the early Celtic period. The Irish scholar, Bob Quinn, writing in his book *Atlantean*, comments:

> In Ptolemaic Egypt, women in childbirth had the habit of keeping by their sides a female figurine called a Baubo. It had the same posture as a Sheela. Its precise function is unknown but as it was a well-fleshed figure it is assumed to have some fertility connotations. I enquired about such a figure in every museum in Cairo but nobody had ever heard of it. This must have been partly because no such daring figure would have a place in Islam; perhaps, also, because German scholars at the turn of the century brought many of the available figurines home with them: the best examples are in Berlin.[8]

Rather than a profanity, Baubos would seem to be nothing more than a remnant from the ancient matrist cults in which the function of motherhood, and therefore those organs associated with it, were seen as sacred.

Taking the overall information available, we may safely assume that these goddess-orientated rites that represented such an important part of life in classical Greece for so many years were highly beneficial to both the initiates and the community at large.

The religion of classical Greece probably inherited many of its features from the old goddess cult of Minoan Crete. In ancient Crete matriarchy had been a way of life for centuries. Women were accorded full sexual freedom, and the goddess was the very core of existence. As Merlin Stone tells us:

> A man became king or chieftain only by formal marriage and his daughter, not his son, succeeded so that the next chieftain was the youth who married his daughter ... until the northerners arrived, religion and custom were dominated by the female principle.[9]

In this woman-dominated society, priestesses were the intermediaries between the goddess and the people, and it was not until later that men were allowed to participate in the rites and ceremonies of the Sacred Bull. As Jacquetta Hawkes remarked:

> Cretan men and women were everywhere accustomed to seeing a splendid goddess queening it over a small and suppliant male god, and this concept must surely have expressed some attitude present in the human society that accepted it. [10]

The self-confidence and security displayed by the Cretan women was also to be evidenced in another characteristic which Hawkes sees as:

> the fearless and natural emphasis on sexual life that ran through all religious expression and was made obvious in the provocative dress of both sexes and their easy mingling — a spirit best understood through its opposite: the total veiling and seclusion of Moslem women under a faith which even denied them a soul. [11]

Closely associated with the goddess in ancient Crete was the cult of serpent worship. Of the many Cretan/Minoan figurines that have found their way into today's museums and private collections, perhaps the best known is that of the goddess (or her priestess) wearing an elaborate garment with a layered skirt, the bodice of which allows full exposure of her breasts. Her arms are extended sideways, the hands grasping two serpents; on her head is a form of crown or coronet, surmounted by the figure of a cat. In fact, the serpent connection with the goddess may be evidenced more in the old Cretan religion than anywhere else in the Mediterranean area, as a consequence of which archaeologists have tended to refer to the Cretan deity as the 'Serpent Goddess'. The cat was also one of her shamanic totems.

The serpent motif later found its way into the classical pantheon via the heroic figure of Athene, whose cuirass or breastplate was fringed and bordered with snakes. Athene's serpent or serpents always appeared in her statues, and a special building known as the Erechtheum, which stood in the Acropolis alongside the goddess's own temple, the Parthenon, was believed to have been the home of her own sacred serpent. There is little doubt that although Athene is said to have been born from the head of Zeus, she was a much older divinity whose worship went back to matriarchal times, and who was incorporated into the Olympian pantheon in much the same way that certain pagan deities became absorbed into early Christianity.

In spite of its association with the sun god, Apollo's famous shrine at Delphi was also steeped in the serpent cult as shown in the title of its priestesses, who were known as Pythia or Pythonesses. Coiled around the sacred tripod stool upon which Pythia was seated during the pronouncement of her oracles was a snake known as the Python. A later myth tells of how Apollo slew Python, which may be read as an indication that the patriarchal gods finally effected their takeover of what had previously been the oracular domains of the goddess.

Serpent worship, as associated with the goddess, was also to be found in many other areas of the Mediterranean, for example, among the Philistines, whom some authorities believe to have been a branch of the Mycenaeans. The Uraeus of ancient Egypt, which we have already discussed as featuring in the headgear of priests and rulers, was also personalized in the form of Uatchet or Buto, the 'Goddess of the North', who frequently shared a shrine with the Vulture Goddess, Nekhebet, the 'Goddess of the South'. Serpent deities appeared under many other names both in Egypt and the surrounding countries. The Babylonian Ishtar, for example, in her role as prophetess is depicted as holding a staff around which are coiled two snakes. Since the serpentine power is the receptive or anima quality of the feminine principle, this is hardly surprising.

My own personal experience in healing has also inclined me to the opinion that both 'serpent' and 'dragon' powers, (anima and animus aspects of the feminine psychic economy) are associated with healing. Running a healing group myself for almost twenty years afforded me the opportunity to study healers and those exhibiting healing PK (psychokinetic energies) at first hand. The two aspects of the healing energies clearly work in different ways, which is doubtless one of several messages concealed within the symbology of the caduceus. Chaos and Order are so closely linked that one needs to understand the subtle nature of both, which did not escape the healers of ancient Egypt and classical Greece. Apollo's son Asclepius, deified as the god of medicine, was frequently depicted naked, serpent in hand, his skills and those of his priests at Epidaurus being a legacy, no doubt, from earlier goddess religions.

The equality and liberty enjoyed by women under the benevolent rulership of the goddess may be evidenced in many other early cultures. According to both Euripides and Plutarch, during the classical age of Sparta, young Spartan women were not to be found at home but in the gymnasia, where they threw off their restricting clothing and wrestled naked with their male contemporaries. This was the age when the veneration of Artemis thrived and women rejoiced in their independence.

Following some major catastrophe (probably seismic, corresponding to the Santorini/Thera eruptions seen erroneously in recent times as synonymous with Plato's Atlantis), which precipitated the fall of the old Cretan empire, the Mycenaeans ruled Crete at the Palace of Knossos roughly between 1350 and 1100 BC. Their period of ascendancy predated the Greece of Homer by many centuries and the Homeric Hymns are believed to have been based on folk legends or oral traditions of events that took place during those times. Many of the tales that have come down to us via the classics, which for centuries were viewed as pure myth, have latterly been proved to be factual accounts of historical events, albeit a little embroidered by poetic licence.

The Achaean invasions of Greece in the thirteenth century BC had shaken the foundations of the matrilineal tradition to the extent that when the Dorians arrived towards the close of the second millennium, patrilineal succession became the established rule. These people from the north brought with them the worship of the Indo-Aryan Dyaus Pitar — God Father — who eventually became the Zeus of Greece and the Jupiter of Rome. New temples arose from the foundations of older structures and although the gods that rose with them were frequently males, their rites retained many of the old goddess hallmarks.

Although the Greek sages are credited with great wisdom and knowledge, and the praises of the classical period are sung by scholars of all lands, some lesser known details have failed to reach the textbooks. Pythagoras, for example, received his tuition in ethics from Themistoclea, a priestess of Delphi; Diotema of Mantinea was a tutor of Socrates, while the Delphic Pythia advised sages, politicians and statesmen from all over the then civilized world.[12]

Goddess worship in its numerous guises was, however, to be found in many other areas in those early times. There is ample evidence of an old matrist religion existing in the British Isles and parts of northern Europe long before the Celts carried their conquering banners, and their accompanying pantheons, to those parts. The ancient goddess-orientated religion of Wicca is at the forefront of the neo-pagan revival that is currently sweeping the British Isles and other parts of Europe and the United States. Psychologist Dr Vivianne Crowley, herself a fully initiated Wiccan, remarks:

> As a religion, Wicca offers a variant of what all religions offer — a philosophy of life, a sense of the place of humanity in the cosmos, and a form of worship through which people can participate in the mysteries of the life force and fulfil their needs for shared human activity by doing this with others. Where Wicca differs is that sympathetic and natural magic is an integral part of the religion.[13]

But exactly how far back into the past do the matrist-dominated credos of Wicca extend? What are its precepts, and why should it have assumed popularity in a world so totally different from the one in which it originated? Dr Crowley has answers to these and many other questions, telling us that Wicca worships in the divine way of our ancient ancestors in its acknowledgement of a triple goddess and a dual god. These are, however, two aspects of the one creative force which is neither male nor female but contains, and yet goes beyond, both. She sees the concepts of a god and goddess as expressed in the art of the Palaeolithic or Old Stone Age, as representing an early form of Wicca — the Mother Goddess who ruled over human fertility, and the horned hunting God who controlled the animal kingdoms. With the development of agriculture and the realization of the effect of the moon on the growth cycles of human and plant life alike, womanhood and motherhood assumed lunar associations. Since the moon has three major aspects — waxing, full, and waning — this was likened to the pre-puberty, fertile, and menopausal stages in a woman's life. In terms of the goddess, these were seen as epitomizing her triple aspects as virgin, mother and crone — the cycle of birth, marriage, and death. Since it was necessary to plant the seed in the earth in order to obtain crops, and likewise the seed of the child was planted in the womb, the phallic aspect, as represented by the god, assumed a new and specific relevance.

According to Crowley, between 5500 and 3000 BC the fair-haired Indo-European horse and cattle herders from Asia Minor introduced the concept of a dual god, whose solar aspect was the giver of life, while the Tanist, or dark aspect, who ruled the chthonic regions, embodied the principle of death. This dual deity later combined with the triple goddess to form the basis of the religion of the Celts, some aspects of which have been retained in modern Wicca. Although the Celts are believed to have been of Indo-European origin, and therefore patristically inclined, certain aspects of their religion belie this. For example, goddesses, and women in general, enjoyed an exalted status in Celtic society. There were noted women warriors and queens, and legal disputes were settled by women. The Celts appear to have absorbed their goddess theology from the cultures they conquered, and their devotion to the arts of music, poetry and magic have been well documented by historians from the Roman period, notably Caesar.

Priestesses were also in evidence in the ancient religion of the Druids, which later became associated with Celtica. My research inclines me to agree with Crowley, however, that Druidism had its origins among the Beaker people who landed on these shores as early as 2000 BC. References to them are to be found in several ancient sources, including the annals of the Frisian race that have already received mention.

Crowley sees the triple goddess concept as according with the Jungian psychology of archetypes. The virgin, for example, does not refer to the non-sexual, but rather to the woman who is not owned by or needing a man through whom to express her essential femininity. For the Wiccan man the goddess is the anima: 'that all-powerful, frightening and beautiful figure who beckons him from the portals of his unconscious to make the heroic journey into the psyche to find the Grail, the divine essence of himself.'[14] Many men, she comments, tend to cleave more to a Queen of Heaven than to a Queen of Earth. This is confirmed in the lives of male Christian saints and mystics, who have tended to place a strong emphasis on the worship of Mary, St Ignatius Loyola and St Dominic being prime examples.

Coming to the maternal aspect of the triple goddess, Crowley refers to the appearance of the goddess's daughter. Demeter begets Persephone or Kore, who in turn bears a child to Hades, Lord of the Underworld. 'In Wicca the Persephone figure is Aradia, the Goddess of the Earth, the daughter of the brother/sister marriage of the Sun and Moon.'[15] The final, crone aspect of the goddess is seen by Crowley as conveying an important lesson in relation to the feminine psyche: 'that the feminine should be valued for itself; not because it brings sexuality or power, but because deep within there is an eternal wisdom, for Hecate is also the High Priestess, the keeper of the Mysteries.'[16]

The triple goddesses may be evidenced in many of the early religions. In Greece there was Hebe, the maiden or daughter, Hera, her mother, and Hecate — she of the Underworld. There were also the Three Moerae, the three Gorgons, the three Graeae, and the three Horae. In Viking tradition she appears as the three Norns; among the romans as the Fates or Fortunae; among the Druids as Diana Triformis. As each of her personae was again considered to be a trinity, the number nine was designated as sacred to her in all her forms. Among the Irish she was the three faces of Morrigan — Ana-Babd-Macha — and in both Irish and Welsh mythology there are references to the 'nine sisters' who were the custodians of the Cauldron of Regeneration, the Nine Sorceresses of Gloucester, and so on. Greece had her Nine Muses, who were, no doubt, originally associated with the goddess, but were later transferred to the retinue of Apollo, probably around the same time that the sun god appropriated her oracle at Delphi.

Arabia was matriarchal prior to the arrival of Islam in the seventh century AD. The Annals of Ashurbanipal state that Arabia was governed by queens for as long as anyone could remember. 'The land's original Allah was Al-Lat, part of the female trinity along with Kore and Q're, the Virgin, and Al-Uzza, the Powerful One, the triad known as Manat, the

Threefold Moon.'[17] The pre-Islamic wisdom schools also incorporated the teachings of earlier sources, and later flowered into Sufism. Ibn El-Arabi, considered the 'greatest master' of Sufi mystics, was accused of blasphemy for declaring the godhead to be female!

This phenomenon is not limited to the shores of Europe. In India there was Parvati-Durga-Uma (Kali), and although the Brahmins developed the male trinity of Brahma, Vishnu and Shiva, according to ancient scriptures these three deities were the creations of the goddess. Barbara Walker tells us that the three aspects of the goddess 'were personified on earth by three kinds of priestesses: Yogini, Matri and Dakini — nubile virgins, mothers, and elder women. These were sometimes called "deities of nature". Manifestations of the Triple Goddess were known as The Three Most Precious Ones.'[18]

The Negritos of the Malay Peninsula once worshipped the goddess as Kari, who was also a trinity whom they referred to as the 'three grandmothers under the earth'. The virgin goddess of pre-Columbian Mexico, often designated as the mother of Quetzalcoatl, was one of the three divine sisters.

Owing to the association of the number nine with the great goddess, anything connected with her or her worship has tended to receive 'nine' connotations, for example, the nine lives of the cat which was one of her sacred animals. In Egypt she was Isis, whose daughter was Bast, the cat goddess, while the Scandinavian goddess Freya rode in a chariot drawn by cats. The Greek Artemis was also often identified with Bast, legend decreeing that when the Greek gods fled into Egypt, hotly pursued by the monster Typhon, Artemis changed herself into a cat and, in this form, took refuge in the moon. The Cretan Snake Goddess also carried the effigy of a cat on her head, a sure indication of its totemistic place in her worship. Persecutors of the goddess and her followers have often seen fit to apply their cruelties to felines on account of the close tie between the two. According to Jewish belief, cats were not made by God, the first pair of male and female cats having been 'snorted forth' from the nostrils of a lion on board the ark of the biblical Noah![19]

In time, the three goddesses gave way to the father/

mother/son-daughter trinities, and eventually to those all-male trios that formed part of the patrist tradition and later came to dominate Christian belief to this day — the mother, or feminine aspect being replaced by the Holy Spirit in the form of a *male* dove. However, the Gnostic version featured the feminine Sophia (Wisdom), whose symbol was also a dove. Sophia was once worshipped at the great goddess in Constantinople, and viewed later by many Gnostics as the consort of God. Interestingly enough, the Roman Emperor Constantine, who was responsible for establishing Christianity as the state religion of Rome, seems to have been somewhat unsure about his decision. Legend has it that he hedged his bets by secretly arranging for acknowledgements to the old gods and goddesses to be concealed in the base of his tomb — just in case!

The Romans culled much of their religious tradition from Eastern, Egyptian, Greek, and Etruscan sources. Even the cult of Mithras, which became such a firm favourite with the Roman Legions, was of oriental origin. As Christianity slowly fused with existing beliefs, the various Gnostic cults made their appearance, many of them, like the Ophites, being decidedly goddess-orientated. One of the best known Gnostic references, to which modern psychologists often have recourse when considering the feminine archetypes, is the *Sophia Mythus*, the *Pistis Sophia* (Faith-Wisdom) being one of the sacred books of Gnosticism (see also Chapter 6). Mead tells us:

> As Wisdom was the end of the Gnosis, so the pivot of the whole Gnostic mythological drama was the so-called *Sophia Mythus*. For whether we interpret their allegories from the macrocosmic or microcosmic standpoint, it is ever the evolution of the *mind* that the initiates of old have sought to teach us. The emanation and evolution of the world-mind in cosmogenesis, and of the human mind in anthropogenesis, is ever the main interest of the secret science.
>
> The dwelling of Sophia, as the World-Soul, according to our Gnostics, was in the Midst, in the Ogdoad, between the upper or purely spiritual worlds, and the lower psychic and material worlds. Below the Ogdoad was the Hebdomad or Seven Spheres of psychic substance. Truly hath 'Wisdom built for herself a House, and rested it on Seven Pillars' (*Prov.* ix. 1); and again: 'She is in the lofty Heights; She stands in the midst of the Paths, for She taketh her seat by the Gates of the Powerful

Ones, she tarrieth at the Entrances [of the Light World]' (*Ibid* viii. 2), says the Wisdom in its Jewish tradition.

Moreover, Sophia was the Mediatrix between the upper and lower spaces, and at the same time projected the Types or Ideas of the Pleroma into the cosmos. . . .

It is not surprising, then, that we should find the Sophia in her various aspects possessed of many names. Among these may be mentioned: The Mother, or All-Mother; Mother of the Living, or Shining Mother; the Power Above; the Holy Spirit; again, She of the Left-hand as opposed to the Christos, Him of the Right-hand; the Man-woman; Prouneikos or Lustful One; the Matrix; Paradise; Eden; Achamoth; the Virgin; Barbelo; Daughter of Light; Merciful Mother; Consort of the Masculine One; Revelant of the Perfect Mysteries; Perfect Mercy; Revelant of the Mysteries of the Whole Magnitude; Hidden Mother; She who knows the Mysteries of the Elect; The Holy Dove who has given birth to Twins; Ennoea; Ruler; and the Lost or Wandering Sheep, Helena, and many other names.

These terms refer to Sophia or the 'Soul' — using the term in its most general sense — in her cosmic or individual aspects, according as she is above in her perfect purity; or in the midst, as intermediary; or below, as fallen into matter.[20]

Some schools of Gnosticism saw the Sophia as the twin or syzygy of the Christos, or the feminine aspect or anima of the Christ Spirit, which was essential to its balanced functioning at all levels.

There were several versions of the Sophia Mythus, which varies with the different Gnostic sects, and one could not hope to do justice to them in a short summary. One story, for example, tells of how Sophia herself descends to effect the redemption of mankind, but is unable to achieve this without the aid of her syzygy (polarity), the Cosmic Christ. The reverse was also believed by some — that the Christ Spirit could not carry out its act of redemption without its female polarity — the Sophia. This doctrine is also re-echoed in other traditions, the Qabalistic concept of the Shekinah, for example. This is equivalent to the Hindu *Shakti*, or female soul of God, who could not be perfect unless he was reunited with her. According to a certain Qabalist tradition, it was God's loss of his Shekinah that brought about all the evils. Walker tells us that the Hebrew Sh'kina meant 'dwelling place', intimating that God had no home without her.[21]

Shakti was the Tantric title of the great goddess (Kali Ma) or soul of both man and God. As well as the Qabalistic Shekinah, she was also the Greek Psyche, Roman Anima, and Gnostic Sophia. According to the tenets of Tantric mysticism, union with the Shakti occurred at the moment of death, as she was both the individual and the cosmic goddess, who absorbed both the soul and the body of the dying sage into herself, thus affording the passing soul an experience of unsurpassable bliss. The name 'Shakti' also has other connotations in Tantrism, and can be applied to mortal women. Walker states that 'The Kulacudamani Nigama said not even God could become the supreme Lord unless Shakti entered into Him.'[22]

From the foregoing it may be seen that the absence of the feminine principle, or blocking of its energies, is to a great extent responsible for the plight of our world. As the teachings of the Gnostics appear to contain a heady mixture of oriental mysticism, Greek philosophy, Egyptian theurgy and early Christian theology, the wheat certainly needs to be sorted from the chaff. Leaving aside the Christian elements, however, the various Gnostic versions of the Sophia legend would seem to have points in common with the story of Isis whose syzygy, Osiris, resides in heaven, and without whose power the goddess is subject to the sufferings and evils of this world until such times as her release is effected by her son, Horus. The Gnostic Ildabaoth or Yahweh therefore equates with Set (Chaos) which tends to confirm the ancient belief that the entity responsible for the problems experienced by mankind over thousands of years of evolution is basically male-orientated. And until such times as mankind rids itself of this sharp division between the sexes and reunites yin with yang, the suffering will continue and our search for the god/goddess within us will be thwarted.

Chapter 6
She of Many Colours

DIODORUS Siculus (Diodorus of Sicily), writing about his travels in northern Africa and parts of the Near East in the first century BC, had some interesting tales to tell, one of which concerned the Amazons, the Greek name for the goddess-worshipping tribes of North Africa, Anatolia and the Black Sea area. Diodorus appeared to be particularly interested in the social status of women, and his commentaries on the subject have been much appreciated by feminists in recent years. For example, it was he who reported that the Ethiopian women bore arms, practised communal marriage, and raised their children in groups, thus foregoing the personalized (and possessive!) aspects of motherhood. In those parts of Libya where the goddess Neith was worshipped, accounts of the Amazon women and their feats in the field of battle were carried over into Roman times. Diodorus tells us:

> All authority was vested in the woman, who discharged every kind of public duty. The men looked after domestic affairs just as the women do among ourselves and did as they were told by their wives. They were not allowed to undertake war service or to exercise any functions of government, or to fill any public office, such as might have given them more spirit to set themselves up against the women. The children were handed over immediately after birth to the men who reared them on milk and other foods suitable to their age. [1]

Diodorus also told of the warrior women of Libya who formed themselves into armies and invaded other lands. Wherever they went they set up shrines and temples to their goddess, whose name he does not tell us, but who was probably Neith. Legend has it that in order to facilitate the drawing of the bow, Amazon warriors had their right breast amputated, some scholars being of the opinion that their name derives from *a-mazos*, 'breastless'. However, as Greek and other representations of these women fail to evidence any such mutilations, it has also been proposed that the idea probably originated in the androgyne, the right half of which was depicted as male and the left as female. Some confirmation of this could perhaps be read into the portrayals of Artemis, who was also greatly revered by the Amazons, as coalesced with her twin brother Apollo.

According to Gaius Tranquillus Suetonius (AD 70-122) the Amazons once ruled over a large part of Asia, and the Black Sea was still known as the Amazon Sea as late as the fifth century AD. Libya, which in ancient times encompassed all of North Africa except Egypt, was also Amazonian. The Amazons were believed to have been the first to tame horses, which could account for their earlier military successes.

In Amazonian mythology, their goddess is frequently worshipped as a mare — the mare-headed version of Demeter perhaps, equivalent to the Cretan Leucippe, or the 'White Mare' whose priests were castrated and required to wear female clothing. There would also appear to be a connection between the Scythians and the Amazons, since certain representations of the Great Goddess, notably the Virgin or Artemis aspect, was shared by both cultures.

The part played by the Amazons in the ancient history of Greece is surely emphasized by the fact that Hercules' ninth Labour involved the acquisition of the magnificent girdle of Hippolyte (also called Melanippe), Queen of the Amazons of Cappadocia, who had received the girdle as a present from Ares as a mark of her sovereignty. Several interesting magical and psychological implications are to be found within this tale. Firstly, it was Hercules' ninth Labour, and nine is one of the sacred numbers of the goddess. Secondly, the girdle is reminiscent of the attribute of Aphrodite, the Love Goddess, who embodies various aspects of the feminine principle. The girdle is also a symbol of binding, and Hercules' initiation might well have involved the breaking of the bonds which imprisoned his anima in the submissive mode as a result of his over-emphasized animus.

At the purely historical level, however, Hercules' slaugh-

ter of the Amazon warriors and their queen surely symbolizes the patrist takeover of the Amazonian lands and
people by masculine force of arms. Corresponding legends
are also to be found in the myths of other pantheons,
notably the Celtic champion Peredur's smiting of the Nine
Sorceresses of Gloucester, who were reputed to have been
garbed in warrior style. These may refer to the eventual
defeat of the Amazons and similar female-orientated
cultures.

In the ancient legends there are several references to
islands populated entirely by women, who only chose to
visit neighbouring colonies of men when they wished to
conceive children. Taurus, Lemnos and Lesbos were said to
house female communities of this kind, and were much
feared by the Greeks since it was rumoured that any men
landing on their shores were likely to be sacrificed to the
goddess.

Women warriors are, however, guaranteed to make their
appearance in any civilization, tribe or culture that practises sexual equality, in which case it is highly likely that
the Valkyries, Frisian warriors and those Celtic queens who
rode at the head of their armies could all be classified as
'Amazons'. This particularly applies to the latter, the Celts
being renowned for their expert horsemanship while the
marks and symbols of their Horse goddesses Epona,
Rhiannon, and Macha (to name but three) are still to be
found etched in white limestone on the hills of Britain.
Perhaps the Amazons were, as Dr Philippa Berry has
suggested, 'doomed defenders of a declining matriarchy'
(personal communication) although their military prowess
would seem to be incongruous with the earlier, peace-
loving, pastoral matriarchates to whom such violence must
have been abhorrent.

The Black Goddess

Black Africa has always contained a strong element of
goddess worship which the Islamic influence has failed to
subdue in many places. Luisah Teish, a priestess of Oshun
in the Yoruba Lucumi tradition, whose ancestors came
from Africa, now teaches classes on African goddesses,
shamanism and the Tambala tradition. Luisah's warm,

human, but nevertheless well informed approach has opened many doors (and many hearts) to the conventions of her African ancestors. The Afro-Caribbean tradition, in common with European witchcraft, has been the whipping boy of patrist propaganda for centuries. Catholic and Protestant churches have persecuted, tortured, and killed those who espoused its tenets and over the four centuries when these abominations were rife 80 per cent of the victims were women. The native beliefs of the African slaves were seen as devil worship by the missionaries who, aided by their white masters, did everything in their power to suppress them. Black people were thus forbidden to practise their old tribal religions, mainly on account of the fear factor — man being ever afraid of that which he cannot master or understand.

Harmony with and a respect for the forces of nature and the cosmos formed the basis of black African religion before the Islamic or Christian missionaries made their appearance on the scene. These energies were placated, worshipped and their favours sought through rites of song, dance, chanting, myth, and a profound respect for the ancestors. Most of the old tribal communities were closely knit, which had both advantages and disadvantages in that while there were plenty of loving hands extended during times of trouble those same hands were quick to chastise anyone who transgressed the tribal taboos.

Due deference was paid to those powerful forces beyond the material world that guide, protect, and test us — the gods or *orishas* — into whose realms we may occasionally be transported on the winged back of ecstasy. However, African religion was nothing if not thoroughly terrestrial, as a result of which all its paraphernalia and the impedimenta of its rites were centred on the immanent, sensual, tactile, erotic, and practical. Things had to be *seen* or *represented* in order to be understood, hence the elaborate regalia of the witch doctor, priestess or shaman/shamaness.

Luisah Teish was born in the city of Voudoun, New Orleans. Her earliest memories were of being 'tipsy', the name given in the African-voudou tradition to that stage of mind that precedes possession — due, no doubt, to the sensation being not dissimilar to that experienced when one is slightly drunk. Today we would call it an ASC or altered state of consciousness. In her enlightening and heart-warming book *Jambalaya*, Teish tells the story of her life, her career, and her 'memories' of and studies in the religion of her black African ancestors. In 1961 she was awarded a scholarship to study dance under the direction of Madame Katherine Dunham at the Performing Arts Training Centre in East St Louis, Illinois, which afforded her the opportunity to study the dances of Africa and the Caribbean Islands and later perform them on the public stage. It was during this period that she learned the names of the *Loa* (Haitian deities) and *Orisha*. Her esoteric studies also took her through the ancient Egyptian religion into which she was initiated, when the magical name 'Luisah Teish', which means 'adventuresome spirit', was conferred upon her. Since then she has also studied psychology and religions ancient and modern.

Her book is a mine of information on the goddess religions and status of women in the old traditions of western Africa. In addition to explaining the old African beliefs concerning the hereafter, the world of spirit, the gods, and allied phenomena, she supplies her readers with practical, everyday ways in which they can realize these truths to their own benefit, as well as that of the Earth herself and all other life forms. Her well grounded, no-nonsense approach accommodates the emotions, needs, and aspirations of ordinary people as well as those whose spiritual aspirations are of a more exalted nature.

Regarding the role played by women both in the divine and human context Teish writes:

One of our limitations is language, and unfortunately sexist language has insisted on labeling this totality whose intelligence gives birth to us all as *he*. Let us exercise dynamic temperance by balancing this popular myopia with an examination of *NaNa Buluku*, the supreme deity of the Fon (Dahomey).

The world was created by One god, who is at the same time both male and female. This creator is neither Mawu nor Lisa, but is named NaNa Buluku. In time NaNa Buluku gave birth to twins who were named Mawu and Lisa, and to whom eventually dominion over the realm thus created ceded. To Mawu, the woman, was given command of the night; to Lisa, the man, command of the day. Mawu, therefore is the moon and inhabits the west, while Lisa, who is the sun, inhabits the east. At the time their respective domains were assigned to them, no children had yet been born to this pair, though at night the man was in the habit of giving a 'rendezvous' to the woman, and eventually she bore him offspring. This is why, when there is an eclipse of the moon, it is said that the celestial couple are engaged in love-making; when there is an eclipse of the sun, Mawu is believed to be having intercourse with Lisa.[2]

Teish emphasizes the importance of exploring gynandry, the male concept of god having been responsible for the oppression of women over the centuries. She points out that since female characteristics are primarily exhibited by all foetuses, masculinity being a secondary development, one could assume the prototype for humanity to be female rather than male. This theory has now been confirmed by the latest studies in genetics.

Jambalaya contains a comprehensive list of the ancient deities of Teish's ancestral Africa. These include the divinities, both male and female, of Ghana, Dahomey, Yoruba, and Ibo. In a chapter entitled 'Beneath Mary's Skirts', Teish highlights the plight of the slaves who, upon finding some basic element to be missing from Christianity, were obliged to reshape it to fit their native religion by continuing to worship their own deities under the cover of the Marian principle.

The cult of the African or Black Goddess has, however, survived to this day, albeit in the disguise of certain personalities venerated by the patrist-orientated religions that have assumed the mantle of power over the popular 'collectives'. In Christianity she is the Black Madonna or Black Virgin, whose statues adorn many churches to this day. Ean Begg provides us with a comprehensive list of her most famous shrines, citing an old verse that dates from 1629:[3]

Oettingen for Bavaria	Quod Bavaris Ottinga
Hal for the Belgians	Quod Belgis Hala
Montserrat for Spain	Quod Serra Montis Hesperiis
Alba for the Magyars	Quod Hungaris Regalis Alba
For Italy Loreta	Quodque Laurentum Italis,
But in France, Liesse	Laetitia Francis illud est
Is our joy and ever	et erit suis.
shall be.	

To this list Begg adds Chartres, Le Puy and Rocamadour in France, Einsiedeln in Switzerland, Oropa in Piedmont, Our Lady of the Pillar in Zaragoza, and Our Lady of Guadalupe and all the Spains. There were (and still are), he assures us scores of others. But why should the Virgin Mary, who was undoubtedly a Jewess, be depicted as black? Since theologians and historians have tended to fight shy of the question, those researchers who have seen fit to investigate the phenomenon have either sought the answers within what they see to be the archetypal symbology involved, or looked back to corresponding pagan goddesses from the pre-Christian past.

Theologians tend to explain away the colour of the Black Virgins by suggesting it could be the result of candle smoke, exposure to the elements, or general ageing. This argument carries no weight however, since there is seldom any accompanying discolouration in the clothing and ornamentation, while the colour of the faces and limbs on other sacred images of a similar period and age, which have been subjected to exactly the same treatment, have failed to turn black. When asked why a process of restoration has not been applied, the answer is usually that the faithful have become accustomed to the sooty appearance, with which they feel comfortable and secure, and to effect any changes might prove confusing for them.

Begg tells us that there are a few other saintly figures who occasionally appear as black, but these usually have chthonic, funerary, or occult connotations. A series of suggestions have been proffered as to why the Virgin Mary should be shown as black. These include: 1) living in a hot climate she might have been sunburnt; 2) the statues were carved by people who were themselves dark-skinned; 3) the European sculptors assumed those who came from Palestine to be black-skinned; 4) prototypes of the Black Virgins were made from ebony, basalt, metal, or some very dark wood, these being copied exactly by artists who came later. The last contention is hardly valid, however, since ebony was not in use in Western Europe until the thirteenth century, and most of the Black Virgins are carved in wood — oak, apple, olive, pear or cedar being the most favoured.

The subject of Black Virgins appears to be something of an anathema to the bastions of the Roman Catholic heirarchy. According to Begg:

> There was no mistaking the open hostility, when, on 28
> December 1952, as Moss and Cappannari presented their
> paper on Black Virgins to the American Association for the
> Advancement of Science, every priest and nun in the audience
> walked out.[4]

The French Order of the Prieuré Notre-Dame de Sion,
which has been in existence since the twelfth century, has
chivalric, religious, and occult features. Its chief aim seems
to have been the restoration of the Merovingian bloodline to
the throne, but it is also closely connected with the Cult of
the Black Virgin, and has staunchly supported equal rights
for women over many centuries. It has counted several
women among its Grand Masters, one of the earliest being
Iolande de Var (1428-83 in Begg's account; 1420-83 according to Baigent, Leigh and Lincoln).

The Prieuré received considerable publicity in recent
years through the Baigent, Leigh, Lincoln book *The Holy
Blood, and the Holy Grail*, which proved such a success
that the authors followed it up with *The Messianic Legacy*.
David Wood added the dimension of sacred geometry and
the science of numbers to their theories in his book
Genisis, which is deeply concerned with the Creatrix
principle in the form of the goddess Isis, which he was able
to trace back to Egypt and Atlantis through the application
of his highly specialized discipline.

Concerning the connection between the Prieuré, the
Black Virgin, and Isis, Begg tells us:

> The Grand Master of the Prieuré 1981-84, Pierre Plantard, is
> reported as saying that the Sicambrians, ancestors of the
> Frankish Merovingians, worshipped Cybele as Diana of the
> Nine Fires, or as Arduina, the eponymous goddess of the
> Ardennes. The huge idol to Diana/Arduina which once
> towered over Carignan, in north-east France, between the
> Black Virgin sites of Orval, Avioth and Mezières, near to
> Stenay, where the Merovingian king and saint, Dagobert II,
> was murdered in 679, points circumstantially to a link
> between the two cults. In this connection Plantard mentions
> that one of the most important acts of Dagobert, when he
> acceded to the throne after his Irish exile, was to continue the
> ancient tradition of Gaul, the worship of the Black Virgin. The

Black Virgin, he insists, is Isis and her name is Notre-Dame de Lumière.[5]

Although Isis is frequently referred to by scholars as 'She of the Many Names', is there any special reason why Plantard and his successors should accord her an Egypto-African connection rather than associating her with European goddesses, such as Cybele, Diana, or any of the Celtic deities that were much favoured in pagan Gaul? The answer would seem to lie in the character of St Mary the Egyptian, believed to be a version of the Magdalene and also one of the titles of the Black Virgin.

Begg takes his readers on an instructive if somewhat labyrinthine tour of ancient goddesses, early saints, Gnosticism, Catharism, Arkites, and Troubadours. It was particularly heartening to note his allusion to the obvious conflict that existed between Mary Magdalene and Peter. Elaine Pagels also highlighted this basic rift in the early Church:

> Furthermore, as we have seen, the *Gospel of Mary* depicts Mary Magdalene (never recognized as an apostle by the orthodox) as the one favored with visions and insight that far surpass Peter's. The *Dialogue of the Saviour* praises her not only as a visionary, but as the apostle who excels all the rest. She is the 'woman who knew the All'.[6]

Pagels also cites the *Gospel of Philip* which tells of the rivalry between the male disciples and Mary Magdalene, described as Jesus' most intimate companion:

> the companion of the [Savior is] Mary Magdalene. [But Christ loved] her more than [all] the disciples and used to kiss her [often] on her [mouth]. The rest of [the disciples were offended by it . . .]. They said to him, 'Why do you love her more than all of us?' The Savior answered and said to them. 'Why do I not love you as [I love] her?'[7]

Begg refers to the passage in the *Pistis Sophia* (Faith-Wisdom — the Gnostic Gospel that deals with the post-resurrectional teachings of Jesus, as referred to in Chapter 5) in which Mary tells Jesus of her fear of Peter: 'Peter makes me hesitate, I am afraid of him, because he hates the female race' and adds the comment:

> If we think of this polarity not in personal terms but as two traditions within Christianity, what we see are the church of

Peter, catholic, orthodox, male dominated and victorious, and the rival church of Mary, Gnostic and heretical, worshipping a male/female deity and served by priests of both sexes. [8]

A possible Black Virgin association may be read into a vision of the Sophia experienced by the Sufi mystic Ibn El-Arabi, while on a pilgrimage at the Kaa-ba in Mecca. Housed within the Kaa-ba is a black meteorite, supposedly given to Abraham by the Archangel Gabriel and placed there by Mohammed. This black stone, which is credited with feminine connotations, is highly revered by Muslims.

Much of Begg's work bears the hallmark of his own varied career since leaving Oxford — army officer, headmaster, Dominican friar, hotel and restaurant inspector, and Jungian analyst. However, the conclusions drawn by myself, and doubtless other readers, can be briefly and succinctly summarized in a single sentence: Black Virgins were undoubtedly inherited from the old goddess cults that once dominated Europe and the Middle East, the memories of which have been preserved, albeit unconsciously, in the hearts of the people.

There are several ways in which the Black Virgin phenomena can be interpreted psychologically, but rather than lean on Begg's analysis, sound though it be, I would like to suggest that a clue might possibly be found in the bipolar or sister cults which I have discussed in some detail in Chapter 5. While Isis was the light or visible aspect, her sister Nephthys was the dark or concealed side of the moon — the hidden or unconscious Self, the 'shadow' perhaps. The same polarity can be seen in Inanna and Ereshkigal, Eve and Lilith. Sometimes it is easier to face the lower, earthly self than its transcendental sister. The so-called whoredom of Magdalene, the sensuous expression of sexuality so often associated with women's rites, courtly love, and matrism generally, are more easily absorbed and understood at a certain stage of spiritual development where the importance of the corporeal appears to take precedence over more exalted principles or ideologies. The recent sexual freedom has given full rein to the archetypal Dark Goddess, who has undoubtedly played an important role in the development of the human psyche in that she has helped to free it from the religious straitjacket which defines natural processes as 'sins'.

On the other hand, the Light Goddess (Isis or the Higher Self) now demands her rights. Through her sister we have experienced the body, now it is necessary that we experience the soul or spirit, but with a moderation born of inner knowledge and mental control. By keeping the two in balance we may thus learn the lessons and reap the benefits to be gained from both. It is a recognized psychological fact that over-zealous religiosity and sex are closely linked, frenzy and ecstasy being but a hair's breadth apart. Perhaps we need the Dark Virgin as much as we need the Virgin of Light, which is why the Sophia herself descended to Earth before assuming her position in the 'middle regions' or central point of *balance* between the two poles, and therein lies the mystery. There would appear to be parallels between the Sophia Mythus and the Isis story which prompt one to consider that the Redeeming Principle is, perhaps, the feminine rather than the masculine aspect of the Christos, call it Sophia, Isis or whatever.

I do not see Black Virgins as being necessarily of African origin, although the goddesses in whose image and likeness they were carved may well have come from the African continent via Egypt. They may refer to Isis, as Plantard claims, but are just as likely to allude to her hidden sister Nephthys, the Egyptian Magdalene who lay with her sister's husband and conceived the psychopompos, Anubis, to whom the gods granted safe right-of-way through all the dark regions. They may even descend from the dark and dazzling Hathor?

Feminine Menstrual Rites

The importance of the role played by women in the propagation of the species and therefore the ensured continuance of the tribe, gave rise to the veneration of the female genitalia in many parts of the ancient world. Attempts were therefore made by men to emulate the feminine pudenda, notably the practice of subincision. In many tribes this mutilation followed that of circumcision, the interval between the two operations varying from five to six weeks. As Eliade points out, this mysterious operation has caused ethnologists and psychologists a number of problems, but seen in the ancient Creatrix religious context it easily falls into place. The first consideration is the idea of bisexuality, or perhaps a folk or genetic memory of some androgynous state that existed in aeons past. The second consideration pertains to the religious value of blood. Concerning the practice in Australia, Eliade tells us:

> According to Winthuis, the purpose of subincision is symbolically to give the neophyte a female sex organ, so that he will resemble the divinities, who, Winthuis asserts, are always bisexual. The first thing to be said in this connection is that divine bisexuality is not documented in the oldest Australian cultural strata, for it is precisely in these archaic cultures that the gods are called Fathers. Nor is divine bisexuality found in other really primitive religions. The concept of divine bisexuality seems to be comparatively recent; in Australia, it was probably introduced by cultural waves from Melanesia and Indonesia.
>
> However, there is an element of truth in Winthuis' hypothesis, and that is the idea of *divine totality*. This idea, which is found in a number of primitive religions, naturally implies the coexistence of all the divine attributes, and hence the coalescence of the sexes. [9]

Eliade further asserts that the novice's ritual transformation into a woman during his initiation is a common phenomenon among other cultural areas, and cites the Masai, the Nandi, and the Nuba in Africa; the South African Sotho; the Arioi Society in Tahiti; and other instances in New Guinea and the Torres Strait.

The flow of blood during subincision rites appears to have been of the utmost importance to those tribes in which it was practised. Blood has always held some mysterious association among primitive peoples, who have tended to associate it with the life force; hence the use of red ochre in ceremonial rites of all kinds from birth to death. Likewise, a woman's menstrual flow was deemed sacred among many pagan and pre-Christian communities. For a woman to lose blood at the time of her menses was considered to be healthy, as it rid the body of 'bad' blood, and those evil spirits associated therewith. The men of the tribe therefore sought to emulate this through the practice of subincision.

In their book *The Wise Wound*, Penelope Shuttle and Peter Redgrove draw the reader's attention to the 'Song of Songs', a piece of goddess awareness which by some strange quirk of fate found its way into the Bible (Song of Solomon, Chapter 4):

I am black, but comely, oh ye daughters of Jerusalem . . .
I am the Rose of Sharon,
And the lily of the valleys . . .
As the apple tree among the trees of the wood,
So is my beloved among the sons . . .
Also our bed is green . . .

This is followed by the response from the ardent male who is, no doubt, eager to effect his entrance into this bower of blissful promise!

How beautiful are thy feet with shoes, O prince's daughter!
The joints of thy thighs are like jewels,
The work of the hands of a cunning workman.
Thy navel is like a round goblet, which wanteth not liquor:
Thy belly is like a heap of wheat set about with lilies.
Thy two breasts are like two young roes
That are twins . . .
Now also thy breasts shall be as clusters of the vine,
And the smell of thy nose like apples.

The sexual allusions in the foregoing are obvious, while its Tantric associations are hardly in keeping with the rest of the Old Testament. The 'liquor' referred to is, no doubt, the white or love-juices discharged by women during the fertile days of their cycle, but there is also the red flow of menstruation. The Rabbis considered this to be 'unclean', and consequently sex during that period was strictly taboo because it attracted Lilith, the Dark Bride of Adam, and could therefore induce the birth of monsters or children with peculiar abnormalities. It is interesting to observe the different attitudes adopted towards menstruation — wisdom or evil, light or darkness, hygienic or unhygienic.

Ancient rites and customs exclusive to the female sex have tended to receive less historical coverage than those which are purely male-orientated, although most of the early rites of priesthood and shamanism were open to both sexes. Some of the more secret puberty rites have been less accessible to ethnologists, mainly because they were often individual, and involved the young girl being removed from her family and isolated from the community, the initiation beginning with the break or rupture of the hymen.

The entry into the segregatory state is usually precipitated by the onset of menstruation, which makes for the individuality involved. The length of isolation varies from culture to culture, from three days (Australia and India) to 20 months (New Zealand), and several years in some cases (Cambodia). As the individuals come together, the girls do eventually form into groups, usually under the direction of an older female relative (India), or an old woman of the tribe (Africa). The girls are fully instructed in the secrets of sexuality and fertility, taught the customs of the tribe and those of its religious traditions that are relevant to their future role within it. Certain tribal secrets are not made available to women, just as the secret knowledge relayed from woman to woman is not readily imparted to the men of the tribe. The education given covers both religious and secular duties to the society in question, while also emphasizing the sacrality of women. Each girl is then ritually prepared for her specific role as a creator, and her responsibilities as an adult female. When the time is deemed fit, the young girls are solemnly exhibited to the entire community with a ceremonial announcement that the mystery has been accomplished and they are *shown* to be an adult, which means assuming the modal expression and full responsibilities of womanhood.

Eliade writes:

To show something ceremonially — a sign, an object, an animal, a man — is to declare a sacred presence, to acclaim the miracle of a hierophany. This rite, which is so simple in itself, denotes a religious behaviour that is archaic. Perhaps even before articulate language, solemnly showing an object signified that it was regarded as exceptional, singular, mysterious, sacred. Very probably this ceremonial presentation of the initiated girl represents the earliest stage of the ceremony. The collective dances . . . express the same primordial experience in a way that is at once more plastic and more dramatic. [10]

Oriental Woman

So far little mention has been made of the Orient, China and Japan in particular. For a long period of relatively recent history different religions co-existed in the vast lands of China, the main three being Buddhism, Taoism and

Confucianism. The Chinese *yang* principle is male, hot, dry, and active while the *yin* principle is female, cool, moist, and passive. A balance between these two was viewed by the Chinese as being essential to spiritual growth and understanding. Quan Yin was the eponymous Great Mother of China — 'The Lady Who Brings Children', the embodiment of the *yin* principle. As Chang-O, the moon goddess, she adopted her lunar abode in order to escape the wrath of her husband, I, the Excellent archer, after she had swallowed a drug of immortality which had been given to him by the gods. Quan Yin was also credited with great healing powers, her famous healing shrine at the Temple of Miao Feng Shan (Mountain of the Wondrous Peak), situated about 40 miles from Beijing (Peking), still attracts long lines of pilgrims. People suffering from every kind of sickness travel there to seek her healing energies in much the same way that Christians visit Lourdes.

The goddess Tara, seen in some branches of Buddhism as representing the Great Mother, enjoys recognition far beyond the East. Known from India to Ireland, the etymological root of her name connects with the Hebrew 'Terah', Gaulish 'Taranis', Etruscan 'Turan', Welsh 'Taran' and Irish 'Torann', to name but a few. In India she was one of the most revered pre-Vedic goddesses, equating with the ancient Earth Mother. The plain of Tara in Ireland was the traditional place at which the kings of old Ireland were crowned, while it also provided an assembly point for several ancient Celtic festivals.

The Kali Ma, or Dark Mother, who is the Hindu goddess of creation, preservation and destruction, although better known in her destructive mode also has her benign side. My own feelings concerning these many-aspected deities is that there is a reflective or mirror-like quality about them in that those who invoked them or sought their aid were likely to contact the corresponding aspect of their own psyches, be that the shadow (id), practical/rational, or transpersonal. Once again, like attracts like; we create our deities in our own image and likeness, seeing in them our own conscious and unconscious fears, hostilities, and hopes. The divinities of Hinduism are numerous and complex, but suffice it to say they can be seen to correspond with other deities worldwide of similar historical periods, which more than confirms the 'single source' theory favoured by many researchers and scholars.

A remnant of the past that has come through to present times is the Living Goddess of Nepal, a tradition which goes back more than 600 years. Each Living Goddess is chosen between the age of two and four, and remains a deity until the age of twelve. The candidates for the job are put forward by their parents. The children have to be beautiful and physically perfect, and their courage is put to severe tests to ensure that they are fit for the role. Each candidate is placed in a dark room, lit only by a flickering tallow candle, her only company the hacked-off heads of wild beasts. The winner is she who sheds no tears nor cries for her parents. As the Living Goddess she is worshipped by the king of Nepal, his government ministers and millions of his subjects in the mountainous country south of the Himalayas between India and Tibet. The child elected for the role receives no education and is allowed to emerge into daylight just seven times a year so that the common people may see and worship her.

Upon reaching puberty, the Living Goddess loses her innocence and with it her value as a deity to the Nepalese. She is then released back into the outside world where her chances of marriage are remote, for there is a legend which says that any man who marries a Living Goddess will be dead within six months. It seems a pity that these pathetic little girls should be required to suffer such deprivations in the name of the goddess, but old traditions die hard and even the female ones are not necessarily kind and caring. The Nepalese would, no doubt, tell us that the spirit in question obviously chose the role as part of its karma, knowing full well the disciplines and deprivations involved, so in the final analysis who are we to judge?

In Japanese mythology we meet the Sun goddess, Amaterasu, and her two brothers, Susano the Storm god and Tsuki-Yomi, god of the moon. An older myth, however, refers to the last two of the seven generations of gods as Izanagi and Izanami. Izanagi washed his left eye and gave birth to the sun, Amaterasu, and then he washed his right eye and gave birth to the moon, who assumes a female gender in this version of the tale. There are points of comparison between this myth and that of the right and left eyes of Ra, one of which was allocated to Horus and the other to Sekhmet or Hathor, and later to Bast.

The Americas

The Amerindian tribes of North America vary as regards their approach to both the goddess and the equality of women. In *Daughter of Copper Woman*, Ann Cameron renders a moving account of life among the women of an Indian matriarchal, matrilineal society in western Canada. The patrist settlers, with their twisted, pseudo-religious ethics, inflicted the most terrible suffering upon these gentle people who lived close to Gaia, observing her laws and so benefiting in mind and body. Perhaps a few poignant paragraphs may serve to illustrate the psychological suffering endured by a female society deprived of its natural rites and dignity:

> And then new men arrived. Men who never talked to women, never ate with women, never slept with women, never laughed with women. Men who frowned on singing and dancing, on laughter and love. Men who claimed the Society of Women was a society of witches.
>
> 'Thou shalt not suffer a witch to live,' they insisted, but the people would not allow them to kill the women of the society.
>
> Instead, the priests had to be content to take the girl children. Instead of being raised and educated by women who told them the truth about their bodies, the girls were taken from their villages and put in schools where they were taught to keep their breasts bound, to hide their arms and legs, to never look a brother openly in the eye but to look down at the ground as if ashamed of something. Instead of learning that once a month their bodies would become sacred, they were taught they would become filthy. Instead of going to the waiting house to meditate, pray and celebrate the fullness of the moon and their own bodies, they were taught they were sick, and must bandage themselves and act as if they were sick. They were taught the waves and surgings of their bodies were sinful and must never be indulged or enjoyed.
>
> By the time the girls were allowed home to their villages, their minds were so poisoned, their spirits so damaged, their souls so contaminated they were not eligible for candidacy in the Society of Women.
>
> The boys were taken away, too, and taught that women were filthy, sinful creatures who would tempt a man away from his

true path. They were taught women had no opinion that counted, no mind to be honoured, no purpose other than to serve man.[11]

Many tribes were completely male-dominated, especially those which delighted in fighting for its own sake. Even among these tribes, however, 'Changing Woman', a female deity associated with the moon, was the most divine member of the Navajo pantheon and enjoyed dual status both as 'Turquoise Woman' and 'White Shell Woman', and her sacred jewel was the much prized turquoise. The goddess was certainly in evidence among the Zunis, their following prayer having survived to this day:

Dawn old Woman
Dawn matrons
Dawn maidens,
Dawn girls . . .
Perhaps if we are lucky
Our earth mother
Will wrap herself in a fourfold robe
Of white meal.[12]

The last line doubtless alludes to the moon, although not all Amerindian tribes considered the moon to be feminine. To the Haida of Canada, for example, the moon was Roong, who took a man from earth to keep him company. In his periodic struggles to free himself, the captured man swings the pail of water which he carries, which causes the rain to fall upon earth.

The Hopi Indians of Arizona hold sacred the binary star Sirius, which they called 'Blue Star Kachina'. The Hopis share with the ancient Egyptians and several African tribes the belief that beings from the Sirius system visited Earth in prehistoric times. Since the large blue-white star of this binary system is always seen in the feminine or goddess context, an acknowledgement of the feminine principle would appear to feature strongly in the beliefs of those cultures which favour its worship.

Among the Eskimo deities the goddess Sedna reigns supreme. Sedna lives beneath the sea with her husband who, according to some sources, is a dog. Eskimo shamans, both male and female, often undertake astral visits to her palace beneath the waves to present a plea for help, or ask a favour on behalf of the people of the tribe. The connection with the deep sea and the murky depths of the unconscious is obvious, while Sedna's dog probably shares a common origin with Merlin's Black Dog of Celtic myth, or Anubis, son of the Egyptian Dark Goddess Nephthys who also rules over the waters.

The native peoples of Central and South America appeared to favour dual-aspected deities: Hun-Ahpu-Vuch and Hun-Apu-Mtye (grandfather and grandmother) of Guatemala and Tamagostad and Zipaltonal of Nicaragua, for example. However, from Honduras there comes a rather different tale:

> A white woman of matchless beauty came down from heaven to the town of Cealcoquin. There she built a palace ornamented with strange figures of men and animals, and placed a stone in the chief temple with mysterious figures on three of its sides. It was a talisman which she used to conquer all her enemies.
>
> Although she remained a virgin, she gave birth to three sons; and when she grew old she divided her kingdom with them. Then she had her bed carried to the highest part of the palace, and disappeared into the sky in the form of a beautiful bird. [13]

While subscribers to the 'lost continents' theory will doubtless read Atlantean significance into that one, it could also be seen to present something of a tasty platter to believers in UFOs which, after all, are not recent phenomena — if we are to accord any credence to the legends of the Hopis and other tribes from different parts of the world.

There was a touching programme on BBC-2 television on 17 November 1989 which featured solo circumnavigator Dame Naomi James' voyage to Oceania. Her ports of call included Tonga, Samoa, Tahiti, and Bora Bora, and what she found obviously disturbed her as much as it must have troubled many ecologically-minded and sensitive viewers. She found that the environmental, political, and racial turmoil of this once beautiful paradise had been shattered by a succession of missionaries and others seeking to impose the Western work ethic, with its accompanying standards of competition, unnatural morals, and patrism upon a simple, happy, matrilineal people whose natural values had stood them in good stead for centuries. Her search for the old ways — those crafts, rites, and beliefs that had previously sustained these people — was thwarted. They were no more. The melodious Polynesian voices that had previously sung the old native chants were now heard only in Christian churches ranging from Fundamentalist to Roman Catholic. Dame Naomi listened, and was sad. 'What had happened', she asked, 'to a people that were once great?' Having studied the philosophy of Huna, which is psychologically and metaphysically as sound as anything we have today, I could not help but agree.

Archaic totemism evidences little if any signs of sexual preference or supremacy, nature spirits or animistic objects selected for veneration being accorded both masculine and feminine identities. Patrist programming obviously failed to penetrate the psyches of these simple folk who were doubtlessly more impressed by their immediate surroundings, which they saw as reflecting their own genders — both male and female.

Chapter 7
Women in Religion

THE roles open to women within the confines of established religions have been somewhat limited over the past few centuries, and only the less orthodox have tended to open the doors of their ministries to women on an equal basis with men. In spite of this, many women have found great solace and fulfilment in the mystical and service aspects of religion, their humility and endurance acting as a beacon for those who have elected to follow in their footsteps. Many of the prejudices encountered in orthodoxy go back a very long way, as we shall see, and although liberalism has, to some extent, found its way into religious thinking and practice there is still a strong fundamentalist tendency which does little to enhance the status of women generally. Women who have elected to serve their chosen deity via the path of one of the major world religions suffer particular discrimination.

Judaism

To this day, Jewish males are taught to offer this daily prayer: 'Blessed art Thou O Lord our God, King of the Universe, who has not made me a woman!'[1]

The two nations of Judah and Israel formed part of an isolated patrist society, whose religion was devoted wholly to the worship of a male deity. This was Yahweh or Jehovah, the name of God artificially constructed from the vowels of *Adonai*, 'the Lord', with the Hebrew consonants YHVH (yod-he-vau-he), known as the Tetragrammaton. The original idea behind this encodement was to avoid speaking the real name of God, as it carried a curse. There were, in fact,

many variations of the name in several Semitic dialects —
Yahu, Jah, Jeud, Ieu, Yahweh, Jahveh, Yaho and Iao, while
another version was Yeshua or Jeshua (Latin: Jesus, Joshua
or Jeud). Walker sees it as related to the name of the
Canaanite moon goddess Yareah, who was possibly
androgynous in her original form. The Canaanite mother
goddess Anat of Elephantine also had a husband named
Yahveh. Walker comments:

> The name of god pronounced Jaho, Iao or Ieuw was applied to
> Zeus-Sabazius as the nocturnal sun; a Lord of Death under the
> earth, like Saturn. Jews called him Sabbaoth, 'Lord of Hosts'.
> His Latin name comes from the same roots: Iu-piter, 'Father
> Ieu', that is, Jupiter or Jove. [2]

How these people came to adopt a patrist religion and a
social structure that was out of keeping with that of the
surrounding nations is still hotly debated, although one
cannot fail to observe the Indo-Aryan derivations in the
above-mentioned etymology, Zeus being the Greek form of
the Sanskrit *Dyaus Pitar*, 'Father Heaven'.

Merlin Stone refers to the Ammonites of Canaan, a
people with whom the Hebrews were in repeated conflict
and whose women acted in official capacities. Stone quotes
the archaeologist B. Landes, who wrote: 'the superior
position of women [was] in agreement with nomadic
practice.' [3] The Queen of Sheba (c.950 BC), for example, and
other female monarchs, were known to have led Arab states
and tribes, a fact that was attested in the eighth and seventh
centuries BC.

The status of the Israelite women in those times
contrasted strongly with the economic, legal, and social
position of the women in surrounding cultures. Scriptural
texts refer to Israelite laws as dating from the time of Moses
(c.1300-1250 BC), these being strictly observed until the fall
of the northern kingdom of Israel in 722 BC, and the
southern kingdom of Judah in 586 BC. The same laws are
still extant in the Old Testament of the Judaeo-Christian
Bible to this day. Stone gives us the following observations
from archaeologist and priest Roland de Vaux, taken from
his book *Ancient Israel*:

> The social and legal position of an Israelite wife was inferior
> to the position of a wife occupied in the great countries round

about . . . all the texts show that Israelites wanted mainly sons, to perpetuate the family line and fortune, and to preserve the ancestral inheritance . . . a husband could divorce his wife . . . women on the other hand could not ask for divorce . . . the wife called her husband Ba'al or master; she also called him adon or lord; she addressed him in fact as a slave addressed his master or a subject, his king. The Decalogue includes a man's wife among his possessions . . . all her life she remains a minor. The wife does not inherit from her husband, nor daughters from their father, except when there is no male heir. A vow made by a girl or married woman needs, to be valid, the consent of the father or husband and if this consent is withheld, the vow is null and void. A man had the right to sell his daughter. Women were excluded from the succession.[4]

No women priests or priestesses were allowed in the Hebrew faith, a distinction which did not exist in other cultures in the Near East. The Assyrians, for example, favoured priestesses, while there was a hierarchy of priest-esses in Phoenicia, including a high priestess. Taking this into account it is little wonder that Peter was so hostile to Magdalene (see Chapter 6), while something is to be said for the person of Jesus (assuming there to be some substance in the Gnostic gospels) in accepting female disciples, one in particular with whom he may well have enjoyed a warm relationship. But as theologians would doubtless hasten to assure us, apocryphal and pseudo-epigraphic works carry no credence among orthodox scholars, and cannot therefore be seen as relevant to the canon of Christian teachings.

In addition to the fact that Hebrew law denied women entitlement to money, property, or the right to engage in business following divorce, a woman could be stoned or burned to death for losing her virginity before marriage. Should she fall victim to a rapist, she was forced to marry him, and if she was already betrothed or married she was stoned to death *for having been raped*. This inequality of the sexes was carried to such an extreme that upon death the body of the husband was placed at a higher level than that of his wife, so that her inferior status was also upheld after her death.

Queenly figures did, of course, occasionally slip through the patriarchal net, although those who did, notably Queen Maacah, were usually accused of 'heathen' or 'pagan' practices somewhere along the line. In 842 BC Athaliah, daughter of Queen Jezebel, laid claim to the throne of Judah which she managed to hold for six years, during which time she set about re-establishing the pagan religion, much to the horror of the Hebrew priests. Hebrew law forbade women to rule alone, but in spite of this it took a violent revolution to bring about her eventual dethronement. Athaliah's grandparents had been the high priest and priestess of Ashtoreth and Ba'al in Sidon, where they also reigned as king and queen. The murder of their daughter, Jezebel, who was also closely identified with the ancient religion, could therefore be seen as a political assault against the worship of the goddess.

Fundamentalism is by no means limited to any one faith, however, and although in the present age certain branches of Judaism have become liberalized, there are still many who prefer to adhere to the old ways and archaic laws. Whether or not one subscribes to Judaism, it is still a joy to see and hear Rabbi Julia Neuberger on our television screens, although, no doubt, there are many extremists within her own faith who raise their hands heavenwards in horror every time she speaks!

Some of the sexual taboos of Judaism, including abstinence during the period of the menses and following childbirth, were highlighted in a 1989 television series about menstruation. Jewish women are considered 'unclean' for 7 plus 33 days after the birth of a boy, and 14 plus 66 days consequent to the birth of a girl (the mother apparently takes on the girl-child's uncleanliness). Several Jewish women who were interviewed on the programme seemed perfectly happy with the arrangement, seeing in it a chance for husband and wife to come to know each other as people, rather than as sexual objects. Sincere friendships resulted from adherence to this ancient law, we were told, and there seemed little doubt that some, if not all of the women concerned were quite content with the Hebraic law on this issue.

Christianity

It is sometimes forgotten that much Christian doctrine comes from Judaism. Accustomed to seeing romanticized pictures and statues of a blond, blue-eyed Jesus, many Christians fail to recall that he was a Jew, and therefore steeped in the religion and laws of Judaism. Sometimes one cannot help wondering whether modern Christianity is based on the teachings of Paul rather than those of Jesus, since so much credence is placed upon the Pauline texts, especially among theologians. Christianity, of course, has many branches, not all of which agree among themselves. With such diversity it is little wonder that there is a deal of confusion as to what the founder originally taught or, indeed, who he was and how he lived.

Much of what appears in the Old Testament of the Bible is purely Hebrew myth, and therefore no more or less valid than the mythologies of any other ancient nation. On the subject of Jesus I am more inclined to give credence to the writings of Jewish scholars, such as Geza Vermes and the late Hugh Schonfield. Vermes, writing in *Jesus the Jew*, helps to throw light on the much debated problem of the women in the life of Jesus. He remarks on the complete silence in the Gospels concerning the marital status of Jesus and that no wife is recorded as having accompanied him in his public career — or even stayed at home. Such a state of affairs was, according to Vermes, 'sufficiently unusual in ancient Jewry to prompt further enquiry, for the Hebrew Bible, though it prescribes temporary sexual abstinence in certain circumstances, never orders a life of total celibacy.'[6]

As regards the married state or otherwise of the Hassid, or Rabbi, according to some authorities rabbinical literature suggests that in those days it was considered the religious duty of every man to enter the state of marriage for the purpose of procreating children. Vermes cites an instance when Rabbi Eliezer ben Hyrcanus, at the end of the first century AD, compared deliberate abstention from pro-creation to murder, as did his contemporary Simeon ben Azzai. The latter being himself unmarried, however, it was only natural that his colleagues should accuse him of not practising what he preached! Among the Hassidim, or holy men, devoutness, fear of sin, humility and sexual absti-nence were seen as essential to the reception of the holy spirit and the gift of true prophecy.

Women were apparently declared taboo to soldiers on campaign, and participation in any act of worship entailed

abstention from intercourse on the grounds of ritual uncleanliness which was believed to last until the following
evening. The same taboo also applied to contact with a
menstruating woman, as we have already discussed. Sexual
life among priests and those involved in Temple rites
therefore called for a disciplined regulation of sexual
activity. The Essenes, on the other hand, with whom Jesus
is believed by some esotericists to have studied, while not
excluding women or marriage (other than during the
42-year-long eschatological war) appear to have followed a
strictly celibate path.

Philo, Pliny the Elder, and Josephus all commented freely
on the subject of the Essenes, the latter translating their
celibacy as pure misogyny. The Therapeutae, or Egyptian
branch of the Essenes was believed to consist of celibate
men and elderly virgins. Writing on *The Contemplative Life*
Philo has this to say concerning the women Therapeuts:

> And women also share in the banquet, most of whom have
> grown old in virginity, preserving their purity not from
> necessity (as some of the priestesses among the Greeks) but
> rather of their own free-will, through their zealous love of
> wisdom, with whom they are so keenly desirous of spending
> their lives that they pay no attention to the pleasures of the
> body. Their longing is not for mortal children, but for a
> deathless progeny which the soul that is in love with God can
> alone bring forth, when the Father has implanted it in those
> spiritual light-beams, with which it shall contemplate the
> laws of wisdom. There is, however, a division made between
> them in their places at table, the men being apart on the right,
> and the women on the left.[7]

The only women to feature prominently in the New
Testament are Mary the Virgin, who conceives a child
without having sex, and Mary Magdalene, traditionally
viewed as a prostitute because, no doubt, she had sex
without conceiving a child. We would seem to be faced
once again with those two aspects of the goddess — the
maternal Eve and the licentious Lilith. The scant and, no
doubt, prejudiced account of the activities of Mary
Magdalene provided by the scriptures fails to show her in
what Christians would no doubt term a 'moral' light. There
is, however a school of thought that designates her as the
wife of Jeshua bar Josephus, but because it was not seen fit

to permit knowledge of his role in the conception of children, she was conveniently relegated to a less favourable position in the society of the time.

Many feminist writers express strong opinions regarding the role played by St Paul in the denigration of women in the early Christian church. This is little wonder, however, when one encounters such statements as: 'For a man ought not to cover his head, since he is the image and glory of God; but woman is the glory of man' (1 Cor. 11:7). Walker suggests Paul's antipathy towards women leads to a suspicion that he might well have been linked to the early Christian practice of voluntary castration, recommended by Jesus for 'the kingdom of heaven's sake' (Matthew 19:12). After all, Paul was a Roman citizen and a noted admirer of Roman culture, and the self-castrated god Attis was certainly popular in Rome in those times. Tertullian suggested that eunuchs might well gain easy access to heaven and there are passages in Paul's writings which suggest he was inclined in this direction: 'They that are Christ's have crucified the flesh with the affections and lusts' (Galatians 5:24). As Walker points out: 'He often mentioned, but never described, his mysterious "infirmity" which he called a "light affliction, which is but for a moment" though it would bring him eternal glory' (11 Cor. 4:17).[8]

While Walker's observations may or may not be correct, many feminists are of the opinion that Paul did untold harm to countless generations of women, both Christian and otherwise, and to Christian doctrine.

With this background, it is little wonder that St Augustine (AD 354–430) declared women to have no souls, as a consequence of which medieval scholars debated whether they might not first have to be changed into men by God in order to qualify on the day of resurrection.

The recent altercation in the Anglican church on the subject of the ordination of women has, no doubt, caused much soaring of blood-pressure on both sides. Clergy and laity alike are divided in their views, to the extent that many priests have threatened to dissassociate themselves from that particular branch of Christianity if the motion to ordain women is passed by the General Synod. The biologist Rupert Sheldrake wrote a controversial article for the *Guardian* (5 September 1988) entitled 'Forget Women

Priests, Bring On The Priestess'. What would a Christian priestess be like, he questioned? No different from a woman priest would be the logical answer, but as he points out:

> At present most supporters of the ordination of women react strongly against the idea of priestesses. They prefer to think of 'women priests' for several reasons. First, priestesses sounds pagan. Second, women should be called priests for the same feminist reasons that poetesses should be called poets. And third, what is being proposed is that women should enter a previously all-male priesthood, and fulfil the same functions that men have performed in the past. It is not being suggested that as women they could be priestesses, and as such bring a radically new element into the Church.

Sheldrake then goes on to comment on the resurgence of interest within the Women's Movement in goddesses and the feminine aspects of the sacred, which he sees as a distinctively feminine divine principle which calls for recognition rather than denial. This can perhaps be found, he suggests, within the Trinity of the Holy Spirit, since the word for spirit in Hebrew is *ruah*, which is feminine. Backing his argument with scriptural references he calls his reader's attention to the role of Magdalene as the first witness to the Resurrection and concludes his argument with the statement:

> Perhaps Marian priestesses may soon emerge within the Church. I for one would welcome this development. But in any case, if we have women priests, who will be able to stop them turning into priestesses in fact, if not in name?

Whether one elects to acknowledge, or serve, the creative principle in masculine or feminine form is hardly germane to the issue of women's rights. Perhaps, as Sheldrake suggests, if Christianity was to drop the concept of the 'Holy Spirit' and reinstitute the Sophia, either as the Bride of Christ, or as his mother, this would help to gain acceptance for the idea of gender equality.

The Catholic church has canonized many women, although some women would appear to be unhappy with the idealized feminine images presented in Christian sainthood. Equally, it has spawned many great women Christian mystics whose exemplary lives and spiritual values have served as an inspiration to both men and women alike.

Simone de Beauvoir, in *The Second Sex*, remarks:

> Queen Isabella, Queen Elizabeth, Catherine the Great were neither male nor female — they were sovereigns. It is remarkable that their femininity, when socially abolished, should have no longer meant inferiority: the proportiion of queens who had great reigns is infinitely above that of great kings. Religion works the same transformation: Catherine of Siena, St. Theresa, quite beyond any physiological considera-tion, were sainted souls; the life they led, secular and mystic, their acts, and their writings, rose to heights that few men have ever reached. [9]

I find it strange that a branch of Christianity that denies sexual expression to its priests and eschews the idea of women in the ministry should have kept alive the feminine principle in the person of the Virgin Mary. Not that I am at all convinced about her 'virginity' on both logical and metaphysical grounds, but since this constitutes an argu-ment that is irrelevant to the present subject matter it is better left for discussion at another time. Mary seems to make visionary appearances somewhat frequently, her Lourdes visitation probably being the best known. In her book, *Mother of Nations: Visions of Mary*, Joan Ashton also lists:

> Our Lady of Good Counsel, Genazzano, Rome.
> Our Lady of Czestachowa, Poland.
> Our Lady of Guadalupe, Spain.
> Our Lady of Haddington, Scotland.
> Our Lady of Mount Carmel, Palestine.
> Our Lady of Perpetual Help, Rome.
> Our Lady of Reconciliation, Walsingham, England.
> Our Lady of Salette, France.
> Our Lady of Sion, Israel.
> Our Lady of Victories, Paris.
> Our Lady of Willesden, England.
> Our Lady of the White Kirk, Scotland. [10]

One cannot help wondering whether these many mani-festations of Mary were not, in fact, aspects of the Great Mother or one of the old goddesses, translated into Christian terms by the beholders, since they knew no other.

We must finally consider — and this applies to other religions as well as Christianity — those who have chosen to live their lives in solitude or service: the monks and nuns of this world. I have frequently heard nuns criticized as being 'sexually unnatural' or 'frustrated old spinsters'. Unfortunately, the stories and 'disclosures' of those who have taken the veil and latterly 'escaped' have done little to enhance the general picture of life behind the convent walls. Of course, there are open orders, and many dedicated women have been able to go about their tasks of caring and serving, either privately or publicly, without the stigmas or innuendoes associated with a segregated life where members of one sex live in close contact.

Perhaps there are times during our evolutionary journeys when we may need to undertake a life of silent contemplation or selfless service, during which we eschew the pleasures of the flesh and the world generally. Or, we may seek sexual segregation in order to make contact with a particular aspect of our psyche, the anima or animus, perhaps, unhampered by the false emphases favoured by currently popular collectives. There is nothing unnatural in this as long as it is not generated by false beliefs or the insistence of others, in which case it is likely to cause psychological disorders or somatizations that are frequently the outcome of subconscious dichotomies.

Islam

According to Merlin Stone, Mohammed is said to have stated, 'When Eve was created, Satan rejoiced',[11] which is surprising, since historical accounts indicate that the Prophet did not appear to have been unduly upset by the women in his life. He married his first wife, Khadijah, at the age of 25. She was described as 'a rich and noble widow of matronly virtues' who brought him domestic content and happiness. Shortly after the year of the Hegira (AD 622) he married A'isha, who was then little more than a child, but who, we are told, 'acquired and maintained great power over him'. From his first wife he had two sons and four daughters. The sons unfortunately died early. One daughter, Fatima, married Alibar Abu Talib and it is from this union that the Shiite Muslims trace their descent from Mohammed.[12] A Muslim dynasty known as the Fatimids ruled over parts of North Africa and Egypt between AD 909 and 1171. The Fatimids claimed the Caliphate through descent from

Fatima, who died in 632 and is considered by Muslims to be one of the Four Perfect Women, and her husband who was one of the first to embrace the Islamic faith.

In the seventh century Mohammed brought an end to the national worship of the Sun Goddess, Al Lat, and the goddess known as Al Uzza, and installed the worship of Allah as the supreme god. Many of the old legends and attitudes of the Old and New Testaments of the Bible were subsequently incoporated into the Koran. For example, Sura 4: 31 tells us: 'Men have authority over women because God has made the one superior to the other and because they spend their wealth to maintain them. So good women are obedient, guarding the unseen parts as God has guarded them.'[13] In spite of this, however, to this day there exists an Arabic mystic system which preserves a Tantric form of goddess and woman worship, namely Sufism (see Chapter 8).

Walker tells us that Islamic mosques still bear signs reading: 'Women and dogs and other impure animals are not permitted to enter.'[14] One wonders whether this also refers to cats, since the Prophet was, according to tradition, extremely fond of them. The story goes that while living in Damascus he had a cat called Muezza, who used to curl up inside the sleeve of his robe. On one occasion, when the Prophet had to go out, it is said that he cut off his sleeve rather than disturb the cat's sleep. Mohammad was often seen preaching from the highest tower in Mecca, holding the cat in his arms. In her book *Cult of the Cat*, Patricia Dale-Green assures us: 'Mohammedans still treat cats well: the animal beloved of their Prophet is allowed freely to enter Mosques, and the killing of cats is illegal.'[15]

Hinduism

According to the Hindu Code of Manu V: 'A woman must never be free of subjugation.'[16] This statement aligns Hinduism with those other patriarchal structures that rely upon the subjugation of the female for the continuation of their power. As Christina Feldman observes, the scriptures of world religions may differ in their spiritual credos, but when it comes to their beliefs concerning the role of woman they are unanimous: *she is inferior*.

The patrist takeover of the goddess-worshipping Dravidians by the Indo-Aryan Brahmins has already received ample coverage in an earlier chapter, although to this day much store is placed upon the importance of boy-children in India. This is understandable, since Brahminism still constitutes the most powerful force within this religion. However, the old goddesses are still worshipped among the Hindus, Brahma having taken something of a back seat.

There would appear to be a connection between Brahma and the Hebrew Abraham, whose name means 'Father Brahm'. The patrist-orientated emphases in both religions certainly bear some striking similarities. The legend of Jonah, for example, was prefigured by the Hindu story of Candragomin. Brahma's wife was Sarasvati, goddess of music, wisdom and knowledge, the creator of the Vedas. It was she who invented the devanagari alphabet, Sanskrit, which suggests that at some point in the distant past women played a vital intellectual role in the culture of the Indian sub-continent. Larousse refers to the theoretical starting point of Indian mythology as encompassing three different factors — Munda, Dravidian and Aryan — and comments that the former two have left no direct traces in very early times, only appearing later through the medium of Brahminic literature — the Vedas. Since Brahminism is predominantly patrist, any references to an earlier matrist society is probably biased and cannot, therefore, be relied upon for accuracy. A few goddess-orientated beliefs have, however, found their way through to the present day. The nature of the goddess Kali is one example, which, when viewed in the wider mythological context, can be seen to represent the combined principles of destruction and regeneration, so essential to evolutionary progress. She also has her equivalents in other pantheons, the Egyptian Sekhmet and the Irish Morrigan, for example. However, it seems paradoxical that Hindu women on the whole play a very subordinate part in Indian society, which appears to have very little connection with the strong and powerful role model symbolized by Kali.

Although some women, notably the late Indira Gandhi, may be seen to feature in the politics of the East, we hear little, if anything, concerning their activities in the area of

the Hindu religion due, no doubt, to their subservient
position within that faith. In spite of this, it has been the
practice of yoga, championed mainly by women, that has
helped to open the way to a knowledge and understanding
of the deeper spiritual mysteries behind many of the beliefs
that originated in the old pre-Brahminic goddess cults of
India and surrounding nations.

Buddhism

The mystical tenets of Buddhism are said to carry the
notion that it is not possible for a female to attain the
control of the Crown Centre, or 'thousand petalled Lotus',
which is believed to be indicative of supreme enlightenment; she has to move further along the evolutionary path
by reincarnating as a male before she can handle such
exalted energies! In the 'Sutra on Changing the Female Sex'
the Buddha makes this quite clear:

> The female's defects — greed, hate and delusion and other
> defilements — are greater than the male's ... You [women]
> should have such an intention ... Because I wish to be freed
> from the impurities of the woman's body, I will acquire the
> beautiful and fresh body of a man.[17]

Tsultrim Allione, who was herself ordained as a Buddhist
nun tells us:

> When the Buddha's aunt, Mahaprajapati, who had nursed him
> in his childhood when his mother died, approached him
> asking that women be admitted to the Buddhist monastic
> order, the Sangha, he refused her. Then she and a group of
> women shaved their heads and followed him to another town,
> and with the intercession of the monk Ananda he finally, with
> reluctance, admitted women to the order, on condition that
> they take eight extra vows. These vows were all orientated
> towards keeping women under the control of the male
> monastic community. For example, the first of these vows is
> that any nun, no matter what degree of knowledge or
> realization she possesses, must treat any monk, even the
> rudest novice, as if he were her senior.
>   By admitting women into the monastic community,
> creating a community of nuns, the Buddha said that the life
> of the Sangha would be shortened by five hundred years. The
> women were thought to have an uncontrolled sexuality and
> longing for motherhood.[18]

Christina Feldman, who spent five years in India studying Buddhist philosophy and meditation in both the Mahayana and the Theravadin traditions, tells us that the elders of Theravadin Buddhism proclaim that women may not assume the role of a fully ordained *bhikkuni*. Instead, it is suggested to those women wishing to pursue this path that they explore their inner potential for service and humility.[19] However, she hastens to assure us: 'We are dispossessed of our own power and effectiveness only as long as we are possessed by our own belief in the source of power lying in centres and structures outside ourselves.'[20]

Despite claims made by Buddhist ascetics that Buddha had charged the true sage never to see or speak to a woman and avoid feminine creatures like the plague, it only took a few centuries for the worship of the goddess to reassert itself via Tantra, in which the Bodhisattvas were conveniently provided with Shaktis who would welcome them to a heaven of eternal bliss, sexual and otherwise! Buddhist legends highlight the constant tension that existed between the sensual and ascetic elements, while later generations of monks sought to destroy the goddess and all she stood for. In the words of an old Buddhist hymn: 'This time I shall devour thee utterly, Mother Kali; for I was born under an evil star — and one so born becomes, they say, the eater of his mother.'[21] However, the female Bodhisattvas and Dakinis still feature prominently in the higher initiations of Mahayana and Vajrayana Buddhism.

The name 'Dakini' is said to mean 'skywalker'. Tsultrim Allione refers to the Dakini as 'the most important manifestation of the feminine in Tibetan Buddhism.'[22] The Dakinis were Tantric priestesses who were believed to embody the spirit of Kali Ma in her role as the Angel of Death. Although the Dakinis were mostly older women, young women were occasionally found among them as the representatives or embodiment of the divine Shakti, who planted the kiss of peace on the lips of the enlightened ones. Dakinis were present at the time of death, when they offered comfort and hope to the withdrawing spirit. However, there were also fierce Dakinis who represented violent or painful departures. Since they were so closely associated with death, their rites of passage and subsequent funerary preparations were frequently held in cemeteries or cremation grounds. As this is a subject that demands a much longer commentary than I have space to include, those readers wishing to pursue the study in depth are recommended to Allione's book, *Women of Wisdom*, several pages of which are devoted to its explanation.

Tara, the female saviour of Buddhism, has already been discussed in an earlier chapter. The name Buddha is purely titular, and means 'Enlightened or Blessed One'. As such it is comparable to the Christos, 'the Anointed One'. The Buddha who appeared in the fifth century BC, who is credited with the founding of Buddhism, counted among his names Gautama, Sakyamuni and Siddhartha, the last of which is again titular and means 'rich in yogic power'. Incidentally, the Buddha's key initiation under the Bodhi Tree is believed to have been given by the Earth Goddess herself.

Correspondences between Eastern religions such as Buddhism and Hinduism and Christianity are to be found in tales of virgin births. China's Shin-Mu (Mother of Perfect Intelligence), for example, 'miraculously conceived her first-born son, a Saviour and spirit of the grain. Her infant "came like a lamb, with no bursting or rending, with no hurt or harm," and was tenderly adored by sheep and oxen.'[23] But then similar myths also appear in other mythologies such as those of Egypt and Greece, albeit differently presented.

Chapter 8
Magical and Mystical Woman

WOMEN have always been associated with mysticism, magic, and similar 'right-brain' pursuits, but since there have also been male magi, mystics, shamans, medicine men, witch doctors and the like, this naturally raises the question: are women more psychically gifted than men? Traditionally it has been believed that because woman was weak at the physical level, on which she played the receptive or subservient role, she was powerful on the psychic or spiritual planes. Jung evidently found sufficient evidence of this to warrant the following observation:

> Wholeness consists in the union of the conscious and the unconscious personality. Just as every individual derives from masculine and feminine genes, and the sex is determined by the predominance of the corresponding genes, so in the psyche it is only in the conscious mind, in the man, that has the masculine sign, while the unconscious is by nature feminine. The reverse is true in the case of a woman. [1]

In commenting on the feminine principle, or Eros, Dr M. Esther Harding, while concurring with Jung, was careful to emphasize that it functions in man as well as woman. She tells us:

> But while in woman her conscious personality is under the guidance of this principle, in man it is not his conscious but his unconscious that is related to the Eros. His conscious personality, being masculine, is under the masculine rule of Logos. In the unconscious, however, he is given over to the 'other side'. There his soul, which mankind has consistently regarded as feminine, rules. This feminine soul of man is the anima. The nature of his anima, and his relation to her determine the nature of his relations to women and his own

inner relations to that spiritual realm over which the anima rules.[2]

A brief look at the functions of the two brain hemispheres, so much discussed in modern psychology, might help us to recognize some of these masculine/feminine references in anatomical terms. These two hemispheres, which are joined by the corpus callosum, have become associated with different kinds of mental activity. The left hemisphere, which operates in what I refer to as 'inner', or linear, time is generally concerned with logic, analytical abilities, mathematics, and day-to-day practical matters. The right hemisphere, which governs creativity, spatial perception, musical and visual appreciation, and intuition, tends to function in 'outer' time, or a state of timelessness — hence its strong connection with the paranormal. The third player in the psychic drama is believed by many researchers to be the hindbrain, or rhombencephalon, the portion of the embryonic brain from which the metencephalon, myelencephalon and medulla oblongata develop. The hindbrain's association with primeval development has recently been linked with the collective unconscious on the one hand, and certain instinctive awareness patterns on the other.

Metaphysically speaking, these three areas of the brain are seen to correspond to the reasoning, intuitive, and instinctive aspects of our nature respectively. Their role in the evolutionary drama is obvious: we commence our cycle using only our instincts or hindbrains, after which we become aware of our left-brain logic and how it can be applied to make life more comfortable for us at the physical/material level. Having exhausted this rather limited range of expression, we experience the realization of right-brain intuition through which we can make contact with energies, essences, and intelligences both immediate and external to our material environment. We may observe the same pattern repeated in our stages of development within one life cycle. From the instinctive patterns of childhood we progress to the logical reasoning of maturity, and thence to the intuitive wisdom that comes (or should come) with age. Earlier cultures sometimes related these phases to the maiden, mother and crone aspects of the Triple Goddess.

If women are believed by psychiatrists and metaphysicians to be more powerful, or to function more effectively via their right-brain hemispheres, while men excel in activities of the left brain, does this mean that the psychic realm is the prerogative of the female sex? Unfortunately, the term 'psychic' is all too frequently used to describe a whole range of preternatural activities such as extra-sensory perception, altered states of consciousness, out-of-body experiences, prescience, psychometry, clairvoyance, astral projection, trance mediumship (channelling), and several other modes of paranormal perception which are known collectively to the psychologist as 'cryptaesthesia'. The recent contribution of semantics from the various schools of psychology and parapsychology have added to the confusion, with the result that many of these terms have come to mean different things to different people.

My own study of the broad spectrum of mystical pursuits that shelter beneath the metaphysical umbrella has indicated four basic definitions:

1. The psychic or mediumistic person, who is telepathically receptive or sensitive to other minds, incarnate or discarnate, or energy frequencies totally alien to his or her immediate environmental programming. Genuine psychics are also able to tap the collective unconscious which exists independently of time and space — hence their ability to 'see' the past and future.

2. The occultist or magus, who strives to manipulate cosmic forces or subtle energies by the use of mind or willpower, a skill which is slowly (and often painfully) mastered by means of a series of disciplines known as initiations.

3. The mystic, who is frequently of religious leanings and extends his or her faith a step or more beyond the accepted dogmas of orthodoxy, choosing to seek both within and without for the answers to life's enigmas. Illumination may well be experienced during this observatory process, but the knowledge gained is not necessarily employed in the practice of either psychism or occultism.

4. The shaman, who is usually gifted with healing PK (psychokinetic energy), tends to make use of 1, 2 and 3 depending upon the needs demanded by the occasion.

The preponderance of women in the world of mediumship and psychism is really no more than a carry-over from the old village 'wise woman' who dispensed herbal remedies, gave counselling where necessary, and frequently maintained shamanic contact with the 'ancestors'. Many such women were later labelled 'witches', regardless of whether they actually practised the 'Old Religion', and for anyone with a political or personal axe to grind, the finger of accusation proved a totally devastating and mostly fatal weapon. As a result, many harmless and innocent women met their ends in horrendous ways.

Cambridge parapsychologist Dr Carl Sargent, and the famous psychiatrist Professor Hans Eysenck, have the following to say regarding the differences between men and women where the psychic faculty is concerned:

> Virtually every survey in existence shows a major sex difference in relation to spontaneous psi (psi experienced in everyday life). Women tend to have more ESP experiences than men or, to anticipate the argument, they *say* they do, while men are in the majority as 'senders'. This looks suspiciously like a reflection of the well-worn masculine/feminine stereotypes — passive males, intuitive females receiving messages and dynamic, dominant males sending them (the popular image of telepathy is that the 'sender' sends a signal to the 'receiver'). There may be a real difference, or simply a bias in responding to surveys. Both women and men are more likely to report experiences which conform with stereotyped sex roles. Women report more ESP experiences generally, especially in the passive role of 'receiver'. Men, on the hand, report fewer experiences, with a strong bias towards those in which they play an active role.
>
> Most experimental investigations of sex differences in ESP have focussed on children, but for every experiment in which girls have outshone boys to a degree inexplicable by chance, there is another experiment which shows the reverse.
>
> Research with adults has not yielded any clear, simple sex difference either . . . we cannot totally rule out the possibility that there may be a basic difference between the sexes in ESP ability. Nevertheless, dozens of experiments have failed to discover it, in which case it is perhaps reasonable to assume

that there is no difference, in fact. That does not mean that social mythology will not manufacture a difference or two.[3]

What our learned friends did discover, however, was that *the most accurate* psychism came from stable extraverts, which kills once and for all the myth that those thus gifted — and the finger is inevitably pointed at women — are unstable or hysterical neurotics.

At the inaugural seminar of my own Institute of Transpersonal Sensitivity in California in the spring of 1989, experiments I carried out in various types of sensitivity/psi/PK tended to confirm Eysenck and Sargent's findings, since those present of both sexes (all of whom were qualified in sociology or one of the psychologies) displayed equal talents.

In so far as paranormal gifts are concerned, while it is conceded that women are, on the whole, less physically strong than men, there does not appear to be any empirical evidence that this weakness is compensated by additional energies or magical powers during OOBEs (out-of-body experiences) or ASCs (altered states of consciousness). This must not be taken as 'gospel', however, since parapsychology is still in its infancy and the technology it employs at present may, in time, be replaced by more sensitive instruments.

During the many years I spent training both men and women in the practical, ethical, and spiritual manipulation of PK and allied psychic phenomena, I observed that these talents were *not* decided by sex, but more by the anima/animus emphases in their personalities. A man with a well developed anima usually made an excellent psychic or 'receiver', and a woman whose animus was in evidence could become a first-class 'sender' or occultist. Experience has tended to show that reliable ESP requires a blend of both right-brain intuition and left-brain logic, the latter being essential to the rational evaluation of the extra-sensory input. I basically agree with Eysenck and Sargent: stable extraverts, men *or* women, with a balanced anima/animus, are the best and most reliable to deal with at the metaphysical level.

As regards those 'basic differences' which are so strongly emphasized by experts such as Harding and Whitmont and, indeed, Jung himself, I am inclined to think that the ancient Greeks understood our psychology perhaps a little better than we do. Let us take the Female Warrior archetype epitomized by the goddess Athene as an example. One cannot conceive of such a woman being weak or submissive at the material level. However, we will be according that aspect of our study more space in Chapter 9 by taking a look at how it has worked with well known personalities from the past who have exemplified a particular feminine archetype, and again in Chapter 10 when I shall be proffering my own interpretation of the various manifestations of the feminine psyche.

Those who do subscribe to the idea that woman's power lies in being an initiatrix on the 'inner planes' tend to believe that by neglecting to value her gifts of wisdom and intuition men have failed to be transformed fully by her influence, resulting in a patristic society overly committed to a sterile rationalism and a mechanistic view of life. The imbalance is obvious to any thinking person: things are not as they should be. Women do not enjoy equal status with men. My critics will doubtless counter with the argument that men and women cannot be equal because they are 'different'. They may certainly *appear* to be different at present, but *should* they be?

Leaving sociology aside for one moment, let us turn our attention to the magical and mystical role women have played over the years since Constantine (AD 285-337) established Christianity as the state religion of Rome, and how the goddess herself has fared during this period of spiritual gloom. Due to ignorance on the one hand, and erroneous religious indoctrination on the other, the words 'magic' and 'occult' are calculated to conjure up illogical fears in many people, which is a pity since the word occult simply means 'hidden' — that which is not normally perceived with the fives senses. 'Magic' derives from the Greek words *magus* (magician) and *mageia* (magic), which are merely permutations of the words *mog*, *megh* and *magh*, which in Pehivi and Zend (both archaic languages of the East) signify 'priest', 'wise' and 'excellent'.[4]

Mythology is rich in tales of female magicians, from Circe the Enchantress of Greek legend to the Celtic Morgan le Fay. The Nine Maidens who tended the Cauldron of inspiration and regeneration, which appears in the myths of many ancient traditions, were also credited with great physical powers, such as the raising of storms, in addition to their gifts of second sight.

As patrism slowly spread its suffocating cloak across the face of womanhood, women were less able to function as magi, although as seers their help was often sought privately. Yet in spite of all this the goddess still managed to make her presence felt in other ways, albeit subtly. The Middle Ages abounded with strange, pre-Christian tales which were transmitted orally from generation to genera-tion in much the same way that African tribal history is passed on. The Druidic concept of Keridwen's Cauldron, the initiatory properties of which had been long since forgotten, surfaced again in the cup of the Holy Grail. Feminine mysteries were also believed to be concealed within the concept of courtly love, with its strange blend of the erotic and the spiritual. According to some researchers, courtly love derived from the Arabian mystical system of Sufism, which preserved a Tantric form of goddess and woman worship. As the troubadours and bards sang the praises of courtly love, so the Sufi poets sang of its spiritual signifi-cance as exemplified in the female form of Fravishi, or 'Spirit of the Way'. The universe, they claimed, was co-alesced by the feminine forces of motherhood and sexuality. The extreme patrism of Islam, however, obliged them to disguise their doctrines in a mystical system of allegorical symbols. Sufi doctrine ordained that mankind can find spiritual fulfilment through the expression of love and the realization that woman is a ray of the Deity. Walker tells us that the word Sufi contained:

> in enciphered form, the concept of Love. Deciphered, it reduced by the Arabic numerological system to three letters: FUQ, meaning 'that which is transcendent'. Under the same language system, the title of the singer was Ta Ra B, which picked up the Spanish suffix — ador — and became 'troubadour'.[5]

The suggestion is, therefore, that the Moorish-Saracen tradition that emanated from Spain and the Middle East following the Crusades contributed to the rise and sub-sequent popularity of courtly love which swept across

Europe during the twelfth and fourteenth centuries. This goddess-orientated love cult stood out in stark contrast to the patrist severity of Islam. The Sufism of today, however, has adjusted its concepts to accommodate Christian prayer, and certain pagan/animistic schools of belief, in addition to its own fundamentalism.

Oddly enough, from the romantic and somewhat magically suspect background of courtly love, there emerged a Christian saint in the person of St Dymphna. The story runs thus: A brick containing the words *ma dompna*, 'My Lady', was found buried near the coffin containing the bones of an unidentified man and woman. Although this was undoubtedly the traditional address of a medieval poet or troubadour to his beloved, the 'lady' tag was seen to contain religious connotations and the Dymphna cult soon gathered momentum. She was later designated the patron saint of the insane, an asylum near Gheel being named after her, and to this day her help is still sought by Roman Catholic women suffering from emotional problems.

The servants of the goddess limped painfully through the next few centuries. Although paganism and other goddess cults were still kept alive, albeit secretly, those prepared to show allegiance to her frequently went in fear of their lives. Persecutions and inquisitions abounded, and the barbarous tortures that were inflicted upon both men and women who appeared to stray from the straight and narrow path set by the two branches of the Christian Church are well recorded. Whitmont cites the 'witches' hammer', the *Malleus Maleficarum*, compiled by two Dominican friars and explicitly authorized by Pope Innocent VIII as the judiciary standard, binding upon judges and princes for adjudication of witches. Between 1486 and 1669 it reached 30 editions from the leading German, French and Italian presses, and was implicitly accepted not only by Catholic but also by Protestant legislatures. Hence, it was the standard of judgment from the fifteenth to the seventeenth century.[6]

Witches — a term generally employed in a derogatory sense to any believers who do not subscribe to the accepted credos of orthodoxy, including pagans, psychics, shamans, mediums, occultists, Wiccans, subscribers to the tenets of ancient religions and followers of the goddess — are frequently accused by fundamentalists of Satanism or devil worship. Since genuine Wiccans, and most other pagans for that matter, do not acknowledge the existence of the Christian concept of Satan, they are hardly likely to worship him. The tragedy lies in the fact that many gullible people are taken in by some of the calumnies reported in the sensationalist media, and their lives are often adversely affected as a result. It would seem that religious persecution is as rife today as it ever was, albeit concealed beneath the cloak of respectability.

Although the Craft of Wicca has always been associated with women, there are just as many men who embrace its tenets these days. Vivianne Crowley remarked to me recently that the type of man who is drawn to Wicca, and similar goddess-orientated faiths, is usually at a stage in his spiritual development where he is searching for his own anima, or seeking to effect the final balancing needed for true individuation. I have noted how among Wiccans one often meets younger men married to older women (and very happily, too) — a tradition that dates back to the old matriarchal days when the high priestess and priest represented the Great Mother and her son/lover.

The fifteenth, sixteenth and seventeenth centuries saw the rise of many magicians of note, most of whom were males. This does not mean that there were no women working in this field, but rather that it was more dangerous for them to declare themselves. It is reputed, for example, that Queen Elizabeth I attended the magical circle of the famous Elizabethan mage Dr John Dee, whose astrological advice is believed by many to have been responsible for the British victory over the Spanish Armada. A later male martyr to the cause of the goddess was the monk Giordano Bruno, who fought to re-establish the religion of the goddess Isis, for which impiety he was burned at the stake by the Church in February 1600.

The less restricting climate of post-Reformation Europe witnessed the inception of many of the magical societies such as the Martinists, Illuminati, Rosicrucians, and Freemasons. Some of these were goddess-orientated, others not. Freemasonry, for example, which is just as strong today and has recently received a great deal of hostile publicity in the popular media, is exclusively for men. This brings me to the very thorny subject of 'women's rites' and 'men's rites'.

In primitive society, where the roles of women and men were quite distinct, separate rites for the sexes made sense. Both men and women contributed differently towards the well-being and continuation of the tribe, which was naturally of prime importance. However, since we no longer live in a tribal society, separate rites and social practices are seen by some women as too segregatory or divisive, and no longer essential. They could therefore be seen to represent a retrograde step in transpersonal sexual relationships, equality and sharing constituting more important factors in the psychology of the Aquarian Age. In spite of this, many women do prefer to have their own separate rites and practices, so in the final analysis it comes down to a matter of personal preference.

Although the various schools of religious belief have spawned some notable mystics over the ages, the overall metaphysical accent in the Occident has tended towards the magical, whereas the Orient has proved fertile ground for the mystic. Many explanations for this have been proffered over the years which are not, however, germane to our subject matter. Suffice it to say, in recent times there has been a uniting of Eastern and Western metaphysical beliefs in which women have played a major role. However, women have featured prominently in certain Eastern mystical traditions in the past, notably Taoism, and the wealth of wisdom and enlightenment contained in the teachings of these great adepts certainly merits inclusion.

A beautiful and deeply moving tribute to women's spirituality is contained in Thomas Cleary's translation from the Chinese: *Immortal Sisters: Secrets of Taoist Women*. The tradition of female Taoist adepts is as old as Chinese myth and history, and the author has selected the writings and poems of six such saints from the fourth to the twelfth century to demonstrate the sublimity of their lives and work. The best known was Sun Bu-er, who passed into folklore as one of the famous Seven Immortals, and whose character appears in countless popular novels in China. Cleary introduces his book in these words:

> Among the images of Asian society most familiar to the average westerner is that of the subservient role of women. Enforced weakness of woman in society is not, of course peculiar to Asia, or to past times; and indeed the globalization

of awareness of this fact has figured prominently in modern attempts by East and West to understand and interact with one another.

In East Asia, the systematic suppression of women is apparently due in the main to the influence of state Confucianism, a conservative ideology that has dominated the Chinese body politic for twenty-two centuries. In this context, state Confucianism means the official perversion of the teachings of the ancient philosopher Confucius (ca.500 BCE), which was instituted centuries after his death and was traditionally bent on keeping political power in the hands of a male elite embracing fixed ideas. To this end it attempted to suppress free thinking, imagination, social change, and inklings of the spiritual side of humanity.

In stark contrast to this is the more ancient tradition of Taoism, a far more comprehensive way of life and thought in which the importance of the feminine element in human life is strongly emphasized, and which mythically and historically counts very many women among its greatest figures. The present volume [*Immortal Sisters*] is an account of the teachings of some of the outstanding women of knowledge enshrined in this most ancient of scientific traditions, illustrating the inner process by which they cultivated their unusual wisdom and power.

The prominence of the feminine in Taoism, both literally and symbolically, is sometimes explained by the great antiquity of Taoism, with roots in ancient society prior to the establishment of patriarchy as a dominant organizational pattern. Whatever the truth of this may be, the importance of females and feminine associations in Taoist lore has transcended the influence of social structure throughout the ages.

As is well known, symbols such as the Mysterious Female and Mother Earth are fundamental to Taoism, representing essential pragmatic aspects of the teaching. Furthermore, while the practicalities symbolized by the Mysterious Female and Mother Earth are regarded as indispensable for all practitioners, regardless of gender, women are said to have a particular talent for them. Therefore it was considered especially easy for women to attain the essence of Taoism even under the rigorous conditions of patriarchal society.[7]

In the final chapter, entitled *Spiritual Alchemy for Woman*, the author tells us:

In the science of essence and life, men and women are the same — there is no discrimination. In sum, what is important is perfect sincerity and profound singlemindedness. An ancient document says 'Only perfect sincerity in the world is capable of ruling.' A classic says, 'The perfection of single-mindedness is that whereby one may heed the order of life.' . . .

Lao-tze said: 'The singleminded energy is most supple, able to be like an infant.' This is the perfection of true harmony . . .

The Master of the Jade Moon, a spiritual alchemist, said, 'When husband and wife meet in old age, their feelings are naturally affectionate . . .'

The reality behind all these sayings is spirit and energy being together, which means mind and breathing being together.[8]

The spiritual effects of the alchemical blending of the yin and yang are explained in the kind of abstract profundity one has come to associate with both Taoism and esoteric Buddhism. The six 'Immortal Sisters' whose insight and enlightenment grace the pages of this small volume are: Wu Cailuan, Fan Yunqiao, Cui Shaoxuan, Tang Guangzhen, Zhou Xuanjing, and Sun Bu-er.

Wu Cailuan was the daughter of Wu Meng, also a distinguished Taoist and civil administrator of the late third and early fourth centuries. She studied at a special centre for feminine alchemy, where she attained the Way. Fan Yunqiao was a woman of the third century whose husband, Lieu Gang, was also a Taoist adept. She is reported to have been endowed with great magical powers of the type we would probably call PK (psychokinesis). According to legend she and Lieu, like Wu Cailuan and her husband, 'ascended into heaven at the same time'.

Of Cui Shaoxuan little is known other than that she was the daughter of a government officer in northern China. Tang Guangzhen, however, was a woman of the Song Dynasty (AD 960–1278) who was apparently afflicted with a female disorder that miraculously healed following a dream in which a Taoist adept gave her some medicine. Soon after, she and her husband went to study with another Immortal Sister, and there is a strange tale of how she was offered immortality but temporarily refused it on the grounds that her mother was still alive and would need Tang to care for her in her old age.

Sun Bu-er, whose name means 'peerless' was born in AD 1124. She had three children and did not take up singleminded Taoist practice until she was 51 years old. Sun's husband, Ma Danang, had already entered Tao discipline having made the decision to so do following a strange dream he experienced at the age of 45.

Zhou Xuanjing and her son Wang Chuyi were both disciples of the eminent twelfth-century adept Wang Zhe, founder of the northern branch of the Complete Reality school of Taoism. On the eve of her son's birth she 'dreamed that she was surrounded by a scarlet mist, a characteristic and auspicious sign.' Her son was accepted as a pupil of the great Wang Zhe at the youthful age of 20 and was later summoned to instruct two emperors, while his mother was conferred with the title 'Free Human of Mystic Peace'. The sheer metaphysical breadth of Zhou's understanding is outlined in her answer to the question as to why spiritual immortals who had transcended the mundane world should concern themselves with such things as making rain. Immortal Sister Zhou's reply was:

'Those who have now attained to spiritual immortality but cannot as yet live in heaven number in the thousands. They are all in various places on earth accumulating virtue, carrying out practical undertakings so that they may eventually make the ascent.

'Some of them take care of rivers and lakes, some of them manage the hidden government, some are in charge of mountains. They work to benefit ten thousand generations, to rid the earth of what is harmful, to heal the sick and eliminate problems, acting mercifully toward the troubled and uplifting the fallen, rescuing the weak and helpless.

'Their hidden works are carried out in secret, their virtuous deeds are practised covertly. Such is their range that they cannot be encompassed in one generalization. But the spiritual immortals do not take pride in themselves, and are wary of becoming known to the public; therefore worldly people do not get to hear about them.'[9]

To do justice to the sublimity and profundity of the spiritual teachings of these women would require a greater literary talent than mine by far, so perhaps we should let their poetry speak for them. The following two verses by Sun Bu-er I found particularly meaningful:

Gathering the Mind (The same for men and women)

Before our body existed,
One energy was already there.
Like jade, more lustrous as it's polished,
Like gold, brighter as it's refined.
Sweep clear the ocean of birth and death,
Stay firm by the door of total mastery.
A particle at the point of open awareness,
A gentle firing is warm. [10]

Protecting the Spirit.

There is a body outside the body,
Which has nothing to do with anything produced by
    magical arts.
Making this aware energy completely pervasive
Is the living, active, unified original spirit.
The bright moon congeals the gold liquid,
Blue lotus refines jade reality.
When you've cooked the marrow of the sun and moon,
The pearl is so bright you don't worry about poverty. [11]

While on the subject of women's spirituality, one cannot fail
to observe how those women (and this probably applies to
men, too) who display the hallmarks of esoteric wisdom or
mysticism are eagerly accepted and supported by the
general public, as long as they practise their asceticism
within the confines of one of the major religions. For
example, when I tell people my cousin is a Roman Catholic
nun they are inclined to say: 'Isn't that wonderful, there are
too few women like her in this modern world.' But were I to
tell them that one of my dearest friends, who is among the
few truly spiritual people I have ever met, is a practising
pagan who acknowledges the goddess, it would be an
entirely different matter! In other words, many of us are
conditioned by the major religions into believing that no
one can possibly attain to a spiritual understanding of
the divine unless they do so within the auspices of set
religious dogmas, many of which, having been decided by
men, are completely out of touch with the realities of
today's world.

Returning once more to the theme of 'Magical Woman', it
should be borne in mind that not all magical traditions are
goddess-orientated. To embark on a description of the many
systems extant would demand a book in itself, so let me use
a few examples to illustrate my meaning. The goddess

certainly features strongly in Celtica, while Wicca, which is noted for its goddess associations, also has a god, so one can take one's choice. The Norse tradition, although overtly patrist, carries some strong matrist (probably Frisian) overtones which, when explored, reveal the gateway to the power of the sun goddess. Although ancient Egyptian magical and mystical beliefs favour both male and female deities, the magical law of polarity being deemed essential to the balance of the universe, its Siriun overtones are suggestive of a powerful goddess influence.

The last hundred years have seen a resurgence of women in the religious, mystical and metaphysical arenas. Mary Baker Eddy (1821-1910), founder of the Christian Science movement and the newspaper *Christian Science Monitor*; Helena Petrovna Blavatsky (1831-91) whose Theosophist movement, founded in Russia in 1850, became a popular study and pursuit in late Victorian times; and Annie Besant (born Annie Wood, 1847-1933), who was as famous for her work as a social reformer and free-thinker as she was for her association with Blavatsky's Eastern-inspired doctrines, and who later became founder-president of the Indian Home Rule League (1916) and president of the Indian National Congress (1917) — to name but three. Bearing in mind the social order in which these women were born and raised, whether or not one approves of their doctrines, it took a great deal of courage to stand up and speak out in a male-dominated society in which men and women, although not totally segregated, existed in entirely different worlds.

More recently the mantle of 'Priestess' fell upon Violet Mary Firth, better known as Dione Fortune, whose occult writings both in novel and textbook form are selling as well today as they were when they were written in the 1930s. Firth was born on 6 December 1890 in Llandudno, Wales, the daughter of a solicitor. Perhaps due to her strange career in the field of magic, there have been many spurious accounts of her start in life, which one of her biographers, Alan Richardson, has fortunately refuted. She died in Middlesex Hospital on 8 January 1946 of leukemia, an illness believed by some who knew her to have been a somatization of a dichotomy between two sides of her nature.

For those who would like to read more about this modern

mystic and occultist, *Priestess* is the title of Richardson's biography. Her mantle is as yet unplaced on the shoulders of another, although there are, I am given to understand, several contenders for her crown.

Chapter 9
History Speaks

WOMEN saints and mystics we have generously acknowledged, but there are many other areas in life aside from the transcendental in which women have shown themselves to be equal to, and sometimes better than men. Although I dislike the idea of men and women being in constant conflict, each trying to outdo the other, and prefer to think of people as individuals, some of whom are blessed with one talent, others with another, it would seem that I am somewhat out of tune with the world at large where this issue is concerned.

Women who have excelled in areas of life normally sacrosanct to men are looked upon as freaks, totally undeserving of the title 'woman' with all that implies to the chauvinist male. Such women have often adopted masculine values in order to be acknowledged in a patrist world. Nor is this a phenomenon of our present age: a succession of Athenes have ruffled the pages of history, leaving their very distinctive mark for us to digest and try to decode. But does this overt expression of the animus affect those women whose destiny it has been to assume that particular role? And what effect has it produced in the men who have seen fit to follow those queens and warriors of the past, whose deeds are guaranteed to excite our admiration on the one hand and, perhaps, give us cause to fear our own sleeping powers on the other?

Mohammed is reputed to have said: 'The men perish if they obey the women', and 'No people who place a woman over their affairs prosper.'[1] However, the Prophet appears to have made several similar statements, which have not been borne out by history. On the contrary, as Antonia Fraser points out, 'a Warrior Queen or female ruler — has often provided the focus for what a country afterwards perceived to have been its golden age; beyond the obvious example (to the English) of Queen Elizabeth I, one might cite the twelfth century Queen Tamara of Georgia, or the 15th century Isabella of Spain.'[2]

Celtic mythology abounds with glorious warrior queens who underwent initiatory rites as terrifying as anything experienced by their Herculean counterparts: Rhiannon, the Welsh Horse goddess who was patron of Justice; the Gaulish mother goddess, Epona; and Macha, an eponymous deity of the capital of Ulster, who was forced, while pregnant, to run a race against the horses of Conchobar at Emain Macha. She succeeded in the contest, but died subsequently while giving birth to twins. There were others; Don or Dana, Brigid, the Morrigan, Anu and, of course, Queen Medb (Maeve of the Irish Ultonian heroic cycle). But then this is hardly surprising since Celtica was primarily a matrist society which accepted dominant male gods comparatively late in its history. Perhaps these great women were real people whose deeds later became mythologized, like Helen of Troy, who was for many years viewed purely as a figment of poetic imagination.

In her informative book *The Warrior Queens*, Antonia Fraser refers to the fact that the United States have so far failed to produce a Warrior Queen either in fact or fiction, in spite of the strong feminist lobby that has insisted on equal rights across the whole sociopolitical spectrum. When a woman did finally appear on the Vice Presidential scene, the reaction was one of unease, which might be read by members of other nations as implying a reluctance to practise what is preached. Fraser suggests that this might be due to a lack of hereditary monarchy and cites Gibbon:

> In every age and country, the wiser or at least the stronger, of the two sexes has usurped the powers of the State, and confined the other to the cares and pleasures of domestic life. In hereditary monarchies, however, and especially in those of modern Europe, the gallant spirit of chivalry, and the law of succession, have accustomed us to allow a singular exception; and a woman is often acknowledged the absolute sovereign of a great kingdom, in which she would be deemed incapable of exercising the smallest employment, civil or military.[3]

Were he alive today, Edward Gibbon, whose *Decline and Fall of the Roman Empire* has been a standard reference book for many years, would doubtless observe many similarities between the Rome he studied and the United States of America. Nor has this comparison escaped the eagle eyes of those psychics who specialize in probing the historical (and prehistorical) past. I can recall in the late 1960s reading an article in a pamphlet sent to me by one of these small, privately funded organizations that burgeon from time to time, burn brightly and are soon forgotten, which suggested that the senators of ancient Rome now occupied similar chairs in the American Senate, while those military geniuses whose names carry weight in the Pentagon would look just as well in a toga, or the traditional garb of a Roman officer. In fact, the particular publication, if I recall, presented the reader with a facsimile of ex-President Nixon thus clad!

The Romans did not favour women rulers, so it must have been somewhat of a shock for them when they came up against Queen Boadicea whose chariot, incidentally, was *not* armed with scythes as popular illustrations might suggest. Unlike those other mythical heroes of British legend whose existences cannot be proved, Boadicea was completely real. Fraser refers to the fabulous King Arthur, much loved of Celtic magicians, as 'no chivalric monarch if he did exist but a sixth century Romano British commander who survives by virtue of an image which is itself spurious.'[4] I am rather grateful for this comment since I have incurred the wrath of certain traditionalists by suggesting that Arthur, or Arcturus, was a title which preceded both Celtdom and Christianity by many centuries, and could not be blamed on a sixth century British monarch, whose existence was highly dubious anyway.

Since the name 'Boadicea', as taught in our schools, is inaccurate, 'Boodicea', 'Voadicea', 'Bunduica', and 'Bundica' have been suggested as possible alternatives. Tacitus' Boudica is seen by some as more befitting to the great Iceni queen who led the AD 60-1 rebellion against the Romans, although the legendary character will, no doubt, continue to be known as Boadicea.

The Frisian Warrior Queen who, according to the *Oera Linda Book* was the original Min-Erva (surnamed

Nyhellenia), later deified as Athene, has already graced our pages and, no doubt, many other Frisian women warriors also slipped unrecognized into the pantheons that were formed between the fourth and the second millennia BC. The same can be said of those Amazonian queens who defied the patrist onslaught and who were not famous simply because they were related to, were an appendage of, or inherited their position of power from a male member of their dynasty or tribe.

I have no intention of supplying a series of potted biographies of these great women from the past who have, by their own personal power, magnetism, imagination and talents, transcended the barriers and restrictions placed upon their sex by the society and times in which they existed. What I would like to do, however, is to bring a few of their names and deeds to the notice of my reader who can, should she or he be interested, tackle the detail via the excellent research and erudition of Fraser, Bancroft, and other able biographers.

Semiramis, or Sammu-ramat, was the Babylonian widow of the Assyrian king Shamshi-Adad and mother of his heir. Upon the death of her husband in 811 BC she held the reins of state until her son was old enough to assume the mantle of kingship. During that short time she appears to have exerted sufficient influence to merit being named among the great queens of the past.

Cleopatra — a character much favoured by claimants of past-life memories — was born in late 70 or early 69 BC. The daughter of Ptolemy XII Auletes, and one of his six acknowledged children, she is believed to have carried Macedonian, Persian and Syrian, rather than Egyptian, blood. Her story so caught the popular imagination that it became immortalized in the works of the great bards and writers.

Zenobia of Palmyra was another widow who, like Boudica, chose to challenge the might of Rome. Perhaps it was her fervent belief that she was descended from the mighty Cleopatra that gave her the courage. Fraser sees her as: 'part of a discernible pattern of pre-Islamic Arabian queens with military connections, many of them coming from her own homeland or areas adjacent. The researches of Nabia Abbott have revealed at least two dozen of these formidable ladies over six centuries, following the visit of the Queen of Sheba to Solomon in the tenth century BC. Various origins have been ascribed to this fabulous queen including south Arabian and Abyssinian: more important, she exemplifies 'the exercise of the right of independent queenship among the ancient Arabs.'[5]

One cannot help wondering why the swing from matrism to patrism in the Arab countries and those surrounding cultures that have embraced Islam should have been so drastic and pronounced. Knowledge of the ancient ways must surely be resident genetically in these peoples unless, as I suggested in the earlier chapters of this book, the overriding external influence is stronger than their natural inheritance. One of the experiments I carried out with my class of 'professionals' in California in the spring of 1989 involved a 'projection' or psychic look into the origins and motivations of the various creeds that dominate our planet at the moment. Allowing for the 'experimenter effect', everyone present — men and women — was in complete accord on what they 'saw' — it was *frightening*!

Eleanor of Aquitaine certainly left her mark on twelfth and thirteenth century European history. Originally married to Louis VII of France in 1137, she later became the wife of Henry II and mother of Richard I, later known as Coeur de Lion. According to legend, Eleanor appeared on one occasion dressed and armed as an Amazon, in the company of her serving ladies who were similarly, if less ostentatiously attired, to encourage the faithful to join the Crusade which she and her female *entourage* were bent upon accompanying. She frequently clashed with the male authorities of her times and Henry made several attempts over the years to curb her powers.

Matilda, Countess of Tuscany, was devoted to the worship of St Peter, with whom she appeared to feel some close affinity. In fact, her piety (and, more probably, the number of men-at-arms in her service) earned her a personal missive from Pope Gregory VII in the latter part of 1704 which read: 'To you, my most beloved and loving daughter, I do not hesitate to disclose any of these thoughts, for even you yourself can hardly imagine how greatly I may count upon your zeal and discretion.'[6] Matilda was born in northern Italy in 1046 and apparently lived to a ripe old age, in spite of her strange combination of piety and overt militarism.

Queen Tamara of Georgia was one of the few women rulers to succeed lawfully to her father's throne — in the year 1184. What is more, she was welcomed by the populace which must have sensed her to be one of those rare monarchs who was destined to add to the prestige and dominions of her country. However, she also earned herself the reputation of being something of a Messalina, which hardly endeared her to her more pious subjects! Her peoples were seen to bear many similarities to the vainglorious Celts, being lovers of music, the arts, fine apparel and jewellery, as well as excellent fighters.

It was during the reign of Queen Isabella of Castile that Christopher Columbus set forth on his epic voyage of discovery which was destined to open up the New World. In fact Isabella, as well as Ferdinand of Aragon, was instrumental in providing the necessary backing. However, although a queen by right of succession, in due deference to Salic Law she was seen more in the context of a powerful partner in the victories and achievements of her husband Ferdinand, rather than as a Warrior Queen in her own right. Isabella's third daughter was Catherine of Aragon (1485-1536), whose first husband, Prince Arthur of England, left her a widow. She later married his younger brother, Henry VIII, and their subsequent divorce caused Henry's break with Roman Catholicism, which precipitated the English Reformation.

Elizabeth I of England needs no introduction. Enough has been said, written and filmed of her life and achievements. Strangely enough, she made no attempt whatsoever to better the lot of women in her time, which evoked an article in *Feminist Review* of 1980 in which Alison Heisch saw Elizabeth I in terms of those women who are 'honorary males', and as such do not involve themselves in the status of the women of their time. Having discussed this subject with several women who have managed to achieve the distinction of honorary male, I can confirm that they have no wish for any change in the status quo that might deprive them of their newly won 'privileges'.

As Simone de Beauvoir has cogently pointed out, however, these great queens were neither male nor female predominantly — they were *sovereigns*, which would suggest that when a woman is vested with a certain degree of power, some other impersonal, non-sexual element in her psychology takes over. This transformation is not, of course, limited to manifestations of temporal power, as it can also be observed in the great woman mystics, teachers and reformers, past and present. In esoteric terms it relates to the placing of the kundalini (serpent) energies which obviously cannot be focused in two places at once — something has to go.

There are many strange tales, both historical and conjectural, concerning the private life of Elizabeth I, the truth or otherwise of which we may never know. While her single-mindedness was guaranteed to anger her ministers from time to time, she can surely be forgiven on the grounds that her competence as a ruler *par excellence* carried her country into the forefront of the nations of her day.

From the feminist viewpoint, one of the finest expositions on the character of Elizabeth I is undoubtedly Philippa Berry's *Of Chastity and Power*. It combines Renaissance scholarship with feminist literary criticism to reject former accounts of the 'cult' of Elizabeth, which presented both the Queen's gender and her marital status as unproblematic. In this scholarly work, Dr Berry, Fellow and Lecturer of King's College, Cambridge, employs readings of key Elizabethan texts by Lyly, Ralegh, Chapman, Shakespeare, and Spenser to show that while Elizabeth's combination of chastity and political and religious power was repeatedly idealized, it was also perceived as extremely disturbing.

By placing these texts within the wider context of European culture and history, Dr Berry illustrates how the figure of the unmarried Queen implicitly challenged the masculine focus of Renaissance discourses on love and absolutist political ideology, subverting the philosophical division between spirit and matter upon which Renaissance ideas of women were founded. Her exploration of the potent combination of themes of sexuality and politics with classical myth and Neo-platonic mysticism offers a radical reassessment of the status of 'woman' as a bearer of meaning within Renaissance literature and culture.

The underlying psychology behind Dr Berry's chastity-power theme, which is vital to an understanding of certain aspects of the feminine principle, will be re-echoed from time to time during the ensuing chapters.

The Warrior Queens of the past have not all been European or even Middle Eastern. Jinga Mbandi (c.AD 1580–1663), later known as Queen Jinga of Angola, led her armies, albeit unsuccessfully, against the forces of an unwelcome occupying power in much the same way as the Celtic Boudica. Jinga's two principal kingdoms were Kongo and Ndongo in central West Africa. Her enemies were the Portuguese, whose slave markets in Angola were proving a goldmine to their operators. Although she was associated with many strange and brutal practices, these were not out of keeping with the customs of her time. In much the same way, the activities of other earlier monarchs of both sexes might be viewed as barbaric by today's standards, while our own morals and civil procedures will no doubt merit severe criticism in years to come.

Nineteenth century India saw the Rani of Jhansi leading her men in the course of the Indian Rebellion — 'mutiny' to the occupying British. The exact date of Lakshmi Bai's birth is unknown, although rough estimates place it between 1830 and 1835. Her original name was Manukarnika, and her unusual temperament apparently manifested at a very early age in the tomboy-like childhood characteristics frequently displayed by future Warrior Queens. She certainly maintained a tradition of intelligent, free-thinking women from the Indian sub-continent that has surfaced in our present day and age in such figures as Indira Gandhi, Mrs Bandaranaike, and Benazir Bhutto. Concerning her death on the field of battle, the following comments were found in a small locked notebook which was found among the property of Lord Canning after his death:

Rhanee of Jhansi. Killed by a trooper of 8th Hussars, who was never discovered. Shot in the back, her horse baulked. She then fired at the man and he passed his sword through her. [7]

The Warrior Queen is, however, but one archetypal manifestation of the goddess within woman. There are others, less obvious but equally plaintive. Joan of Arc, for example, was not a queen, and yet her actions surely qualify her for the 'warrior' title. Walker refers to her as ' "Joan of the Bow" — Joan the Huntress — also called La Pucelle, "The Maid," a traditional title of a priestess in the fairy religion.' [8]

There would seem to be conflicting views regarding the voices she heard, although Joan herself stated that she received her mission 'at the tree of the Fairy Ladies' at the centre of the Dianic cult at Domremy. In 1429 ecclesiastical judges accepted her angelic voices as genuine, and announced that she had been divinely appointed to save France. This decision was later revoked by the Bishop of Beauvais, and in 1431, when she was only 19 years of age, she was burned as a witch at Rouen wearing a placard which referred to her as a 'Relapsed Heretic, Apostate, Idolator'. The 'idolator' aspect, however, was never explained. Joan remained a popular national heroine until she was finally canonized by Pope Benedict XV in 1920.

Modern psychiatry has tended to relegate Joan, along with other historical characters who 'heard voices', to some division of the schizophrenic category. Likewise, one could easily adopt the role of devil's advocate and observe that there is little difference between the Joans of this world and those mediums who demonstrate regularly at Spiritualist churches throughout the world, or the current crop of channellers whose disembodied spirits or extraterrestrial 'guides' regularly tell us how to live better lives, put right the wrongs of our society, or save Gaia from total destruction. There is, of course, a fine dividing line between mental illness, self-delusion, and genuine mystical guidance, so a little incredulity does not go amiss. My own feeling concerning the Maid is that she was probably a natural psychic with pagan leanings, who strove to keep on the right side of the reigning sacerdotal establishment by placing her 'quest' within the Christian context.

While on the subject of France, the French writer and philosopher Elisabeth Badinter reminds us that discussions on the subject of women's equality were well afoot in France as early as 1673, when Poulain de la Barre put forward one of the most revolutionary of all propositions: the equality of the sexes! De la Barre, a disciple of Descartes, saw this equality to be total since men and women were endowed with the same reasoning power and are similar in almost every respect. She tells us:

Feminine nature is so intrinsic a part of human nature that Poulain dreamed of seeing women having access to all occupations in society: professors of medicine or of theology, ministers of the Church, '*generalles* [sic] in the army, or *presidentes* of Parliament.' By reducing the difference between the sexes to the minimum, Poulain wove bonds of fraternity between men and women and restored woman to the bosom of humanity. [9]

She goes on to speak of Denis Diderot, who pitied women their troublesome and painful bodies, and felt that in compensation for their lives of prolonged physical suffering they should be decently educated and accorded some degree of compensation by receiving a fairer acknowledgement of their special talents. Diderot's old friend, Madame d'Epinay, failed to see things in the same light, however. Followed shortly afterwards by Condorcet, she opined that since there were more resemblances between the sexes than dividing issues, simple equality might be better valued than a pedestal or altar. Regarding the alleged inability of women to create, Condorcet asserted that he did not believe in it and commented, albeit tongue in cheek, that if only men capable of inventing were admitted to office, there would be many vacant places, even in academies.

> 'There is no difference between women and men that is not a product of education,' he asserted, and to prove his point he demanded a common syllabus of education for both sexes, whose aim was 'to teach individuals of the *human race* what would be useful for them to know in order to enjoy their rights and fulfil their duties.' [10]

Needless to say Condorcet's plan got nowhere, the argument in favour of happiness through the equality of the sexes being rejected by the men of the Assembly, who were more taken with Talleyrand's Rousseauist arguments than Condorcet's equality ideology. In fact, it was a long time before such issues finally made their way into the national legislations of the major powers, and the age-old warriors and queens gave way to the expression of other, more subtle feminine archetypes.

For many years women were precluded from the kind of artistic or academic training that would render their talents acceptable to the establishment, which naturally resulted in a dearth of women artists, architects, scientists and composers. Had a woman of great innate talent incarnated in, say, the sixteenth, seventeenth or eighteenth centuries, there would have been little opportunity for her to perfect her gifts, let alone express them publicly. Interesting, witty, and entertaining females were obviously to be found among the monied and titled classes, but few of these ever achieved fame in what were considered to be essentially male areas of expression. What woman could do, safely within the confines of the home, was to write. Sometimes these observant and often moving notes took the form of diaries that contained enlightening and revealing comments on the social conditions of the age; poetry followed quickly in their wake, and eventually the woman novelist stepped into the public arena. Literary woman had arrived!

One of the first militant feminists to seize upon this literary outlet as a platform for her beliefs was Mary Wollstonecraft (1757-97), seen by many as the 'Mother of Feminism', whose manifesto entitled *Vindication of the Rights of Woman*, published in 1792, certainly rocked the boat of eighteenth-century society. Mary's activities in France during the period directly following the French Revolution, the disillusionment and despair that resulted from her first limerant relationship, her eventual marriage to a fellow radical, William Godwin, and her death from septicaemia at the age of 38, brought on by the birth of her daughter Mary, later to become Mary Shelley of *Frankenstein* fame, are all well recorded. As a tireless reformer, social worker, and militant feminist, she stands head and shoulders above many of the better known names that succeeded her.

The novels of nineteenth-century women writers such as Jane Austen (1775-1817) and the Brontë sisters Charlotte (1816-55), Emily (1818-48), and Anne (1820-49), are noted for their incisive social satire, and wit, and for their fine observation of the manners and morality of the period as seen *through the eyes of a woman*. Considering that in Victorian times men and women existed in different worlds, and for the single woman marriage was the ultimate aim, a talented woman needed to be both single-minded and brave to hold up against the prevailing climate of opinion. But the slow and laborious trek towards equality had started and the path was being carefully paved for the arrival of the suffragette movement proper.

Women slowly started to become prominent in other fields of human endeavour: Josephine Butler in social reform, Florence Nightingale in nursing, and Dorothea Beal in education, to name but three, while the final barrier — science — was soon to come tumbling down. Maria Skodowska (1867-1934), later to become Madame Curie, the Polish chemist famous for her co-discovery of radium, had studied science in Paris in 1895. The hallowed portals of academe were slowly and grudgingly opening to women. From now on the names come too thick and fast on both sides of the Atlantic for me to include without omitting someone of importance whose area of activity is perhaps less known outside the sphere of their special skill.

It has been commented that the women who have most distinguished themselves have never been the most beautiful or the most gentle of their sex. Why should this be? Male analysts would, no doubt, see compensatory factors in this, but the evidence shows that a beautiful face and body can be a hindrance to a woman with serious work in mind, as many have found to their cost.

History has spawned its heroines as well as its heroes, and they have been numerous: the Grace Darlings this side of the Atlantic and the Molly Pitchers the other. But my bouquet goes to those unsung heroines whose names we have never heard and never will, but whose bravery has equalled anything we may read about in our myths and sagas. Only yesterday someone asked me whether I had included Queen Victoria among my historic queens and warriors, to which I replied that I had not. My questioner wondered why. A great leader and mother Empress figure Victoria might well have been, but as a woman she was no warrior, and in common with other rulers who have been vested with great temporal power she paid little attention to the demands and sufferings of her own sex. In *The Victorian Woman*, Duncan Crow gives a vivid account of the damaging effects that the laws of the time had upon women. For example, until 1857 a woman could not sue for divorce (except by an Act of Parliament — a privilege usually reserved for the aristocracy); until 1881 the legal right of a husband using physical force to restrain his wife from leaving the marital home had never been questioned; until 1884 a wife could be imprisoned for denying her husband his 'conjugal rights'. He tells us that:

> The Christian religion, too, was a powerful force in pro-
> claiming and maintaining women's inferior position. On its
> Judaic inheritance it had erected the myth that women's
> subordinate place was a punishment for the original sin of Eve.
> It worshipped the words of Paul that 'man is not of the woman
> but the woman of the man'.[11]

During the Victorian period men and women were not only
expected to attend church every Sunday, but Bible readings
in the home, organized prayer meetings, listening to ser-
mons and strict observance of the Sabbath were to be found
in many homes. Women were also obliged to fight hard for
even the slightest social reform. For example, in 1876, when
Annie Besant defended a pamphlet on the use of contra-
ception, both the Government and the Church came out
against her.

Of course, one cannot blame all the ills or injustices
against women on an apparently unconcerned British
Queen, as the lot of women was grim in most parts of the
world, for which the blame must once again be placed fairly
and squarely on the shoulders of the popular religions.
Stone cites Russian-born George St George, who suggested
that the Church played a major role in the inferior status of
women in pre-revolutionary Russia:

> Dominated by Judeo-Christian tradition, churches held the
> key to woman's prison. Since God made his original covenant
> with man, man's position is paramount and unassailable.[12]

Simone de Beauvoir is quick to sanction this premise:

> Man enjoys the great advantage of having a man endorse the
> code he writes; and since man exercises a sovereign authority
> over women it is especially fortunate that this authority has
> been vested in him by the Supreme Being. For the Jews,
> Mohammedans and Christians among others, man is master
> by divine right, the fear of God will therefore repress any
> impulse towards revolt in the downtrodden female.[13]

De Beauvoir then tells us that according to French law,
obedience is no longer included among the duties of a wife.
Those women who have sacrificed the comforts of life to
face a hostile world made such civil laws possible, but while
the religions are still opposed (sometimes violently) to
woman's equality and freedom, the battle still rages.

Part II
The Present and Future

Chapter 10
Dragons and Serpents

L ET us now take our leave of past scenarios and turn our
attention to the women of today. Have the endeavours of
our sisters over the ages really borne fruit, or were their
efforts in vain? Are we women (and our menfolk for that
matter) really in charge of our own lives, or are we directed
by some devious programming, genetic or otherwise, which
decides how we may or may not express ourselves or
command our own destinies?

Modern woman has, to some extent, been freed from
many of the duties and social encumbrances that befell her
sisters in times past. She has been accorded equal opportunities (on paper, anyway); she is able to enter any of the
professions, apart from certain branches of the major world
religions (albeit in lesser ratio to her male competitors); and
she has a degree of sexual freedom not seen since the old
days of matriarchy (or has she?) How, therefore, is she coping
with these seeming beneficial innovations that have somehow conspired to alter the rhythm of what is considered to
be 'normal family life'? These and other questions will be
analysed in this and the ensuing chapters.

Woman's 'equal' opportunities are not really so equal if
one bears in mind that there is a destructive psychological
element involved which starts to work against her from a
very early age. For example, a woman I know who has a
doctorate in Zoology and who teaches science at a private
school for girls, tells me she has no problems with her
science students. They are bright, intelligent, able and
confident — until they come face to face with their male
counterparts from the boys' section of the same school,
when they are subjected to the kind of derision which is

calculated to demoralize them totally, and often causes them to question and even abandon their chosen calling.

Let us take university life. Here is an anecdote which was told to me by a Cambridge honours graduate in Classics, who is totally sympathetic to our cause. A certain professor always started his lectures with the words, 'Well, gentlemen!' Since his disquisitions were nothing if not boring, the attendance at his classes slowly dwindled until one day he arrived for tutorials to find only six women present. Upon entering the lecture hall he took a quick glance round before commenting, 'I see there's nobody here today,' and then promptly left!

How a woman fares in any field of endeavour will, of course, depend on her basic nature and how well she handles her particular talents and energies. Psychologically speaking, women can be grouped and sub-grouped, so let us start with what my experience has shown me to be the initial grouping as endorsed by the sages, scholars, analysts and physicians of the past.

Feminine energies can be expressed overtly or covertly, hence we have the DRAGON and the SERPENT — the primaeval Tiamat and Uatchet, also known by many other names over the ages. Many of those strong, energetic women whose lives and deeds we have examined in the previous chapter are easily recognizable as Dragons. The Dragon emphasizes the animus in a woman, and it is through this overt channelling of her Dragon energies that she is able to compete in a man's world. Warrior women — the Athenes, Minervas and Boudicas — were all Dragons. We have all met them in our everyday lives — those organizing ladies who inevitably run something, whether it be the local Women's Institute, a social event, a commercial enterprise, or some public office that demands an outward display of strength. Those brave women who were the advance guard of the suffragettes exhibited Dragon power; likewise those of the modern feminist movement. Dragons are usually fearless, outspoken, and willing to take a chance. There are several of them in both our government and opposition parties. In fact, I would suggest that being a Dragon is a *sine qua non* for political success, as far as any woman is concerned.

Next come the Serpents, who can be equally as strong as their Dragon sisters, but in a different, more subtle way.

Their energies are, like the Kundalini, sinuous and mutable. Whereas Dragons are quite straightforward, with Serpents one has to watch out as they tend to weave about and, like the fiery salamanders of occult legend, burn brightly one moment and withdraw to an almost dying ember the next. For this reason it is always advisable to be prepared for any turn of events when dealing with Serpent power, as most Snakes usually keep a trump card tucked away somewhere beneath their beautiful skins. Snakes hate confrontations, but if forced out into the open their aim can be precise and their venom deadly. The Chinese astrologers, in commenting upon the nature of those born during the Year of the Snake, describe them as being both peaceful and artistic, enjoying the gifts of music and humour, and having the power to bewitch. Snakes, they tell us, are wise, intelligent and deep-thinking, but their intellect is restless and they are essentially guided by their intuition. The Dragon and Serpent themes are, of course, embracing of both virtues and vices, and which of these predominate will depend very much on the spiritual maturity of the individual.

We have already discussed in an earlier chapter the commonly held belief that men are at their strongest on the material level, while women are more powerful at those subtle levels that cannot be perceived by the five senses — a notion I have seen fit to dismiss on the grounds of personal observation and experience. I would like to replace this concept with the Dragon-Serpent theory: *Dragons work better at the outer or material levels, while Serpent power is strongest on the inner planes.*

In the Old Religion snakes symbolized the inner wisdom that is termed 'intuition'. They were also associated with the lunar gods: Cernunnos, Hermes, and Thoth, for example, the implication being that Serpent energies are more powerful in the world of the mind and the imagination, while also carrying healing PK. Dragons, on the other hand, are better able to utilize their animus energies to advantage on the Earth sphere. Dragons and Serpents can also be seen in the bi-polar context. Ereshkigal, for example, is essentially obscure and serpentine, contrasting with her draconian sister, Inanna. I am inclined to think that it is this serpentine nature in woman that gave birth to the old metaphysical concept of woman being more powerful on the subtle planes, since in times past few Dragons outside of the Amazons and Warrior Queens have found sufficient outlets for their natural energies to warrant either occult or public acknowledgement.

Now let us examine our elemental natures. Specific qualities in human terms are ascribed to each of the four elements. Fire, considered by occultists to be the senior element, is associated with creativity, ardour, raw energy, valour, and loyalty; Air with intellectuality, speed of thought, communication, detachment, and inventiveness; Water with the emotions, feelings, receptivity, under-standing/sensitivity, and sympathy; and Earth with thrift, acquisition, conservation, and practicality. The ancient sages saw Fire and Air as 'masculine' forces and Water and Earth as 'feminine' energies. However, in terms of modern psychology they would be better applied to the animus and anima and the Dragon-Serpent modes as follows:

FIRE	Animus	Dragon	Introvert
AIR	Animus	Dragon	Extravert
WATER	Anima	Serpent	Introvert
EARTH	Anima	Serpent	Extravert

Dragons who are either fiery or airy, and Serpents who are watery or earthy, tend to be easily recognizable, as the respective elements emphasize their basic natures. But fiery Serpents or watery Dragons are a different kettle of fish. For example, the latter would tend to exert their drive via the emotional mode, while the former would use their creative strength behind the scenes. Similarly with airy Serpents and earthy Dragons, the former tend towards intellectual subtlety and the latter towards practical management.

Fiery Dragons can be very intense, and although they may appear to assume the reins of office with ease they seldom wear their hearts on their sleeves. Airy Dragons, in contrast, are able to detach themselves from the emotions of those over whom they have gained a position of authority, en-abling them to go about their extraverted business without undue stress. Watery Serpents are frequently tossed hither and thither on the emotional tides of life, their ability to plumb the depths of the deep unconscious rendering them fair game for dominant males on the one hand, and causing them to be their own worst enemy on the other. They are, however, seldom without a creative talent of some kind. Earthy Serpents or Dragons probably fare the best in the long run because they are more closely in touch with Gaia and are thus able to handle the 'things that are Caesar's' with cunning and ease respectively, while giving the outward appearance of being practical or efficient.

How can we recognize our elemental natures, and from where did we acquire them? The horoscope can be very revealing when it comes to understanding one's own (and others') elemental qualities. For example, an absence of planets in Water signs in a chart will indicate a corresponding absence of feeling and emotion, while the person who lacks the support of the element of Earth will be hard pushed to cope in the practical world of money-making. The horoscope, however, only shows us the elemental qualities we have to work with in this life. There is also a belief that we are spiritually akin to one or other of the elements and that the pattern or quality of that element will predominate through many, if not all, of our earthly lives. But now we are entering the metaphysical world of reincarnation, which is the subject matter of other books.

The Western tradition teaches that women have a closer relationship with the four elements, but I have not found this to be necessarily so; it depends on the individual woman. Several men I have known and worked with have been able to enter the fabled Mountain Cavern, with its elemental associations and goddess overtones. Serpent symbology features strongly in Hermeticism, what is termed the hermetic Way being concerned with mind, which is the half-way house between spirit and matter. Dragons, on the other hand, occur in those traditions which emphasize the yin and the yang.

Woman, like man, is imbued with instinctive, emotional, logical, and intuitive qualities, which can be equated with the four elemental attributes. She is body, mind, and spirit, which means she is capable of functioning at the material, psychological, and transpersonal levels. Some women, however, are unable to bring their spiritual resources to bear in their present lives, so they find themselves thrown back into the arena of the material world (with its limited knowledge of the human psyche, especially in its transpersonal frequencies) wherein to resolve their problems and imbalances. But this does not and cannot work! Separating one segment from the whole inevitably causes a void that cannot be filled by the gifts, qualities, or energies of the other two. That many women have come to realize this may be evidenced in the women's spirituality movement which is fast gaining momentum. The irony of this is, of course, that in order to understand one's own spirituality one needs to come to terms with one's own animus, which means acknowledging who, what, and why we are, and how we stand in relation to the other sex with which we share this planet.

And so we proceed with the analysis, but first there are still a few further factors to be taken into consideration. Carl Jung, in his Introduction to Esther Harding's book *Woman's Mysteries*, comments on the compensatory aspects of the unconscious that are brought to bear when one aspect of the psyche becomes overemphasized. If, for example, we try to effect an outward display of either the anima or animus that goes against our basic nature, personality-wise we are likely to exhibit exaggerated tendencies in the opposite direction. In other words, we are not totally ruled by what we observe immediately around us or what life has taught us by experience to date, because there are certain inner features which come to the fore at given periods during our lives, and it is these archetypal forms and our individual response to them which render each of us unique. Should we fail to be true to our basic archetype, whichever that may be, then we are likely to encounter psychological problems that may either stay resident in the mental sphere, or somatize, as the archetype will inevitably out!

It is important, therefore, that we take a hint from the ancient Greeks and come to know ourselves — our *real* selves, that is, not some false persona that we may have elected to adopt in order to fit into some section of society which may suit our material convenience but in which we are spiritually ill at ease. The social conditioning factor has, in my opinion, caused more mental and physical illness than might be imagined. Too many square pegs have been forced into round holes, distorting their original, pristine shape, the archetype they brought into this life in order to gain the experience their psyches deem necessary for their

ascent to the next rung of the ladder of spiritual development. As a consequence, the karma of that life has not
found fulfilment and they are beset with illnesses both
physical and psychological. Anyone who has worked with
older terminal cancer patients will attest to what I am
saying. And this, I am told, applies more to women than
men.

During counselling sessions terminally ill patients tend
to let go of their emotions, hidden fears, and frustrations.
With some it has been a life of subservience and drudgery
that has given rise to the despair which 'allowed' the
entrance of the final illness. With others, it was the love they
never had, or the child they always longed for which never
came. Some women tell of a great talent which had been
acknowledged by the experts, but which they forfeited for
the love of a man who later left them with small children
to raise alone.

The story may go something like this: 'I was greatly gifted
as a child and won a scholarship to art school (music
college/university/drama school or whatever) where I was
doing very well. In fact, my professor singled me out for
private tuition and my first exhibition (recital/term marks/
play) received critical acclaim. Then I met Bob (Joe, Chris,
or Bill) and fell in love.'

A few too many drinks, a cosy night together, an ensuing
pregnancy, and the reticent male does the 'right thing' —
with freedom in mind a year or so later. The end of what
could have been a brilliant career; the result, one very
dissatisfied and bitter lady. Many women who have experienced this particular scenario have been able to 'get their act
together' at a later date and pick up the threads of their
former career, or a new one. These are usually the watery
Dragons or the earthy Serpents. Fiery Dragons seldom get
caught that way as they tend to look after Number One.
Airy Serpents or Dragons usually endeavour to avoid
complicated involvements in the first place, while watery
Serpents are inclined to look for another man who will take
them, and their child, and provide them with a home. The
irony of this is that because like attracts like, the latter will
more than likely take up with an equally watery and
emotionally unstable partner who is also looking for a
secure prop!

At the other end of the scale, there is the ambitious woman who would dearly love to read medicine, the sciences, or the classics, but whose financial situation or social background precludes her from so doing. Such women, if given the opportunity later in life, tend to gravitate towards complementary disciplines such as alternative therapies, the social services, nursing, or teaching.

I am inclined to think that when a young woman (or young man, for that matter) is confronted with impassable barriers, she has either failed to make contact with her essential archetype, or has deliberately chosen the hard way in order to leave her mind free of the often myopic or tunnel vision programming of academe, so that she can explore the world in some unique, creative way.

In their book *Psychology and Psychiatry*, Consultant Psychiatrist Peter Dally, and Senior Nursing Sister Mary Watkins, who is a tutor for In-service Education and training at a major London teaching hospital, offer the following list of what they assess to be the eight basic personality types (to which I have added my personal comments as applying to women generally).

The Hysterical Personality: predominantly youthful, watery Serpents and airy Dragons.

The Obsessional Personality: immature earthy or fiery Serpents and Dragons predominate here.

The Schizoid Personality: watery Serpents, plus a sprinkling of fiery and airy Dragons.

The Paranoid Personality: fiery Serpents, watery Dragons, and immature airy Dragons.

The Depressive Personality: earthy Dragons and Serpents in the negative mode, with a few watery specimens of both types also present.

The Cyclothymic Personality: fiery and watery Dragons and Serpents who are poised on the threshold of spiritual maturity.

The Anxious Personality: mature earthy and fiery Serpents, or fast-learning fiery Dragons here.

The Narcissistic Personality: Lots of airy Dragons and Serpents, plus a fair number of watery Serpents who are suddenly becoming aware of themselves as unique entities.[1]

Very few people represent any of these groups *in toto*, however, most of us being something of a mixture. Those interested in entering into a more detailed study of personality types are recommended to either the above mentioned book, or my own work: *The Psychology of Healing*.

Introvert/Extravert

The following introvert-extravert complex might also prove of interest to the reader:

INTROVERTED

Passive	Quiet
Careful	Unsociable
Thoughtful	Reserved
Peaceful	Pessimistic
Controlled	Sober
Reliable	Rigid
Even-tempered	Anxious
Calm	Moody
STABLE	UNSTABLE
Leadership	Touchy
Carefree	Restless
Lively	Aggressive
Easygoing	Excitable
Responsive	Changeable
Talkative	Impulsive
Outgoing	Optimistic
Sociable	Active

EXTRAVERTED

Although conditions affecting women have featured prominently in several clinical and psychological studies that link personality factors with disease, not all the conclusions drawn clinically have proved helpful to the feminine cause. Ernst Kretschmer, whose invaluable research in the evaluation of the close relationship that exists between soma and psyche was less impressed by his women patients, tending to read sexual sublimation into any artistic talent or transpersonal experience relayed to him within the confidentiality of the consulting room. On the other hand, his disciple, the distinguished psychiatrist Dr Charlotte Wolff, whom I was privileged to meet socially a number of years ago, nurtured no such fixed ideas. In fact, our conversation revealed a broad and comprehensive understanding of the feminine psyche as related to her specific area of research. Kretschmer and Wolff observed that there were correspondences between physique and temperament which appeared to go hand in hand with certain illnesses. Recognition of the somatic statement therefore helped them to erect a psychobiogram which served as an aid both to psychoanalysis and the diagnosis of future potential problem areas. I shall be dealing with Kretschmer's somewhat chauvinistic views on feminine sexuality in Chapter 12.

The fact that social conditioning or early collective programming has had a damaging effect on the health of many women may be evidenced in various recent psychological and clinical studies. Were we able to express our true archetypes, many of us would not, it seems, be beset with the numerous diseases and complaints, both mental and physical, which are viewed by many as our natural inheritance. Elisabeth Badinter quotes a comment of Diderot, written in the eighteenth century, which is pertinent to the problem: 'I have seen women carry love, jealousy, superstition and anger to excesses that a man never feels.' Badinter continues:

> The reason for such violent transports, which Diderot considered foreign to men, is of an anatomico-physiological order. Woman 'has within her an organ that is liable to terrible spasms, which dominates her and stirs up phantasms of all kinds in her imagination.' It is not surprising, then, that she can pass from hysteria to ecstasy, from revelation to prophecy. Slaves of their uterus and of their fiery imagination, women are 'most extraordinary children' who inspire Diderot with tenderness and pity. He pities them for being what they are — not only doomed to the pains and dangers of childbirth, but also to 'long and dangerous illnesses' when they are past childbearing age.[2]

More women than I could keep count of have voiced the complaint, both privately and publicly, that whoever designed the female body made a pretty bad job of it. Whether or not there is some hidden metaphysical reason for this is debatable, but I, for one, rather suspect there is. However, against all these physical and psychological odds, and the erroneous dogmas to which they have given rise, woman has kept going, and has succeeded.

Chapter 11
Modern Feminine Archetypes

SINCE it is generally believed that archetypes are constant, how can they be divided into 'ancient' and 'modern'? The answer is that they cannot. What happens is this: during specific periods of evolution which, like the astrological Ages, tend to emphasize and in some cases exaggerate certain aspects of the human condition, some archetypes tend to become more accentuated than others.

For example, in the days of classical Greece or Rome women did not hold executive posts in the government or civil service, nor did they participate in such professions as architecture, art, or sculpture. Some of my more erudite readers may well hasten to assure me that the wife of this official, or that great man, did produce an acknowledged work of art, but this would have been the exception rather than the rule. Likewise there were women sages and logicians, as well as those skilled in the healing arts who consulted with and sometimes even instructed the great philosophers and physicians. Some examples are Diotema and Mantinea who were tutors to Pythagoras and Socrates respectively, and Hygieia, Iaso, Panacea and Aegle, the daughters of Asclepius, later deified as the Greek god of healing, who worked closely with their father in his ministrations. Mature souls incarnating into female bodies in such times would have been aware of these limitations, and should they have wished to excel in any field which required a certain standard of education, they would have been obliged to incarnate into the kind of social background which would have afforded them the necessary opportunities.

Thus the stereotyped Greek characters typified by the

goddesses tended to be uncomplicated. Aphrodite, for example, although adept at the domestic arts, was required to confine her talents to the areas of carnal delight. Today an Aphrodite may appear as a love goddess of the silver screen, a pop star sex-symbol, or a writer of salacious literature without necessarily acting out the Hetaira or Courtesan mode in her own private life, or she might even aspire to the love principle at its more elevated frequencies.

Many of the ancient archetypes are, of course, just as valid today as they were in the past, while those which appear limited in the past tense may now be seen to have other, more subtle connotations. Of late a great amount has been written on the feminine archetypes. Books by Harding, Whitmont, Bolen, Gilchrist, and others have supplied the curious woman with a stack of literature to wade through in search of her 'true' self. I have tried it and so have other women I know, but many of us appear to have arrived at the same conclusion: the writers have us all wrong! Can we possibly be the exceptions? Do the experts' stereotypes really exist? I am inclined to think that, broadly speaking, they probably do. This brings us back to my favourite bone of contention — collectives!

The psychology of the collective has long fascinated me for two reasons: first, the dependencies created by major collectives; and second, the suffering they can cause to those who either do not fit in with their requirements, or who are sufficiently individuated to dispense with the need for social strap-hanging. One of the dangers of living in a free society is that many people do not feel sufficiently supported morally and ethically. Old-established ways of behaviour are now considered *passé*, and the tendency, especially among the young, is to be seen as not being 'different'. It takes a strong mind to stand out against the group entity, but it can be done, and many who have tried it and have survived intact are stronger for the experience.

However, while collectives can afford great comfort and security to some they can also pose a threat to others. The id, or shadow — that aspect of the psyche that is kept submerged under the control of conscious discipline — is only too happy to raise its ugly head if given half a chance. Base instincts tend to surface in revolutionary or mob situations when emotion overpowers reason and the process of mass dehumanization gives birth to the 'group entity'. Families, close friends, and people who have been known and respected for years suddenly assume the role of 'the enemy' because they appear to be on the opposing side. Politics and religion are noted dehumanizers and depersonalizers, for they can exert a type of mental influence that encourages the rejection of long-standing relationships, friendships and loyalties to the extent that those who formerly occupied these roles are thenceforth seen as 'scabs' or traitors.

Dehumanization is the name given to the psychological process that takes place when a crowd or gathering of people assumes a group entity. This may be witnessed in witch-hunts, lynch mobs, unruly sports gatherings, and incidences of emotionally or fear-induced mass hysteria. As one reviewer in the *Guardian* remarked: 'This sinister dehumanization is obvious at any political rally, football match or picket line.' My reason for accentuating these factors in a book which is mainly concerned with woman is that women are capable of being equally guilty of these mob reactions. Women's collectives can be very cruel to those who do not conform to the standards decreed by them as the 'norm'. The necessity to establish one's own identity therefore assumes a degree of importance, since it is likely to be the deciding factor as to which collective, if any, one decides to align oneself with. This, no doubt, accounts for the success achieved by those writers who have specialized in this particular aspect of the feminine psychology. My past experiences living in all-female communities taught me that one needs to adopt a very definite stance where women's collectives are concerned; one cannot hover in the middle. One either joins them, or earns their scorn or respect for being an individual, and the latter is no easy task since women are less likely to be taken in by externals than men.

Before we embark on our voyage of personal discovery, however, we should bear in mind the role played by physiology in the selection of the archetype. When our hormones shift dramatically, as they do at puberty and at the menopause, there is frequently a conflict between emotion and reason. Our bodies cry out for the limerant experience, for pregnancy or for sexual experimentation, while our minds point out the folly of such behaviour — how it could ruin our careers, condemn us to a life of homelessness, poverty, and frustration. However, as Dr Jean Bolen points out, behaviour is not determined by hormones alone, but through the interaction of those hormones with the goddess archetypes. From a very early age some women appear to exhibit signs of spiritual maturity or an age-old wisdom that belies their years and enables them to ride the transitional passages from youth to maturity and thence to senior citizenship with an ease and confidence denied to their sisters. There are many metaphysical explanations for this phenomenon, which are too diverse and lengthy to merit inclusion in this book, but with which many goddess-orientated people will already be familiar.

Since some women, when faced with excessive hormonal activity, would naturally react to it in a very different way from others, there are several factors to take into consideration. Bolen tells us:

Pregnancy instigates a massive increase in the hormone progesterone which sustains the pregnancy physiologically. Again, different women react differently to this increase. Some become emotionally fulfilled as their bodies become large with child, and they feel like the embodiment of Demeter, the mother goddess. Others seem almost oblivious to the pregnancy, missing hardly a day of work.

Menopause — the cessation of menstruation brought about by a drop in estrogen and progesterone — is another time of hormonal change. How a woman responds again depends on which goddess is active. For every grieving Demeter suffering from an empty-nest depression, there seems to be — as anthropologist Margaret Mead remarked — other women with a surge of P.M.Z., or 'postmenopausal zest'. This upsurge can happen when a newly energized goddess can now have her long-awaited turn.

Even during monthly periods some women experience 'a goddess shift', as hormone and archetypes interact and have an impact on their psyches. Women who are sensitive to these changes note that during the first half of the cycle they seem more attuned to the independent goddesses — especially Artemis or Athena, with their extraverted go-out-into-the-world focus. Then in the second half of the cycle, as the pregnancy hormone progesterone increases, they note that their 'nesting' tendencies seem stronger and their home-body or dependent feelings become more pronounced. Now Demeter, Hera, Persephone or Hestia becomes the strongest influence.[1]

Bolen's observations are certainly borne out among the many women whom I have either counselled or discussed these matters with over the years. I was particularly pleased to note that Bolen had included Hestia among the home-orientated archetypal goddess figures. So many women tend to see the home in Demeter terms only, the inference being that unless one has given birth at sometime or other, the home is not one's natural habitat. This totally erroneous concept probably grew out of that mythical figure, the Victorian mother, who hovered over her brood like some anxious hen. I have seen some beautiful homes lovingly cared for and well lived in by lesbians, maiden aunts and 'ladies of easy virtue', and some filthy, scruffy hovels inhabited by 'mumsie-types', complete with 'pinny', apple pies in the oven, and babies galore.

Certain archetypes also tend to predominate at given stages in life, the ancient classifications of the feminine psyche applying just as much today as they did in the distant past. Let us take the Triple Goddess, for example — Maiden, Mother and Crone. Although not every woman manages a natural transition from maidenhood to motherhood, the fertility aspect of the feminine psyche will usually find an outlet through other creative avenues of expression. The third goddess aspect, the Crone or Wise Woman, is believed to arrive not so much with age as with the wisdom gleaned from life's experiences in the two earlier modes. The entry into the Crone stage in a woman's life has caused many a former outgoing, extraverted woman to abandon worldly values in favour of meditation or spiritual/metaphysical studies.

In all of these I am in agreement with Dr Bolen, but I also believe that just as we each have a basic sonic or keynote, we also have an inherent archetype which resonates to that keynote. So, no matter how many areas of archetypal experience we may elect to negotiate during the course of one lifetime, all these are inevitably overshadowed by the original, which accords with the nature of our true Essence. So, Nicola, Emma, or Julie may each express themselves through the Demeter archetype in keeping with that which is demanded of them within the collective of which they form a part. Nicola, however, may be a basic Hestia, so she will be by nature quiet and home-orientated, and have no wish to be jetting around the world. Emma's Demeter exterior, on the other hand, may be cloaking a pulsating Aphrodite, and once her children are packed safely off to school and the house has been tidied up, lover boy will pop quietly in through the back door! Julie, however, has married and produced children because her family has expected it of her. Inwardly she is yearning to board a jet clipper and be off to faraway places, which is only natural since she is an Artemis at heart.

If we stray too far from our original archetype we are in for trouble. Subconscious frustrations set in which we fail to understand, and these in turn somatize into those vague but nevertheless real discomforts which the medical profession finds difficult to pigeon-hole. Our basic archetype is inextricably bound up with our karma. Ignore the one and the other is not fulfilled. The secret, therefore, lies in discovering the real self rather than the archetypal identity one has conveniently adopted to fit in with society, accommodate the nagging needs of one's hormones, obtain an easy meal ticket, or hang on to a man who is looking for an escape route anyway!

Although several Jungian analysts, in the company of women writers such as Bolen, have tended to emphasize our involvement with feminine archetypes as exemplified in the goddesses of classical Greece and other ancient pantheons, there is also a school of thought which opines that masculine and feminine archetypes should not be encapsulated in two distinct groupings. In other words, a woman should be able to imbibe masculine archetypes and likewise a man with the goddesses. I have dealt with this in some detail in *Olympus — An Experience in Self-Discovery* in which all twelve of the Greek archetypes, both male and female, are cross-referenced and can equally be cross-utilized. And it does work. I see no reason why we should limit ourselves to the feminine manifestation of archetypal energies, since the development of the masculine side of woman's nature has been such a marked feature in recent years. Perhaps our female city magnates could do with a goodly dose of Hermes, our architects with the steady

confidence and skills of Hephaestus, our musicians with
Apollo's golden touch, and our women ministers with Zeus'
thunderbolt. I can certainly think of a few men who would
undoubtedly benefit from a touch of Hestia, Hera or even
Aphrodite.

M. Esther Harding discusses hidden aspects of the
feminine psyche at some length, proposing that we project
unconscious factors onto inanimate objects, so that when
we see human qualities and characteristics in these they are
not just arbitrary imaginings but reflections of our own
conscious qualities. She suggests that when we regard
natural phenomena naïvely, personifying them as myths
and folk tales, or in the poetic language of art, we are
interpreting Nature according to our *own* nature — in other
words, projecting our own unconscious into the outer
world.

However, I cannot fully agree with Harding on the question of animism. There is ample evidence of the existence
of an intelligent life force in everything from the tiniest
quarks, charms, or super-strings upwards, while Sheldrake's
morphic resonance theory suggests that communication
can take place between particles beyond the barriers of time
and space. This subject has recently been tackled by such
scientific stalwarts as Lyall Watson and Danah Zohar, who
find themselves in agreement with the metaphysicians (and
the ancient goddess worshippers) on this issue.

Jung divided women into four main categories: Mary, the
Mother; Eve, the Temptress; Helen, the Heroine; and
Sophia, the Intellectual. This theme is re-echoed by Edward
Whitmont in *The Symbolic Quest* in which he suggests
that all women unconsciously identify themselves with
the Mother, the Hetaira or Courtesan, the Amazon, or the
Medium. These would seem to be four fairly straightforward if somewhat simplistic categorizations which, if
translated into Greek terms, would appear as Demeter,
Aphrodite, Artemis and Athene. There are, however,
married women who are 'wifely' rather than motherly, as
discussed in Chapter 4.

Cherry Gilchrist, who is closely connected with the
Sophia Network for women, employs nine feminine archetypes in her book *The Circle of Nine* (the number nine
being traditionally sacred to the goddess), these being: the

Queen of Beauty, the Weaving Mother, the Lady of Light, the Queen of the Night, the Great Mother, the Lady of the Hearth, the Queen of the Earth, the Just Mother, and the Lady of the Dance. Gilchrist's approach differs considerably from that of Bolen, or my own for that matter, but she nevertheless contributes a valid, if unusual, approach to the many guises adopted by women during the process of fulfilling their respective archetypal roles.

Since the maternal expression of the feminine mode would appear to predominate among so many women it obviously demands particular attention, which it will duly receive in Chapter 13.

Chapter 12
Women and Sexuality

THE recent appearance of AIDS which, we are told, is likely to assume epidemic proportions in the third millennium if a cure is not soon found, has caused both men and women to take stock of their sexual lives and practices. In early matriarchal societies the sexual experience was not confined to the reproductive mode and the penetration normally associated therewith. The joy to be experienced by full use of the tactile sense, the sheer act of closeness and the warmth of a loving embrace were considered essential to the full and varied expression of the feminine psyche. With the onset of Christianity such 'female vanities' were considered highly sinful. Sex was designed for procreation only, and couplings that were not productive of progeny were viewed with suspicion. Many a childless couple was accused of 'sinning', while sterility, seen in those days as entirely the fault of the woman, was considered to be some kind of a punishment for indulgences in sexual practices not approved of by the Church.

In recent years many women saw fresh hope in the advent of psychology, and although some feminists have tended to view Freudian attitudes as little more than patrist-orientated phallocentrism, others have been grateful to Freud for opening the door of the sexual closet. Freud's former disciple, Carl Jung, however, was quick to recognize the importance of the goddess principle and the role it was destined to play, and although his views on masculine/feminine expression might not meet with the approval of every woman, he certainly paved the way for a more open approach among future generations.

Freud's views on the nature and functions of the libido are

probably the best known of all his studies. Jung, speaking of his early friendship with Freud, wrote:

> It is a widespread error to imagine that I do not see the value of sexuality. On the contrary, it plays a large part in my psychology as an essential — though not the sole — expression of psychic wholeness. But my main concern has been to investigate, over and above its personal significance and biological function, its spiritual aspect and its numinous meaning, and thus to explain what Freud was so fascinated by but was unable to grasp. My thoughts on this subject are contained in the 'Psychology of the Transference' and the *Mysterium Coniunctionis*. Sexuality is of the greatest importance as the expression of the chthonic spirit. That spirit is the 'other face of God', the dark side of the God-image. The question of the chthonic spirit has occupied me ever since I began to delve in to the world of alchemy. Basically, this interest was awakened by that early conversation with Freud, when, mystified, I felt how deeply stirred he was by the phenomenon of sexuality. [1]

As regards the nature of the libido, Jung conceived of this as 'a psychic analogue of physical energy, hence as a more or less quantitative concept, which therefore should not be defined in qualitative terms.' [2]

History has shown us how periods of extreme repression are often followed by a corresponding increase in hedonism, usually seen in compensatory terms but definable with equal validity in the chaos–order sequence. There is a middle path, but before we examine its pros and cons an analysis of the sexual drive is called for, since its variations appear to cause so much consternation. This is especially true among certain established collectives, many of whose members fail to understand the basic biological functions at work behind the scenes, and the enormous effect these can have on libidinous behaviour patterns.

Although at the physiological level sexual impulses appear to be largely governed by endocrine and other biological factors, the brain itself can be seen as the largest sexual organ in the human body. Certain areas of cerebral activity are known to govern the *libido sexualis* to the extent that physiological or psychological traumas can produce over-activity, or perverse variants, or frigidity. In questioning the relationship between symbolic genders and

the meaning of the cultural influences which have pro-
moted them, Whitmont discovered some interesting factors
relating to sexuality and brain hemisphere activity. This led
him to the conclusion that our hormones are also inter-
connected with the development of those brain regions
which control sexual behaviour.

This kind of reasoning tends to be oversimplistic, however, for as I understand it, the purpose of our spiritual
descent into matter is to learn to control the physical and
rebalance it in accordance with the kind of metaphysical
understanding that arises from transpersonal seeking. If
women's and men's hormones are the cause of the war
between the sexes, then we should employ our minds/
willpower to remove that barrier so that peace can once
again reign.

However, the brain is merely the coordinator between the
endocrine system and that intangible factor — the mind.
The brain can be understood as a complex computer, which
has to be programmed. When we do not effect that programming ourselves, either by conscious control, or by virtue of
an aspect of our 'higher selves' which is assisting us in a
particular incarnation, the collective programming of the
zeitgeist and the ethos into which we have been born takes
over the task for us. Now we can break that code and
reprogramme via the methods of education or spiritual
seeking, or we can live with it and remain cosily in tune
with the ways and views of popular collectives. Besides, an
increasing number of anomalies in the male-female system
are beginning to surface, and as the horizons of psychological and physiological knowledge slowly broaden, it
would be unwise to impress the dye stamp of the norm at
this point in time. Generalized polarities can and do apply
in many cases, but I am inclined to think that the old sun-
moon, lingam-yoni, light-darkness, active-passive classifications are likely to give way to other, more cosmic
interpretations as we cross the space-time frontiers of the
Aquarian Age. On the issue of comparative male-female
sexuality, I would therefore prefer to reserve judgment, as I
rather suspect that we are only in possession of a minimal
number of the real facts.

As regards the sexual modes predominant in today's
world, there is little doubt that our libido is greatly influ-

enced by what we see, read, eat or drink, and by what is happening in the chemistry of our bodies. For example, regarding our food intake, Mahatma Gandhi wisely observed that celibacy was not possible — for a man, at least — unless a pure non-meat diet was adhered to. Ancient Eastern tradition divided food into three categories: *sattvic* — pure foods; *rajasic* — foods promoting activity and passion; and *tamasic* — foods that encourage dullness, inertia and depression. *Tamasic* foods, such as sugar, salt and meat are also highly addictive, and over-indulgence in food or drink is often accompanied by corresponding sexual excesses.

Where sexual aberrations are concerned, neurologists and psychotherapists often find it impossible to establish a convincing psychogenesis in many cases of homosexuality and other kinds of what are considered to be psychosexual anomalies, whereas their organic origin may be clearly discernible. In other words, many of us are born the way we are and so have to live with it the best we can, although in cases where there are accompanying physiological factors, complete sex changes have sometimes proved to be the only solution. Genuine deviation is often unfairly judged as libertinism, much to the distress of many gay men and women. A lesbian I know takes great exception to the idea that she or the woman with whom she shares her life are hedonistic Messalinas. Like many other homosexuals, their sexual proclivities are neither greater nor lesser than the 'average' heterosexual couple — if there is such a thing. Gay women are now able to emerge from their closets and declare their preference openly, although in generations past lesbianism was never viewed in quite the same light as male homosexuality.

The sexual impulse is seen as an important, inseparable component of our total make-up. Kretschmer described it as 'a dynamic factor of the first order which can provide a vast amount of power for the psychic apparatus, either directly and consciously or, perhaps more often, in the most complicated commutations, disguises, and metamorphoses — in any case, far more comprehensively than is usually supposed.'[3]

Sexual swings are known to occur as our hormonal balance adjusts in the course of our lives. Just as our archetypal preferences obligingly accommodate these changes, so also do the requirements of our libido. There is a well known popular saying that I have often heard cruelly used against some older women: 'A harlot when young, a devotee when old'. This is seen by psychologists as expressing the dynamic relations between sexuality and religious activity at their lower levels. Kretschmer wrote:

> That a certain kind of bigoted religiosity is in fact a direct form of sexual substitution is quite patent. There are many transitional stages leading from this primitive kind of substitution to true *sublimation*, i.e. the transformation of primitive impulses into dynamically correlated religious, ethical and artistic values.
>
> The transitional stages between crude substitution and sublimation are represented in the religious beliefs of many strange little communities, sects, and conventicles which form round the strongly affective personalities of certain eccentrics, paranoid prophets, and founders of religions. In the relationship between the heaven-sent prophet and his for the most part female adherents, religious veneration and erotic ecstasy are psychologically indistinguishable, in fact they constitute a single feeling. In more educated circles also, the same remarks apply to the comet's tail of female worshippers in the wake of a celebrated revivalist preacher, mystic, or theosophist. One would be inclined to regard the combination of sexual acts and sacramental ritual which characterize the worship of historical sects . . . as a rare curiosity, were it not for the fact even today we can observe the same combination of feeling with almost identically the same ceremonial in modern paranoid conventicles. In the religious rites and ethical ideology of such sects the sexual impulse frequently exhibits the most sharply atavistic ambivalence as a kind of taboo, appearing as something which is both sacred and unclean and possessed of great and mysterious magic power.[4]

However, that was written in the 1950s, and today would be considered unacceptably sexist in certain circles. I do not concur with Professor Kretschmer regarding the preponderance of female adherents, at least not in popular modern 'cults' and their associated minority collectives, although the situation might well have been different in his day.

The connection between sex and religion must naturally include Tantrism and other forms of mystico-sexual practices favoured in the East. During his travels in India, Jung

was shown a pagoda in Konorak (Orissa), which was covered
from base to pinnacle with explicit sexual sculptures.
Seeing a group of young peasants admiring the same, Jung
took issue with the pandit regarding the possible dangers of
the fantasy-inducing aspects of the display, to which the
guide replied: 'But that is just the point. How can they ever
become spiritualized if they do not first fulfil their karma?
These admittedly obscene images are here for the very
purpose of recalling to the people their dharma (law);
otherwise these unconscious fellows might forget it.' As the
two men continued their exploratory walk, the guide added:
'Naturally this does not apply to people like you and me, for
we have attained to a level of consciousness which is above
this sort of thing. But for these peasant boys it is an
indispensable instruction and admonishment.' [5]

Are we then to presuppose that the more spiritually
mature among us are better able to handle these energies
and assume a less carnal and more transcendental approach
toward sex? This attitude should be looked at carefully,
since some people have been known to emulate a spiritual
mode under false pretences in order to give an impression
of piety, which in itself constitutes a psychological danger.

In her book *Sex Is Not Compulsory*, Liz Hodgkinson
postulates that regular sex is often indulged in purely as a
convention. As with any ingrained, ritualistic habit, it can
develop into an addiction, the need becoming insatiable. As
such it constitutes as much a dependency for many people
as drugs or alcohol. Once again we come up against the
libido factor, and although I have counselled many people
who find frequent or habitual sex a prerequisite for a
satisfactory relationship, I have come across an equal
number (if not more, especially among women) who are in
total agreement with Ms Hodgkinson, and could happily
live without it. Hodgkinson writes:

> Married men — or those in a long-term partnership — will
> know just how often they have to beg their partners for sex, or
> wheedle them into it. They may have to use moral and emo-
> tional blackmail, physical force, threats and punishments in
> order to force the other person into agreeing to sex. Even in our
> supposedly sexually liberated days, many women know they
> have to pretend to have a headache, be fast asleep or too tired,
> so that their husbands — people for whom they have long

ceased to feel the slightest desire — will not bother them for sex.[6]

To this I would also like to add — pretending to have an orgasm. Many women I have counselled have told me how their husbands refuse to complete their sexual sessions until they have fulfilled this demand. Since many of them are either too tired, uninterested, or just not at all aroused, it pays them to fake it in order to end the scenario and get some sleep. Trying to force orgasms can create terrible headaches, as many women have found to their discomfort, so why are we required to put up with such unnecessary suffering in the name of 'love'?

Hodgkinson contends that she does not believe there to be 'any such thing as purely *sexual* desire or *sexual* frustration. What we call arousal, frustration, and satisfaction are actually generalized mental feelings that we have in recent times, for some reason, ascribed to the genital area.'[7] She proposes that what people do have is a need for intimacy, to blend with another person with whom they may share their joy or pain. Celibacy, she tells us, has far more going for it:

> Celibacy has come to be regarded with extreme distate, because we have been led to believe that sex is (a) necessary and (b) natural. In fact, it is neither. Apart from its purpose in propagating the species, sex is no more necessary to our daily lives than a glass of whisky or a cream bun. All the celibate people I interviewed during the course of this book have spoken of the benefits of the non-sexual life, and have claimed that it is celibacy, rather than sex, which frees the individual and confers happiness. Celibacy, according to its adherents, can make people stronger in themselves, more autonomous, more self-confident and certainly more creative and intelligent. It also brings about an improved state of physical health.[8]

My own researches have tended to indicate that the path best suited to the majority of women lies somewhere in the middle. Woman is only recently emerging from her cocoon of patrist domination, so it remains to be seen how she will develop given the time, space and opportunity to simply 'be herself'. Males I cannot vouch for, as I have insufficient data to effect a fair analysis, although there are probably statistics available for the asking. Besides, I find men are often reluctant to discuss such matters with female researchers. The fact that some men have adopted a similar attitude, however, may be evidenced in the words of Mahatma Gandhi, who took a vow of lifelong *brahma-charya* when he was 36. He wrote:

> It has not been proved to my satisfaction that sexual union in marriage is itself good and beneficial to the unionists . . . momentary excitement and satisfaction there certainly was. But it was invariably followed by exhaustion. And the desire for union returned immediately the effect of exhaustion wore out. Although I have always been a conscientious worker, I can clearly recall that this indulgence interfered with my work. It was the consciousness of this limitation that put me on the track of self-restraint and I have no manner of doubt that the self-restraint is responsible for the comparative freedom from illness that I have enjoyed for long periods, and for my output of energy and work both physical and mental which eye-witnesses have described as phenomenal. [9]

Hodgkinson suggests that it is more than likely the 'thou shalt not' aspect of physical denial that caused many of us to veer in the opposite direction, whereas if we were able to shed that certain childishness which demands that we automatically oppose disciplines of any kind, we might benefit both physically and mentally. Self-discipline is very much an attribute of spiritual maturity, however, and most of us have not yet reached the exalted spiritual status of a Gandhi or a Mother Teresa.

Liz Hodgkinson is a successful author and journalist. Formerly married, and the mother of two sons, Ms Hodgkinson tells me: 'I have practised what I preached by getting divorced. My former husband also believes that marriage is a complete nonsense, and our relationship is so much better now that the rubbish of legality is not attached to it. There is nobody else involved in either case — thank goodness — and we live happily but separately.' Her views on sex, she assures us, are now the complete opposite of those she held 'a couple of decades ago', since she has observed for herself that 'more frequent physical sex has not added one jot to the sum of the world's happiness. Rather, it has probably been instrumental in compounding the sum of human misery.' [10] I found her book to be one of the best studies on the subject, as it deals with the kind of everyday problems that the professionals tend to dismiss as mundane. Not everyone will agree with her premises, but they certainly strike at the heart of a deeply important aspect of our psychology. The libido finds many different avenues of expression, some of which are relatively harmless, while others do pose a threat to society. This brings us to an escalating problem that faces women in particular in our present day and age — that of rape.

Rape, we are informed by our lawyers and sociologists, is really a crime of violence and not of sex. There have even been cases where the victim has been abused by several men who have egged each other on as though it were some kind of amusement or sport. By the same token we could define wife-battering as a crime of sex, so let us take a deeper look at both. Because the legal profession is dominated by patrism, women rape victims are seldom accorded the credence they deserve, let alone the compensation normally awarded to victims of social violence. So why the difference? Because it is *women* we are dealing with, of course. Now, were a man to be raped it would become a vastly different matter. Some legal authorities have tended to blame women themselves for this injustice which has been precipitated, or so they tell us, by the fact that women have 'cried wolf' on too many occasions in the past to be taken seriously. The same is also said of child abuse, with both the police and the legal eagles frequently rejecting the veracity of the children in favour of the statements of the accused adults. The increase in cases of rape is undoubtedly symptomatic of the period of uncertainty and change through which we are at present passing. This is of little consolation to its victims, however, whose resulting traumas frequently persist long after the initial shock. Incorporated under the heading of rape is indecent assault, which includes forced oral intercourse and other sexual practices which are unacceptable if forced at knife or fist-point, or emotional blackmail of any kind.

Another, and in my opinion more serious manifestation of rape, is that which takes place within the framework of legally accepted partnerships — i.e. marriage. By English law it is not a crime to rape one's wife. In plain language, the price of the marriage certificate entitles a man to sexually abuse a woman as much as he pleases, and she has no comeback whatsoever. Current inquiries have uncovered a network of misery that would shame any civilization.

The enormity of this problem was recently featured in a television programme commissioned by ITV's *World in Action*, entitled 'The Right to Rape' that was shown on 25 September 1989. A recent survey in England and Wales showed that 14 per cent of women were regularly raped by their husbands. More than a million women suffer thus, and probably twice that number if the truth were known, since many are too ashamed to speak of their humiliations. Violence was unveiled as a regular feature of British family life in the lower income groups, with rape committed on a regular basis in one in five less well-off families. In fact, many men are of the opinion that sex on tap is part and parcel of the marriage deal. In other words the married woman is nothing more than a sex slave who is obliged to perform at her 'master's' bidding! Laws making marital rape a crime have already been instituted in the United States, notably in Oregon and Massachusetts.

Marital rape is a 'Cinderella' crime, an invisible statistic, a taboo subject, and far more common than once believed. The women interviewed spoke of feeling degraded, and of seeing their husbands as the most dangerous men in their lives — more feared, in fact, than the 'stranger on a dark night'. More than 22 per cent of women are forced to have sex against their will, while two out of five have accepted forced sex without realizing that they need not put up with it. To say 'no', however, constituted a threat to their person, or even their children. Of 1,000 women interviewed, 96 per cent said that English law should be changed and brought in line with Scottish law, which gives women the right to prosecute husbands who force sex on them. An organization entitled 'Women Against Rape' (WAR) is fighting to have the legal definition of rape broadened to include 'rape through the abuse of power and rape by financial duress, like threatening to harm the children or to throw her out of the house.'

I have heard it remarked that one cannot have sex with those one likes without complicating the friendship unalterably — love, liking, and lust being three different things. It is therefore sometimes advisable to live with one's friends and sleep (or breed) with one's lovers. The present social and financial structure is hardly conducive to this arrangement as far as women are concerned, but perhaps there are more enlightened times ahead.

In discussing this issue with both men and women I have been assured that it *is* possible to find liking, friendship, love, and sex within the context of one relationship, albeit rarely. To those who have been so fortunate as to discover this much prized combination I say 'good luck', and I wish that there was more of it about. But, sadly, it would seem that they are in the minority, which leaves the majority of women suspended in limbo, until such times as we come to terms with our anima and animus and learn to use our Dragon/Serpent powers to best effect.

Another 'crime of violence' against women which is also seen in both a social and sexual context is wife-battering. Liz Gill, reporting in *The Times* on 22 May 1989, referred to the work of Sergeant Colette Paul, who helped to set up Britain's first police domestic violence unit, an idea which is now spreading to many parts of the country. Gill writes:

> They come in to see police sergeant Colette Paul with their smashed faces and bruised bodies and say: 'I'm not one of those, you know.'
>
> Popular wisdom holds that they should be downtrodden drabs, helpless punchbag victims of the rage of a particularly low-life kind of man. Paul does not share this view. For a start, she never uses the word: 'victim' — 'with all its connotations of powerlessness.'
>
> 'Many of them are very strong women, and very brave. They are survivors.
>
> 'We tend to think of it as a working-class problem or a problem of colour or culture, but believe me, it cuts across all classes, all types. I've seen doctor's wives and businessmen's wives and policemen's wives. I've seen a professional career woman beaten up by her computer executive husband simply because she was more successful than he was.'

The sexual innuendoes involved in this particular brand of violence are surely akin to those of rape, but not in the generally accepted sense of the term 'sex', i.e. as associated with the use or abuse of the sexual organs themselves, or those practices normally defined as being of a sexual nature. What we are surely dealing with is a psychological or subconscious hatred of women, based purely on their gender. The excuses used for this kind of behaviour are varied and interesting. Sometimes the motive is pure jealousy, as in the case of the computer programmer cited above. For others it is personal frustration. Some men are brazen enough to maintain that women actually enjoy being beaten but, as Sergeant Paul says, 'I've never come across a single woman who enjoyed being beaten.' And I would fully endorse that remark. I have encountered cases where violent men also beat up their sons — until the boys are strong enough to hit back — but as their violence is mostly confined to members of the feminine gender, I fail to see how these crimes can be labelled as anything else but 'sexual'.

Some readers may wonder why I have included these violent manifestations of misogyny in a chapter about woman's sexuality. It is because so much of the blame is placed squarely on the shoulders of women — the temptresses, hussies, evil ones, those who have caused unbridled passions to rise in the hearts (and loins!) of men since the mythical Eve first seduced Adam with her Serpent power. Rape cases, for example, are frequently dismissed from the courts on the grounds that the victim 'behaved provocatively' in dress or manner, and therefore asked for everything she got.

There is much talk these days about the change in sexual attitudes experienced during and after the menopause. In some women the libido is increased, which is often put down to their new freedom from the fear of pregnancy. Other women, however, appear to lose their sexual drive almost completely, which demonstrates that it is a very individual process, and so generalizations should not be made.

According to Ruby Wallace, writing in the *Guardian*, 5 December 1989, contrary to what many people believe, the libido is considerably heightened during pregnancy. Masters and Johnson reported an increase in desire during the second trimester (15th to 28th weeks) and a decrease during the third (29th week to term). This is hardly surprising, since the whole of the pelvic area increases in vascularity, making the capacity for sexual tension and orgasm much greater. The entire body is flooded with hormones whose effect increases clitoral responsiveness and strengthening of the muscles effective in orgasm.

Breasts and nipples also become more sensitive which is encouraging of stimulating foreplay. Never having experienced a pregnancy myself I asked around a few friends of mine who had. Their opinions differed considerably. Some agreed with Ms Wallace while others firmly declared that the pregnant stage had produced entirely the opposite effect, putting them off the sexual act completely and making them feel 'overly broody'.

Menstruation produces similarly diverse effects, some women claiming to feel their libidos stirring just prior to or during their periods. Others, however, suffer from PMT (premenstrual tension) which is often accompanied by depression, while the period pains experienced by many are hardly conducive to love-making.

Of the many women who have confided in me both privately and professionally over the years, the majority, while admitting to enjoying sex, have secretly confessed that it was the combination of penetration with the loving closeness, cuddling, and foreplay that was most meaningful to them, since it brought them in closer contact and communication with their partner. It is for this reason that the new approach to sexual pleasure (the old goddess ways revived!) which allows both partners to explore, and make the most of each other's sexuality, is proving more fulfilling to many women than the instant penetration employed by insensitive males who often view their advances in terms of obliging the sex-starved woman who, should she see fit to reject such advances, is immediately labelled a 'dyke' or frigid. However, there appears to be a tendency for some goddess-orientated literature to over-romanticize the old 'temple prostitute' concept, which naturally results in an erroneous association of the expression of the feminine libido with hedonism. My own researches tend to suggest that the life of religious whoredom was not always the personal choice of those women who found themselves bound to its service. Anyway, what temple servers did in ancient Crete is hardly relevant to life today, and modern women should not be judged in that light.

Limerance, the term for romantic love coined by Dorothy Tennov, is characterized by involuntariness of feeling and intrusive fantasy, and experienced by *both* sexes. Non-limerants are apparently incapable of understanding the lack of logic displayed by those who are experiencing the limerant condition but in spite of this, 'falling in love' and enjoying the fruits of love has been a source of universal enjoyment (and tears, and anguish, and suicide) since the year dot! Will we carry on doing it? Of course we will — many of us obviously think the risks are worth it.

By the time my readers reach the end of this chapter my views on female sexuality will, no doubt, have become abundantly clear. But in case any of my points have been missed, may I reiterate my belief that women should not be lumped together under any one heading or designation, either sexually, intellectually, emotionally, or spiritually. To me the world is peopled by individuals, and although many may choose to tread the path of life via the group experience, ultimately we are each a unique unit with our own personal identity.

Chapter 13
The Creatrix

SINCE time immemorial the archetypal mother has held sway over the minds and emotions of millions of people throughout the world. Even those religions and ideologies that deny woman due rights or acknowledgements are happy to accommodate her in her maternal capacity. In this respect mankind is no different from many other species that will go to any length to ensure the perpetuation of its kind. It is a natural instinct rather than a logical deduction, since the importance of woman as the Creatrix was acknowledged even before men realized that they, too, played a part in the conception of a child. M. Esther Harding remarks:

> The desire to have physical children is not unrelated to the almost universal desire for immortality. Among primitive people and also in the Orient, one of the chief reasons for desiring children is that there may be someone whose duty it is to perform the burial rites and continue the ancestor sacrifices which are believed to keep alive the spirit of the deceased and further it on its journey in the other land. Among many peoples, too, it is felt that the parents gain a certain kind of immortality through their children who carry on the family name and in whose lives the life of the parents is in a way continued.
>
> In certain very early and primitive myths a distinction is made, however, between the partial, or quasi, immortality of a life lived in the person of the child, and a more direct immortality of the individual himself. The idea seems to be that the divine creative spark in man can either express itself in the creation of a human child or, alternatively, it can be assimilated into the individual himself, creating in him a spirit which is immortal. [1]

For many women, the creation of a child represents the apex of their life's experience, their *raison d'être*. And for some it is not simply the act of giving birth, but the subsequent nurturing and raising of children that constitutes fulfilment for them. Bearing all this in mind, it is little wonder that childless couples who are unable to obtain a baby through the normal, recognized adoption channels are frequently prepared to mortgage their homes or sell everything they possess in order to raise sufficient funds to purchase an unwanted infant on the black market. According to one survey, one woman in eight is infertile, while another report estimated it as nearer one in five.

The recent increase in abortions has made the task of adoption more difficult than ever before. Hospital authorities that appear totally insensitive to the feelings of both sides of this lobby are often to blame for the enmity which must certainly exist between the 'haves' and the 'have-nots'. In fact, it was brought to my notice that at a certain gynaecological clinic the 'terminations' were lined up in chairs on one side facing the 'infertiles' who were seated on the other. The young woman who gave me this information, who was at the time receiving treatment for infertility, told me she used to cry for hours after each visit.

Of course, there are two sides to every story, and just as our young friend had a nice house, generous and kindly husband and no financial worries, so the occupants of the opposing seats may well have been in dire financial straits with no one to care for them or provide a home for their child. A childless couple I knew some years ago tried very hard to adopt a Vietnamese war orphan, but were turned down on the grounds that they 'had no experience'. Instead, a family living nearby, who already had two children of their own, managed to meet the authorities' requirements in spite of the fact that people who knew them well were only too well aware that their intimate environment was hardly conducive to the stable raising of a family at the best of times. A year later, when the husband left home for a younger woman, the baby had to be uprooted and placed in care.

There are two kinds of woman for whom the motherhood issue can cause great mental (and sometimes physical) suffering: those who see the Demeter mode as their one and only objective, but who are unable to have children of their own and are subsequently denied adoption; and those who have already raised a family, but whose children have grown up and flown the coop. Add to these the problems of the menopause and the ensuing period of loneliness and confusion, and we have fertile ground for the growth of neurosis or worse.

Women who have managed to produce families with little or no problem can often be extremely cruel to those who have not. The hurt is, of course, the greatest to those who have tried in vain to secure a pregnancy, while the woman who has deliberately elected to remain childless for reasons best known to herself is less likely to feel the pangs of rejection and ridicule. A television programme in 1986 on the subject of infertility highlighted the fact that in many cases of nervous breakdowns and other psychosomatic ailments suffered among the childless, it was not so much a woman's inability or refusal to have children that was the cause of her suffering, but the terrible stigma that childlessness still carries to this day, especially in certain sections of society, which many women (and men) are totally unable to cope with. Some men even leave their wives for young women because of their inability to produce progeny. The need to 'run with the herd' is so strong with some people that they are incapable of effecting any deep or lasting relationship with a partner whose health or physical make-up might preclude them from child-bearing.

Another factor involved in the infertility issue, and the anguish it can cause some women, is the implied lack of control over their bodies. The fertile woman can choose whether or not to conceive; the infertile woman has no such choice.

This leads me to the question: motherhood — choice or accident? How many times have I heard it said, 'well, little James (Julia) was not planned, of course, and we were really at our wits' end at the time, but now he (she) is here we would not be without him (her).' Life's 'little accidents' have a habit of turning out better for some than others. Today's abortion laws tend to take care of the unwanted pregnancies which, years ago, would have landed the unfortunate girls in the 'workhouse', or worse, although many women view the recent change from 26 to 22 weeks as an infringement of personal liberties. On the other hand, there are many single parents by choice who have elected to pursue the role of motherhood against great odds and without the assistance of a partner. I have also known many single women in the past who would have loved to have adopted a child, but whose single status denied them that right, despite being well qualified through their stable background and lack of financial problems.

The belief that every woman should be a mother is based in the myth of the maternal instinct. Many biologists, psychologists, psychiatrists and sociologists are now of the opinion that the wish to become a mother is a socio-cultural conditioned response and not, as was previously believed, a biological need. In other words, it has been programmed into the feminine gender as a social convenience. This ritual commences in childhood with toys specially designed to accustom the girl child to her future reproductive role. It is followed through in school with the encouragement of more 'feminine' studies rather than the sciences. This attitude is reinforced by parents and peers, and advertising hammers it home at every possible opportunity. Those women who do not conform are viewed either as 'oddballs' or just plain selfish. Tricia Stallings, writing in the *Guardian* (15 December 1987) captures it beautifully in her article 'Nature Never Meant Us To Be Mothers' with the comment:

> Nowhere else do we find such a thorough and complete conditioning process. Yet we are told the desire to reproduce is based on 'maternal instinct'. The ultimate tyranny of a social dictate is the acceptance of that dictate having its origin in nature. This is the case with the so-called maternal instinct.

Many women have simply accepted this conditioning, only to find themselves extremely uncomfortable in the maternal role. There should be some way in which we can seek help or counselling at an early age to determine our correct archetype, because if we pursue the Demeter line in order to conform with everyone else, when we are really an Athene or Artemis at heart, we will pay for it in later life. And what is more, our family will also be dragged through the mire of our suffering with us. As an astrologer, I should probably say that the natal chart is as good an indication as any as to which path we should or should not elect to pursue. However, birth charts are seldom simple in that they tend to show a series of alternatives or bridges that need to be crossed before the true self becomes clearly defined in the mirror of life.

So we follow the crowd willy-nilly. We get married, or live with a man according to our preference, and produce babies because all our friends are out wheeling prams and we feel somewhat left out. The truth slowly dawns, however, and we may find ourselves having to wait until the child or children are well established at school before we can resume our studies again or take up the work of our real choice. There are those who have managed to secure the best of both worlds, but in my experience one needs to be a very special sort of person to give equal attention to the needs of both a growing family and a responsible career.

It has been suggested that women are by nature more security-minded than men because of their need to nurture and provide a home for their families. I do not see this as the deciding factor in the security issue, however, since many women who are either single, married without children, or gay, are just as security-conscious as their Demeter sisters, and more so in some cases. Whether or not a woman has children, she can still be subjected to the indignity of being left stranded after a broken marriage.

Journalist Polly Toynbee commented in the *Guardian*, 9 February 1989, on Sylvia Ann Hewlett's book *A Lesser Life: The Myth of Women's Liberation*, which has been a sensation in America:

The picture she paints of women's lives is grim indeed. Women and children are worse off now than they have ever been. 'Liberation' has brought freedom for men and poverty for women and children. With half of the marriages failing (a third in Britain) women are left to rear their children alone and their earnings are still only 64 per cent of men's (66 per cent in Britain).

Career opportunities appear open to young women but turn to dust as soon as they have children. Women who wish to be equal to men have to choose — as the Victorians did — between love and families, or spinsterhood and barrenness. But half of those who choose family will lose it anyway and become 'displaced homemakers' — alone, poor, and unemployable after divorce.

The family is in crisis. Because of divorce, women have to work, have to maintain their skills. But they are caught straddled between the Fifties cult of motherhood and the Seventies collapse of support for them and their children. Only 10 per cent of divorced women receive alimony and only 30 per cent any support for their children and the sums of money are mainly so small no one could live on them ... Women and children are fast becoming the new poor, as even wealthy, middleclass mothers and children tumble into poverty after divorce. Women become 73 per cent poorer, while their husbands go on to become 42 per cent richer after divorce.

Negative traits in motherhood can be productive of corresponding aberrations in children. In writing on 'The Mother Complex', Jung had this to say:

> The mother archetype forms the foundation of the so-called mother-complex. It is an open question whether a mother-complex can develop without the mother having taken part in its formation as a demonstrable causal factor. My own experience leads me to believe that the mother always plays an active part in the origin of the disturbance, especially in infantile neuroses or in neuroses whose aetiology undoubtedly dates back to early childhood. In any event, the child's instincts are disturbed, and this constellates archetypes which, in their turn, produce fantasies that come between the child and its mother as an alien and often frightening element. Thus, if the children of an over-anxious mother regularly dream that she is a terrifying animal or a witch, these experiences point to a split in the child's psyche that predisposes it to a neurosis. [2]

As Jung has so wisely pointed out, motherhood is not without problems. For example, in the United States where the feminist movement is purported to be at its strongest, some women are still following in the steps of those ancient Greeks who saw fit to expose their girl children. Of course, they do not leave their new-born girl-babies to die of exposure on some windswept mountainside, but the principle is the same in that they are ridding themselves of female foetuses as soon as the sex of the child they are carrying can be determined. At the Fertility Institute in New Orleans, Louisiana, there is the Repository for Germinal Choice, where a woman entering a pregnancy can decide the sex of her baby in advance. The number of women choosing boy-children apparently far outnumber those wishing for a girl. In a country where many infertile couples are being forced to buy their families from among the poor of the Third World the aforementioned seems somehow incongruous.

Motherhood, as we have seen, has both its pros and cons. With the majority of both male and female collectives leaning on women to conform to some outmoded maternal stereotype, we could do without opposition from our own sex. In other words, the individual woman should be afforded the right to choose her path in life without fear of incurring the wrath of those dominant feminine groups whose members delight in giving all their girl-children babydolls for Christmas.

Chapter 14
The Working Woman

MANY successful professional women, and others whose ambitions have been thwarted by circumstances or obstacles laid in their paths, have been vehement in their criticisms and castigations of the society that has been the cause of their anguish or frustration. Since such women are often highly literate, numerous articles have appeared in both specialist and popular publications, while others have voiced their protests in books, lectures, or some other public medium.

Novelist and journalist Joan Smith, in an interview with Angela Neustatter of the *Guardian* (18 April 1989) cited several disturbing incidents that had taken place in her life, which she saw as confirming the idea that British men are decidely misogynist. Neustatter reports:

> At a literary event in Oxford, she [Joan Smith] was asked by a middle-aged man to talk about her latest book. As she began he interrupted her in honeyed tones: 'Oh darling, why bother? I have slept with thousands of women and can tell you they don't want to know about that sort of thing.' When Joan insisted that she and plenty she knew did, indeed, feel the need to understand the forces of male hostility in society, his tone changed and within minutes he began to shout: 'You are demented; you're mad. Take this woman away from me.'

Other women writers commenting on social and psychological inconsistencies in male behaviour towards women have met with similar problems and abuse. Fidelis Morgan, for example, who has published a collection of sayings about women by men through the ages, suggests that there is a certain urgency abroad around the subject.

The woman who is brave enough to face the wrath of the

powerful masculine or feminine collectives and pursue her own path must prepare herself for a rough ride. The arts and entertainment professions would appear to be the most tolerant of the aspiring career woman. This is probably because they usually demand right-brain utilization in both males and females if they are to become artists rather than technicians. We are told that regular use of the right brain encourages the development of the anima in a man and likewise the left brain and animus in a woman.

In medicine it is a different matter, however. According to *The Times* (7 July 1989) the British Medical Association heard at its annual meeting, in July of that same year, that while nearly half the graduates from medical school each year are women, they comprise less than one per cent of general surgeons, and not one female general surgeon had been appointed a consultant in the last five years. The proportion of women graduates is, of course, higher now than it was when those now senior enough for consultant positions were first qualified. However, on present trends it does not seem likely that nearly half the total of consultant surgeons will be women in 20 or 30 years' time. Young women doctors leaving medical school can now expect their gender to weigh against them, probably throughout the rest of their careers. This is a classic example of a common pattern.

The more obvious forms of discrimination against working women are now beginning to disappear, at least from sight. The message has finally penetrated that it is both unlawful and socially unacceptable to refuse a job or promotion out of pure prejudice. This has by no means removed the disadvantages of being a woman in employment, however. There is another layer of discrimination beyond this obvious one that apparently still prevails in medicine, and particularly in general surgery where the training regime could almost have been designed to erect obstacles against women. Its particularly rigid structure makes it ill-suited to those who may require maternity leave or time for other family commitments, while it is also difficult to return to after leave of absence. Appointment panels are therefore given to enquiring from young women doctors what likelihood there is that they might start a family or, if the candidate is already a mother, whether she anticipates repeating the performance.

Fortunately, not all branches of the medical profession are so difficult for the married woman or mother to negotiate. Psychiatry or pathology, for instance, offer feasible alternatives. However, this merely serves to fortify the cycle of discrimination, for it means that women doctors rarely reach influential positions. The hard and fast line taken in the field of surgery suggests a wasteful squandering of investment in training and neglects the particular contribution women may be able to make in this area. What is more, it is unfair to the women doctors themselves, as well as their patients.

Medicine is but one field in which women have met with difficulties. The media is another. Many women presenters and newscasters have complained that they are hired for their bodies and fired for their wrinkles. Men are often seen to retain their 'attractiveness' for up to 15 years longer than women, so male newsreaders, everything being equal, can look forward to a longer working life and fuller career than their female counterparts.

One of the main differences between women who have chosen to pursue a professional life and the men they work with is that a woman is often better able to disperse her energies. Dorothy Wade, reporting in the *Sunday Times* (12 March 1989) in an article entitled 'Feminine Ways to Get on with the Job', tells us that Professor Cary Cooper of the Manchester School of Management, University of Manchester Institute of Science and Technology, has carried out comparative studies of men and women in 65 different occupations — including oil-rig workers, secretaries, dentists, and managers for organizations such as the Manpower Services Commission — over the past ten years. He has found out that no matter what the job, the differences between men and women at work seem to apply. 'Men are always looking up the ladder for the main chance — Women are looking at doing a thorough job and doing the job well.' This is partly, says Cooper, because women are increasingly moving into a man's world. Insecure about their abilities, they have to concentrate on reaching high standards in each task they are set.

Many women have preferred to work at home, although it has been observed that going out to work carries more prestige. Working at home during the child-raising stage must be difficult at the best of times, but the same can also be said of working at home with anyone around.

Many women these days work out of financial necessity rather than choice. However, women from wealthy families often choose to pursue careers, self-expression and need to prove themselves constituting the deciding factors.

While on the subject of 'a woman's place' the question of marriage inevitably raises its head. Upon entering the marital state, woman sacrifices a goodly slice of herself to her husband and children. She may, if she is lucky, be able to retain a portion for herself. Few women enter marriage knowing what it really entails, and an article in the *Guardian* (1 November 1989) by Liz Hodgkinson and Anne-Marie Piper, casts the spotlight on these difficulties and restrictions that we are either blind to or choose to ignore as we walk up the aisle. The problems encountered by women as a result of marriage break-ups featured prominently in the article and Piper supplied the following table which shows clearly the dramatic rise in the divorce rate over the past 30 years:

Year	Marriages	Divorces
1957	346,903	23,785
1967	386,952	43,093
1977	356,954	129,053
1987	351,761	151,007

(Figures from the Office of Population Consensus and Surveys)

Hodgkinson offered several excellent alternatives and suggestions, although most of these are calculated to cause traditionalists to throw up their hands in horror.

Instead of marriage, which constitutes the only contract we ever sign of which we don't know the terms, we would have individually drawn-up, legally binding contracts between people who wished to live together and share their lives. These contracts would not imitate marriage laws, nor bear any relation to them, but would work along the same lines as partnership contracts, with each partner being absolutely equal. There would be no vestige of dependency, protection or ownership implicit in the contracts. Their whole point would be not to decide who does the washing-up or other trivialities, but to make realistic provision for property, finances and children.

If contracts replaced marriage, both men and women would remain legally single for ever. The contracts could apply equally to heterosexual and homosexual relationships, or even perhaps to a group of people living together in a community. For women, there would be no more taking of a man's name, no more 'Mrs' — the concept would simply not exist. And, as legally single people, women could at the very least claim social security benefits in their own right. The notion of a man 'supporting' them would vanish. As would the married person's allowance.

There would, of course, be no divorce as the contracts would simply be terminated to the satisfaction of both parties. If marriage laws are ridiculous, divorce laws, which insist on 'irretrievable breakdown', are even more so. By no means all marriages or relationships that end have broken down. Sometimes the partners just want another kind of life. Sometimes they only wish, like Garbo, to be alone.

Yet however amicable the separation in reality, we still have to pretend that something dreadful has happened to break up the marriage, and that this is a sad and tragic thing. In fact, in many cases, marriages ending are a liberation.

As I see it, contracts would make people more, rather than less, responsible about children because each child would necessitate an alteration in the contract. People would then have to think very carefully about the implications of having children, and both parents would become equally responsible for their care. The idea that women are primarily responsible for small children would disappear. If men wanted children, they would have to be prepared to share their upbringing completely. Do they deserve them?

Partnership contracts — I prefer not to call them 'cohabitation' contracts, as at present cohabitation is regarded as a pale imitation of marriage — would give men and women true equality in our society, far more than any equal opportunity legislation has been able to do.

Such contracts would also do a lot to prevent the continuing discrimination against gay couples, single parents, unmarried mothers. They would also mean that all men and women would be treated, and would regard themselves, as individually operating, single, autonomous, responsible, grown-up individuals, rather than as half of an invisible couple.

The blanket state, legally-binding institution we call marriage no longer reflects the reality of society. It has had its day and now it must go. Does what I'm saying sound radical? I'm not clairvoyant, but I believe I can safely predict that by the end of the next decade, most of the reforms I'm talking about will have either come in or be well on their way. The traditional marriage is crumbling fast, thank goodness, and nothing will ever bring it back.

Brave words, but one wonders what all those vicars will do with their time with no wedding ceremonies to perform! Some women might suffer from finding themselves caught in the crossfire between orthodox religion and romantic traditionalism on the one hand, and the reforming legislative bodies on the other; there would most certainly be casualties.

Two recent studies have shown that employers' attitudes towards women have tended to drive them out of the workplace and back into the home. A survey by the Maternity Alliance reveals that companies are often insensitive to women who take maternity leave. According to a report in *The Times* (19 July 1989), based on the experiences of 243 women returners, only 56 per cent said that their managers reacted positively to the news of their pregnancy. A small number of women added that the pregnancy was seen as an 'inconvenience' by their employers. The experience of a Civil Service employee was cited who was denied special leave when her baby was born with a heart defect. A request to work three or four hours a day until the situation resolved itself was also denied. Sadly, the baby died three days prior to her return to work, after which she was awarded special paid leave.

The key results of a report by Blue Arrow Personnel Services showed that of the 2,000 employers it surveyed, few offered specific inducements for attracting and retaining working mothers. Facilities lacking included career-break schemes, extended leave periods to accommodate pregnancies, workplace or sponsor-shared community nurseries, financial aid towards childcare, flexible working hours, and job-sharing. Many were openly hostile to recruiting older people. Employers, it seems, are failing to tap the vast pool of women returners (estimated to be more than 700,000), which could exercise some effect on the general economy.

The Japanese minister Mr Hisao Horinouchi recently remarked: 'A nation will fall when a woman becomes a ruler.' Jung on the other hand, saw the Age of Aquarius as being one in which women would come into their own. I know in whose sagacity I would prefer to place my trust.

Jenni Murray, BBC presenter of Woman's Hour, recently set out to find what makes women of power tick. She interviewed six women who have reached positions of great power and influence, and examined how they had arrived at their exalted positions, what they have done with the power now they have achieved it, and how being a woman has been significant in what they set out to do. The six women were:

1) Tatyana Zaslavskaya, who grew up under the Stalinist regime and achieved a brilliant academic career in the government think-tank at Novosibirsk. Her report, written in 1983, became the basis of perestroika.
2) Benazir Bhutto, former Prime Minister of Pakistan.
3) Corazon Aquino, President of the Philippines.
4) Eugenia Charles, now 70 years old, who has been prime minister of Dominica for nine years.
5) Gudrun Agnarsdottir, Women's Alliance Member of the Icelandic Parliament for six years.
6) Vigdis Finnbogadottir, the woman President of Iceland.

The 40-minute documentary on Tatyana Zaslavskaya, which Murray made for BBC 2 television was shown in July 1989, and no doubt by the time this book comes off the press the public will have been treated to more of her experiences with these fascinating women.

Politics is by no means the only arena in which women are excelling. Vandana Shiva is one of the world's most prominent radical scientists and a campaigner on the issues of women, ecology and development and on the environmental impact of science and technology policy. She is a quantum physicist turned people's scientist with the passion and conviction of a convert, although her ideological enemies might call her a recidivist. In a review of her book *Staying Alive: Women, Ecology and Development*, published in April 1989, Sara Dunn, writing for the *Guardian* says of her:

Her road to Damascus was the journey back from Ontario, where she did a doctorate in quantum theory, to her native

Uttar Pradesh, northern India; her flash of light was an encounter with rural women of that region involved in Chipko, a mass women's protest against deforestation and resulting ecological destruction. These women, she says, have enabled her to 'learn the world from scratch.'

The daughter of an 'extremely liberated' mother who had been involved in the Indian independence movement and a forester father who nurtured her love for the natural world, Vandana Shiva was brought up in a household where the gender distinctions in Hindi, her native tongue, were considered unnecessary; she used only the masculine forms.

Dunn describes Ms Shiva's book as a scholarly and polemic plea for the rediscovery of the feminine principle in human interaction with the natural world. The feminine principle, Shiva explains, is not a gender-based quality, but rather an organizing principle — a way of seeing the world.

In writing about the working woman, I have not limited my comments to the plight or otherwise of those women achievers who have tackled or are taking on those professions usually considered as male preserves, but rather *all* women who choose or are obliged for some reason or another to work for a living. This may imply either a totally independent state or one contributory to the family as a unit. However, woman's right of choice must always be maintained. We should never look down on our Demeter, Hera, or Aphrodite sisters, and we Artemises, Athenes, and Hestias request a similar courtesy of them. We are all part of one cosmic family. It is unfortunate that there are still women who strongly proclaim: 'I couldn't go to Church if there was a woman preaching,' or 'I wouldn't let my daughter study science, as that won't help her cook the Sunday lunch.'

Men may have littered the pages of history with the carnage of the over-emphasized animus but, to be fair, they have often had strong Dragons or wily Serpents behind them, urging them forward. One wonders how long it will take to break the established mould — if ever!

Chapter 15
Transpersonal Woman

THE women's spirituality movement, a blanket label
which encompasses many different mystical, metaphysical, and extramundane studies, has made its appearance worldwide. Groups of all sizes, from private circles to
major clubs and societies, have mushroomed, each claiming to cater for the transpersonal needs of women.

Since the term 'spirituality' has come to mean different
things to different people, some definitions are called for.
Unfortunately, being 'spiritual' has tended to be seen as
synonymous with being 'holier than thou', and displaying
sanctimonious piety, such as strict observation of the rites
and tenets of one of the major religions. Our words, actions,
and deeds are the real statements of our metaphysical
proclivities. There is no need to belong to an organized body
or fly any particular banner in order to work in harmony
with the higher or transpersonal self. Following a particular
collective or ideal need not, however, preclude those of
group inclination from aspiring to and working with the
finer frequencies, since the final decision lies with the
individual psyche. Thus we may observe the emergence of
saints from the mire of corrupt religions, and the unmask-
ing of charlatans and crooks before their sincere and
unsuspecting congregations. Nor is spirituality necessarily
synonymous with occultism, magic, mysticism, or any of
the other esoteric pursuits which normally shelter under
the supernatural umbrella, although many people have, no
doubt, discovered their true paths during the process of
investigating these highways and byways of the mind.

So what do we mean by women's spirituality, and why
should the transpersonal aspirations and experiences of

women differ so very much from those of men, if indeed they do? If women are, as many esotericists believe, more powerful at the transpersonal level, then the fact that they are awakening to their true spiritual heritage is of great importance, as far as their influence on the world is concerned. What worries me, however, is the possibility of a kind of spiritual 'Berlin Wall' between men and women, which in its divisiveness can do nothing but harm. As I have stated in previous chapters, I am none too happy about these area designations for men and women, experience having shown me that the manifestation of our energies on both the material and subtle planes is more a matter of individuality and spiritual development. However, let us go along with the popular concept and see where it leads us.

Where women have obviously succeeded is in bringing a new awareness into our world, which is fast catching on at all levels and in both sexes. A woman's predisposition to use the right side of her brain, normally labelled 'natural intuition', serves to make her a better receptor to those subtle forces of nature which form the heart and soul of Gaia. Spirituality should not be confined to the fields of meditation, religion or mysticism. If we women are to have any effect on our world, we must take our spiritual concepts into the highways and byways of life, for it is there that our sobering influence is needed, as much as in the temple, cathedral, or ashram. Many women have already been doing this for years, and as the ranks of the women's spirituality movement are fast swelling the caring touch is evidenced in many avenues of everyday expression. It should be borne in mind that manifestations of change at the more mundane levels have a deeper meaning, since their impulse must have originated 'above' prior to becoming apparent 'below'. Either way they are indicative of a slow but perceptible rise in consciousness.

Many women have chosen to express their spirituality in service to the feminine creative principle in the form of the Goddess, and since, as we have already discussed, the major religions tend to frown on the concept of a female deity, this has consequently given rise to a vast expansion in the pagan movement worldwide. Goddess cults and groups have mushroomed, and she has appeared in any manner of names from those under which she was worshipped in antiquity to the new nomenclatures that have arrived via the currently popular spate of channelling and cosmic interests. For some of her followers she is Isis the Magician and mother of Horus; for others she is Athene, Tanith, Keridwen, Sarasvati, Aradia, Brigid, Freya, and so on.

The resurgence of Goddess-consciousness has brought with it a revised interest in the rites and beliefs of those past ages when she was last accorded her true status. An interest in and closer understanding of the other life forms with which we share the planet, an acknowledgement of the life-force in all things inanimate, and other such concepts that would have been ridiculed by people a generation or so ago are now quite acceptable. Writing in *Woman Awake: A Celebration of Women's Wisdom*, Christina Feldman tells us:

> Mystics in every spiritual tradition have endlessly spoken of the inner freedom that is our spiritual heritage. Wholeness, oneness, connectedness and awakening are words used to attempt to describe a dimension of being that is essentially indescribable. They are words to describe a way of living that is an expression of reverence. It is a way of being that reveres the sacredness and dignity of all life, honours the earth, and appreciates the implications of our fundamental interdependence and interconnectedness. Mystics speak of it as a fundamental inner awakening that empowers us to transform our world . . .
>
> The Path of the mystic is directed towards the end of conflict and suffering. It is the path of honouring the innate dignity and spirit in all life. It is the path of honouring oneness and truth above all else. It is a life committed to peace, harmony and compassion. The mystic spurns domination and falsehood. She turns aside from exploitation and lives in accord with the oneness she perceives. Above all she knows the emptiness of the division between inner and outer.[1]

While some women (and men for that matter) seek to serve the Goddess via the performance of intricate rites, overt ceremonies, or physical movements and postures calculated to produce altered states of consciousness, others seek her energies in the strength and grace of a tall tree, the caressing rub of an animal, the song of the wind across the broad plains, the soft rain, the welcome rays of the sun, and the velvet petals of the flower opening its face to greet the morning light.

There is a story by Tagore of a man who became obsessed with the idea of finding God. So determined was he in his quest that he arose quietly one night so as not to disturb his wife and child, and crept forth into the darkness to commence his search in earnest. For years he trod the path of a holy man, denying himself the luxuries of life, but ever intent upon his goal. In time old age descended upon him, and feeling exhausted and sensing that his end was near, he sat down beneath a tree to offer his final prayer. 'O God, I, your ever-devoted servant, have sought you for years in all places, and yet I have not found you. Now I am old and weary, and death hangs heavily over me. Tell me, where have I failed to look?' And the voice of God replied to him: 'My son, you left me the night you left your wife and child.'

We can sometimes become distracted from real spirituality by the paraphernalia of organized religion or the impedimenta of magic to the extent that we forget why we are repeating that prayer, attending this service, or performing that rite. It was recently brought to my notice that a certain group of esotericists spent several weeks arguing about which ritual garments they would wear for the rites that had been devised for them by their leader. Likewise, clerics and divines debate senseless points of dogma for hours to no fruitful purpose. If people must sharpen their intellects, there are surely better fields in which to effect their target practice than the transcendental.

One word which is frequently bandied about in both orthodox religious circles and New Age teachings is 'love', the implication being that spirituality and love are natural twins. Well, it all depends on what one means by love. Since the word is so frequently associated with either limerance or the expression of the libido — 'making love' (fulfilling a biological urge, with or without emotional involvement) — its more transcendental connotations have become somewhat obscured. Affection, appreciation, joy, adoration, friendship, fondness — all or any of these we may bestow on our children, partners, friends, or pets, but the level of feeling which they encompass may not extend to the transpersonal. True spiritual love is boundless, selfless, undemanding, and all-understanding. Women are believed to be more capable of love than men, but perhaps we are confusing love with sacrifice. The two are not necessarily synonymous, although transcendental love does, of course, embrace the sacrificial mode.

The re-emergence of shamanism as a form of devotional expression has been much espoused by women mystics and those seeking their spirituality via the way of the Goddess. Paganism and animism go hand in hand with the shamanic scene and many shamans carry strong healing PK. Shamanic types are inevitably drawn to the animal kingdoms, their totem beasts representing not only an aspect of themselves but also the embodiment of the principles they are trying to convey. (Psychologists would see it in terms of their alter-ego or some cloaked persona which they have adopted to defend the more vulnerable aspects of their personality against the rigours of the real world.) The kind of awareness that accompanies genuine shamanism is not limited to *Homo sapiens* contacts. It has also been realized that the falsely induced frenzied altered states of consciousness (ASCs) of older times, seen as an essential prerequisite for convincing an audience of the genuineness of the possession, are not necessarily the hallmark of true spirituality. Nor do they guarantee contacts with the transpersonal Self or the finer dimensions of the inner worlds. But since it is metaphysically conceivable that all frequencies, like all time, exist simultaneously in the eternal now, compartmentalization only occurs as a result of the subjective experience of a particular period of spiritual development that has become encapsulated in a single pocket of time, which gives the illusion of being isolated from eternity.

Although shamanism may be seen by many as coming into its own during the Aquarian Age, I am inclined to view it in terms of a bridge between Gaia's human children and her other progeny. Eventually, all people will develop the kind of sensitivity which allows them to become aware of the subtle energies that operate around and within our planet. Droughts, earthquakes, and volcanoes will no longer afflict us since we will be well advised in advance as to the probability and location of their occurrence. Pipe dreams? Not necessarily, since many of those who work within the finer frequencies have been alerted to the imminence of that much prophesied evolutionary quantum jump. The present mechanistic culture may well disappear beneath the 'greenhouse' mists to make way for a gentler world, which will be happy to accommodate *real* equality.

Shamanism is by no means the only outlet through which women are seeking to express their spirituality. Many have chosen orthodox religion, and particularly those areas which have previously been sacrosanct to men. Many women are serving as ordained priests in the United States, and despite the face that the more liberal Christian elements in Britain have seen fit to dispense the occasional priestly privileges to a woman, the main Christian bodies operating here have denied us these rights, although the winds of change (or hurricanes, perhaps) are already hovering threateningly on the horizon.

Eastern philosophies are also proving a valuable asset to the women's spirituality movement, and many women have discovered their true spiritual path through the practice of yoga, meditation, or a period in an ashram. Some have, like the personalities we will be discussing in the ensuing chapter, entered strict Orders and engaged in a life of prayer, self-denial, and self-discipline, which they believe has helped them to understand the essential 'self' on the one hand, and the diverse and perplexing contingencies of the world at large on the other. Such periods of deep contemplation have often led a woman to the realization that there is work for her to do in the outside world, as a consequence of which she has exchanged the reclusive life for one of service to the community generally, or to some specific social aspect in which she feels her help is needed.

Spirituality need not necessarily be contained within the 'self'. It can emanate from the aura to encompass those who are fortunate enough to experience its presence. So whether a woman chooses to express her transpersonal self via the Goddess, the shamanic path, orthodox religion, mysticism, magic, or in service to her fellow creatures is of little consequence since it is the basic act of spiritual self-discovery, and how one chooses to use (or share) that knowledge that constitutes life's lesson. For too long men have considered the higher aspects of the spiritual as exclusively their domain. Women have been brainwashed by the major religions into thinking that they are incapable of attaining the spiritual heights, their very bodies proving the stumbling block. It is surely time that we dispensed with this erroneous and highly damaging superstition and acknowledged the fact that 'spirituality' as such knows no gender, and its only bounds are those erected by personal choice and transpersonal awareness.

Chapter 16
Servants of the Goddess

RECENT years have witnessed the emergence of several prominent women in the fields of religion, mysticism, shamanism, magic, and other areas of transcendental study and spiritual service. Selecting which personalities to feature in a single chapter has proven to be no easy task, however. I have therefore sought to include women from a variety of spiritual disciplines, and should a particular favourite of the reader be excluded this is by no means meant as a judgment on my part.

Women saints have always been with us. But what of today? Is the pace of modern life, plus the additional duties imposed upon most women, conducive to mystical or spiritual achievement? Apparently it is, since women mystics and saints are still flourishing. In her book, *Weavers of Wisdom: Women Mystics of the Twentieth Century*, Anne Bancroft refers us to the life and works of 15 of these highly gifted women who have contributed in some way to the spiritual understanding of our present culture. Bancroft herself spent the early part of her life in the Quaker village of Jordans. While her four children were growing up, she became a lecturer in comparative religion, and at the same time began her own quest for spiritual understanding. Over the years she found strength and inspiration in Buddhism and a deepening understanding of Western mysticism, and has written several books on these subjects, including *Weavers of Wisdom*.

Bancroft opens her Introduction to *Weavers of Wisdom* with some lines from *Mysticism* by Evelyn Underwood, whom she sees as one of the foremost Christian mystics of the century:

She opened her eyes upon a world still natural, but no longer illusory; since it was perceived to be illuminated by the uncreated light. She knew then the beauty, the majesty, the divinity of the living world of becoming which holds in its meshes every living thing . . . Reality came forth to her, since her eyes were cleansed to see it, not from some strange, far-off and spiritual country, but gently, from the very heart of things.[1]

Recent scientific discoveries about the nature of the universe and our own planet have, albeit unconsciously, presented us with a blueprint for the supernatural — an equation for the sublime, the spiritual significance of which has somehow escaped the notice of those who seek the transcendental in some mythical heaven which is entirely divorced from all matters earthly.

Bancroft comments:

I came to find that women (although there must be many exceptions) are naturally at ease within themselves; that they find within their own integrated body-mind-spirit a sustaining core of harmony and love, which many men look for in the heavens. Women tend to see all things around them as revelatory, revealing totality and completeness and a numinous quality. To see things in this way a certain attention has to be given, which women are good at. It is not the kind of attention with which one acquires knowledge but rather that which happens when one lets go all concepts and becomes open to what is there. Then what occurs is not so much an understanding as a 'being at one with', even a 'being taken up by', a clarity of expansion and liberation which at the same time seems to be the very deepest sort of relationship.

I discovered that the women in this book seemed to have a relatedness to existence that embraced both the timeless and the immediate present. Certainly many men have this too, but I think it is more apparent in women. In the end I came to feel that conventional, male-dominated religion has perhaps little to offer such women who have discovered their source within themselves. For 'seeking the face of God in the created world', as Meinrad Craighead puts it, has played a very minor part in most of the great religions, particularly those which regard the body and all matter as a necessary evil which the religious must transcend.[2]

'Relatedness' — the integration of spirit and flesh — is the theme of Bancroft's book, and she cites Joanna Macey, who is becoming known world-wide for her work on personal empowerment; Meinrad Craighead, a solitary artist and visionary; psychiatrist Marion Milner, who has gained her personal enlightenment from a profound questioning of existing attitudes; and Twylah Nitsch, who has found her guiding light in her native American beliefs. The contemplative and more intellectual approach she sees as passing beyond the time-space continuum. In this category she places Evelyn Underhill; the poet Kathleen Raine; mystical writer Simone Weil; and Toni Packer, who was influenced by Krishnamurti.

Of the others about whom she writes, two hold Hindu beliefs: Dadi Janki, described as 'one of the realized women leaders of a worldwide spiritual movement'; and the late Anandamayi Ma, whose right to sainthood was acknowledged in India well before her death. Ayya Khema, a European of Buddhist persuasion who became a Theravada nun, and whose work is concerned with radically altering the structure of Buddhist nunhood; the medium Eileen Caddy, co-founder of Findhorn; Irina Tweedie, a Sufi; Danette Choi, a Korean Zen practitioner, psychic and healer and Elizabeth Kübler-Ross, whose spiritual work is concerned with grief, death, the afterlife and the transition thereto. To the above list I would like to add Mother Teresa of Calcutta, whose worldwide acclaim both as a religious mystic and devoted field worker surely accords her a worthy subject for the title of 'saint' in any religion.

It seems that several of these women fiercely denied that they were 'mystics', and Bancroft found herself wondering what they feared from the term or what pride lead them to reject it. I am inclined to agree with her that in the cases of the Christians in particular, there would be the feeling that the title implies an involvement in occult or other supramundane practices. Bancroft therefore gives her own interpretation of the term, quoting from William James's *The Varieties of Religious Experience*: 'The conscious person is continuous with a wider self through which saving experiences come.'

In her book *Shape Shifters: Shaman Women in Contemporary Society*, the American Michele Jamal, an anthropology graduate and practising hypnotist, offers a series of short biographies of some of the better known shamanic personalities on the American (mainly Californian) scene who, she tells us, come from such diverse cultural backgrounds as a Montana Crow Indian reservation, the black south of Louisiana, Latvia in the Soviet Union, war-torn Berlin in Germany, the American Mid-West, an isolated ranch in Washington, the glitz of Beverly Hills, and the suburbs of America. I must confess to being disappointed at the exclusion of any British shamans, since this tradition has been extant in Britain since archaic times, and there are several talented and deeply spiritual practising women shamans who work to keep alight the fire of the Goddess. One can only assume that we are up against the natural reluctance of many Britishers to come forward and speak out, preferring to go about their esoteric activities under less public conditions.

Prominent among Michele Jamal's American shamans is Luisah Teish, about whom I have already written at length in Chapter 6 and shall be including some further comments towards the end of this chapter. Joan Halifax, whose book *Shaman: The Wounded Healer* I prize among my possessions, claims northern European origins. After travelling in Europe and Africa she returned to her family home in Southern Florida to recover from an illness. In the 1970s she married a psychiatrist, after which she spent a period of time working with people dying of cancer. This first-hand view of death caused her to experience many altered states of consciousness, and it was the sum total of these experiences that brought her to the idea that the cradle of the sacred was to be found in the great lineage of the palaeolithic shaman. It was not until 1984 that Halifax experienced her initial burst of the healing energies common to most shamans and as she now tells us: 'One feels no need to build statues to the goddess. One can sit under a tree. One feels no need to create a throne for her to sit on. Her throne is everywhere on this earth.'[3]

The work and experiences of Tsultrim Allione, also chronicled by Jamal, have already received consideration in an earlier chapter. Jamal's profile is extracted from *Women of Wisdom* and lectures by Tsultrim Allione, whose life story is worth reading in itself aside from the spiritual implications and teachings contained therein.

Probably better known in Britain is Starhawk, author of

The Spiral Dance and *Dreaming in the Dark*. She is a well known and highly respected follower of the Goddess who states openly: 'I am a witch, and a witch is someone who practises the Old Religion, a religion we believe goes back to prehistory. It's the religion of the Goddess.'[4] Starhawk is not afraid to profess the practice of magic and the Craft. She is also outspoken on the political scene. Starhawk was born into a Jewish family. She tells us:

> I went through Jewish Bat Mitzvah, and later went to a Hebrew High School, and also the University of Judaism. I know all that has a strong influence on me. The Jewish influence comes more, I think, from the regular Jewish tradition, not just from pre-patriarchal roots. By the time you go back to the pre-patriarchal roots of Judaism, what you've got is basically witchcraft, or paganism. If you're throwing out four or five thousand years of tradition and the history, you're not dealing with Judaism in an honest sense.[5]

Vicki Noble, author of *Motherpeace — The Way to the Goddess through Myth, Art and Tarot*, was also the co-designer of the Motherpeace Tarot Cards. Noble tends to emphasize woman's sexuality as holding the key to her power, and sees feminine sexuality as 'holy'. Her devotion to the Goddess is expressed through body-consciousness; she tells us: 'We need to stop abusing our bodies with all the chemicals and pollutants we put into them. The more in touch we can get with our bodies, the more in touch we get with nature and the earth, the happier and holier and more sacred we will be.'[6] According to an article which appeared in the American magazine *Magical Blend* (Issue 21, January 1989), Vicki Noble has been working with Riane Eisler on an event titled 'Healing the Earth: Gaia Reborn', co-sponsored by Harper & Row and the Gaia Bookstore in Berkeley. 'This event will feature multi-ethnic singers, dancers and ritualists collaborating to raise enough healing energy to reach a "critical quantum leap into new consciousness honouring the Divine Feminine in women *and* men.'[7]

Other notable shamans who receive coverage in Jamal's book include Rowena Pattee, Ruth-Inge Heinze, Larissa Vilenskaya, Petey Stevens, J. Ruth Strock, Sandy Ingerman, Susana Eger Valadez, and Brooke Medicine Eagle.

I should now like to add my small but significant

contribution to the list of those who have chosen to serve the Goddess. The Hon. Olivia Durdin-Robertson and her brother Lawrence, Lord Strathloch, a fully ordained priest in the Church of Ireland, founded the Fellowship of Isis in the 1970s to promote the work of the Goddess and a universal understanding of the feminine principle. Since those early days the Fellowship, which is totally eclectic and has no fixed dogmas, has grown into an international network. The Durdin-Robertsons function from the family castle in the Irish Republic. In spite of their heritage they, like their lifestyle, are totally unpretentious and their doors are always open to their members from all over the world.

The FOI is not so much a group, organization or society as a union of minds, all of whom are dedicated to the return of the feminine principle and the worship of the Goddess in any of her many names and traditions. Olivia herself is now elderly, a shy but dedicated worker whose fragile frame and modest demeanour belie an inner strength and sublimity. She displays none of the sanctimoniousness often associated with spirituality, however, which is one reason why I have chosen to mention her. The other reason — she deserves it!

My next character is also a woman of the people rather than an esoteric teacher, recluse or religieuse. Her name is Margaret Heard, a middle-aged woman who resides with her invalid mother in a London suburb. Heard is an outspoken woman who practises what she preaches, both in her tireless work for animals and the women's spirituality movement in Britain. A follower of the Goddess, Heard works 'in the field', her inner spirituality manifesting in her commitment to bring about a better understanding of women, animals, and all things 'green' and Gaian. Women like Heard are easily overlooked in the search for the unusual and transcendent. She neither courts a following nor sees herself as anything but a simple woman doing what she can for that which she believes in.

Although such names as Dolores Ashcroft-Nowicki, Marian Green, Vivianne Crowley and Caitlin Matthews come quickly to mind, I am deliberately refraining from including potted biographies of women from the more specialized fields of magic, Wicca, and the occult, or those who have risen within the ranks of religious orthodoxy, for that matter. It would be easy to supply lists of names which without qualification would mean nothing to most readers. I have personally received much help and advice from Nerys Dee, Maureen Ballard and Patsy Claridge, all devotees of the Goddess, and dedicated field workers in the healing, feminine, animal and Gaian movements.

I should now like to cross the Atlantic and mention some of those American women who have, in my opinion, contributed to the cause and development of women's spirituality. I fully admit that, since I have few connections in the American academic world, unlike Riane Eisler I am unable to supply my readers with long lists of names of women active in the American feminist scene. From among those whose work I am familiar with, however, I have chosen the following: Maggy Anthony, Nancy B. Watson and Luisah Teish.

Luisah Teish I see as using the exoteric to convey the esoteric. She speaks to her public through the media of objects, rites, and paraphernalia, which are easily comprehended by and readily available to the man/woman in the street. Her work is by no means limited to black people, although she employs the terms and traditions of her black ancestors. In a recent letter she told me: 'My African name is Osun Miwa, "Love Goddess gives me character" and my native American name is "Ravenwolf". She also refers to the connection we both share with 'The Old Country' — Atlantis. 'Yemaya-Olokun — this is our "Mother of Atlantis". Many of the African traditions which are believed to have originated in Atlantis have now been forgotten, although the odd snippet of knowledge has seeped through via the Dogon of Mali, the Bamba, Bozo, and the ancestors of Osun Miwa, in whose heart they have obviously lived on to surface in more spiritually fertile times.

Maggy Anthony's first book to be published in this country *The Valkyries — The Women Around Jung* appeared in Britain in 1990. She also co-authored the book *Moon, Moon*, one of the most popular works on women's mysteries to appear in America in recent years. Two other books, *The Goddess is Alive* and one on a study of dreams, are also in the pipeline.

Maggy Anthony studied at the Jung Institute in Zurich and now works as an analyst and counsellor for the social services in Reno, Nevada, where she specializes in chemical dependency cases. Her spiritual studies extend far beyond the realms of Jungian psychology, however, and are highlighted by a strange experience she underwent during a visit to Rio de Janeiro in Brazil. It was here that she had her first encounter with Umbamba. The full details of Maggy's encounter with this ancient religion are well documented in her *Goddess* book, and as I have no wish to pre-empt her beautiful and moving description of the experience, I will keep my account as succinct as possible.

A friend of hers, who had taken pains to learn a smattering of the Bantu and Yoruba dialects, informed her that she intended to take a group of friends to an Umbamba meeting late one evening. Maggy was asked to wear a skirt rather than trousers as a token of respect for what was, to the Umbambistas, their church. For some unconscious reason she chose a white dress, which she later discovered carried a deep esoteric significance in that faith.

During the course of the rite she entered an altered state of consciousness which was immediately recognized by the officiating priestess who announced: 'She is possessed by the spirit of Lemanja, the most powerful goddess of them all. She is a mermaid and the Goddess of the Sea.' Maggy Anthony later studied the religion and rites of Lemanja, and is one of the few white women who have ever been initiated into her priesthood.

Her experience serves as a reminder that our spiritual heritage or karmic past knows no distinctions of race, colour, or creed. We may pass through the disciplines of many persuasions, practise magical arts in secret glades, or experience the doubts of agnosticism or atheism, as our spiritual inadequacies deem necessary. However outside this planet lies the infinite universe and the realms of timelessness which eventually we will also need to negotiate during the process of our spiritual ascent.

My last American candidate is Nancy B. Watson of San Francisco, who practises as a shaman in the northern European tradition. She trained as a serious actress, but like many women gave up her career for marriage. Later she studied psychology, but ultimately found that her true calling lay in other areas. Her avenues of seeking led into an esoteric understanding of the healing energies of herbs, flowers, and all things that grow; the power of the elements and how they affect our psychology; and the spiritual interplay between the natural and supernatural or esoteric worlds. The healing and balancing properties of her potions, which are concocted with a spiritual understanding of and mutual cooperation with the resident essences or intelligences of the ingredients she uses, are slowly becoming known and acknowledged.

Nancy Watson, like the other women I have chosen to include in this chapter, is an essentially well grounded and integrated personality. In addition to being an able psychologist and a highly proficient astrologer she is also a fine psychic. Her special ability in this field is her talent for dialogue with the plant, animal and mineral kingdoms, with the satyrs and centaurs of Greek magic and other non-hominid cosmic intelligences. It was, after all, the Centaur Chiron who, according to the myth, taught the art of healing to Apollo himself! The popularity of her classes and seminars demonstrates that many women and men in the San Francisco area and beyond are becoming aware that Nancy has the subtle quality of a servant of Gaia and is a harbinger of the type of New Age spirituality that is based more on an awareness of all life forms than on a preoccupation with some vague bodiless state.

Chapter 17
The Return of the Goddess

THE title of this chapter has been the theme for several best-selling books over the past few years, 'Our Lady', and the feminine principle she represents, having assumed a new prominence in many areas of life aside from the religious. The recent revival of many of the old goddess-related religions is but one manifestation of her energies. The Fellowship of Isis, for example, has Iseums in many countries, each with their own priests and priestesses who have been ordained by the Durdin-Robertsons, or those authorized to act for them. These ordination services are esoterically meaningful, and carry strong esoteric significance. In accordance with the eclectic nature of the Fellowship, however, there is no orthodox over-structure or dogma, so it is left for each priest or priestess to carry out his or her duties according to conscience.

There has also been a resurgence of Celtic and Druidic beliefs, although some of these have tended to adopt the sort of Christian overtones that accompany an all-male priesthood. In ancient times, however, male and female Druids worked side by side, a fact which the composer Bellini saw fit to acknowledge in his opera *Norma*.

Although the modern-day revival of the Northern Tradition has tended to be largely the work of men, there are also strong matrist aspects to it which have been less explored. The exaggerated masculine image inherited from the Viking days is really only as old as the patrist onslaught discussed in earlier chapters, while the older sources hearken back to the matrist society of the ancient Frisians. In the old Northern Mysteries women practitioners of the magical arts were known as *volvas* — sibyls or prophetesses

— who practised divination. There was also another role, that of *seidkona* — a woman who engaged in *seidr*. The word *seidr* translates literally as 'seething', and is the name applied to a variety of magical procedures such as soul journeys, shape-shifting and allied shamanic practices. Runic expert Freya Aswynn tells us:

> In old English the names for these women was 'haegtessa'. This terms dates from pre-migration continental Northern Germany. A similar word exists in Dutch, 'hagedisse'. Incidentally, the name of the Dutch capital city, The Hague, is a remnant of this association, for the area was renowned as a centre of female magic. 'Hagedis' is the Dutch word for lizard and I venture the hypothesis that the name 'hagedisse' is derived from a time when our people had totem animals, when the lizard would have been associated with female magic and witchcraft. Lizards being members of the reptile family suggests immediately snakes, which symbolise hidden feminine wisdom as corroborated in other shamanic practices such as that of the Australian aborigines. On the other hand the same word, 'hagedis', may have applied to lizard-like creatures such as salamanders and newts which can live in more than one element in water and on land. Likewise, a haegetessa, like a shaman, can move in more than one element. In occult terms this means the astral plane or the underworld. [1]

We are back to our dragons and serpents again, the lizard or salamander being long associated with the element of fire. The patrons of the haegtessa were Freya, the Norns and Frigga. The Norns were, like their Greek counterparts, the original 'spinsters', meaning spinners of the web of Fate.

Although Odin is seen by followers of the Norse tradition as a sort of northern Zeus, in keeping with many other leading patriarchal divinities he relied very much on the goddesses for assistance. Freya, for example, taught him *seidr*, while he frequently sought the counsel of Frigga. In keeping with all other gods and mortals, he was also subject to the decrees of the Norns while one of his famous ravens, Muninn, was probably female since 'munin' means memory, which is frequently regarded both occultly and psychologically as a female function. Those much-sung Teutonic female warriors, the Valkyries, were nine in number, nine being sacred to the Goddess from the earliest of known times.

The old Northern Feminine Mysteries are a study in themselves, and one to which I could not hope to do justice in a few paragraphs. There are many women today who feel strong affinities with the Northern Tradition, the goddess Freya in her shamanic mode being of particular significance. The cat was her totem animal, and she was traditionally the patron of volvas, who would wear catskin gloves in her honour. Like certain other northern goddesses, Freya was seen to carry solar rather than lunar energies, which are a source of inspiration to many women of today.

Fiction writers have drawn on many Utopian metaphors in their search for an ideal state of existence where wars are no more, and the chaotic, latent, and suppressed energies innate in people are channelled into harmoniously creative avenues of expression, which benefit the community as a whole. The present problem is not merely one of gender, but of the socialization of men and women on a different and more equitable basis. Men and women have lived together on amicable terms in the past, and there is no biological or sociological reason why they should not do so again in the future. Both sexes have the biological potential for many different kinds of behaviour; it has been the rigidly hierarchical roles imposed upon them, usually for religious, social, or political convenience, that have been responsible for stunting their individual growth.

Scientists tell us that we are on the threshold of massive global changes and mutations. These, in turn, are conducive to corresponding metamorphoses in personal attitudes as the old order topples and new realizations dawn. Many women, and men for that matter, share the belief that a fuller acknowledgement of the feminine principle will become one of the dominant features in these changes. Unless we hasten to correct the imbalance brought about by the over-emphasis of those patrist values that are seen by many as the primary cause of the present-day crisis, there will be little hope for the future of Gaia and her children. There is also a school of metaphysical thought which opines that we ourselves are the creators of our own destinies, both individually and collectively. On this very point Riane Eisler writes:

Our invention of tools was both the cause and effect of the

bipedal locomotion and erect posture that freed our hands to fashion even more complex technologies. And, as both technology and society have grown more complex, the survival of our species has become increasingly dependent on the direction, not of our biological, but of our cultural evolution.

Human evolution is now at a crossroads. Stripped to its essentials, the central human task is now to organize society to promote the survival of our species and the development of our unique potentials ... androcracy cannot meet this requirement because of its inbuilt emphasis on technologies of destruction, its dependence on violence for social control, and the tensions chronically engendered by the dominator-dominated human relations model upon which it is based. We have also seen that a gylanic or partnership society, symbolized by the life-sustaining and enhancing Chalice rather than the lethal Blade, offers us a viable alternative.

The question is how do we get from here to there?[2]

Random chance in evolutionary biological systems, or the exercise of the element of human choice? These are the alternatives suggested by Eisler and other erudite writers, scientists, and psychologists, from whose work she quotes. I would like to introduce a third factor — the cosmic influence.

The concept of a world mind, into which we may all make our input, has recently gained a decree of credence. We are told that if we all pull together we can save Gaia, and in so doing ensure a safer and better planetary environment for future generations. In other words, the old parochial attitudes are slowly giving way to a kind of Brotherhood of Mankind within the embrace of Gaia. But just as the atom is but one manifestation of the microcosm, as against the planetary macrocosm, so is our planet itself but a microcosm in the macrocosmic solar system, the solar system thus related to the galaxy and so on ad infinitum. The isolationist view may have lessened as far as national barriers are concerned, but what of the universe beyond our planet, which we are only just beginning to explore?

Those of us who tend to look outwards are frequently criticized on the grounds that there is plenty with which we should concern ourselves in our immediate environment. But there have always been visionaries and pioneers, and were we all to spend our time and energies endeavouring to cope with the complexities of earthly existence we would probably still be troglodytes. And there is another factor to consider: looking inwards is not always the answer. It is sometimes necessary to look outwards in order to understand the inner problems. During my days as a healer, I frequently observed how people with nagging health or social problems often miraculously recovered when they took up healing themselves, or engaged in some activity external to their own environment and its related problems. Distancing ourselves from what might appear to be insoluble problems often provides those very answers that elude us when we are too involved with them. Travel, we are told, broadens the mind; likewise mental travel broadens the spiritual horizons. So one does not need to take to the road, air or sea in order to gain a clearer perspective, it can be done by mental detachment or simply stretching the mind.

The breaking down of male dominance with its competitive and belligerent overtones will be no easy task, and I cannot see it being achieved through any form of overt feminism. Most women have, I think, observed that one of the best ways to encourage a man to adjust to new ways of thinking is to let him believe that it has all been his idea. I am seeing this happen all around me at the moment. Men, as well as women, are channelling dolphin, leonine, tree, and other animal, elemental, and plant essences normally associated with Goddess-orientated shamanism. At psychic fairs there are now almost as many men practising as mediums or readers as women. Among young people in particular, the distribution of household and other menial tasks differs considerably from the conventions observed in such matters by the older generation. As Eisler comments:

> These new ways of imaging reality for both women and men are giving rise to new models of the human psyche. The older Freudian model saw human beings primarily in terms of elemental drives such as the need for food, sex, and safety. The new model proposed by Abraham Maslow and other humanistic psychologists takes these elemental 'defense' needs into account but also recognizes that human beings have a higher level of 'growth' or 'actualization' needs that distinguish us from other animals.
>
> This shift from defense needs to actualization needs is an important key to the transformation from a dominator to a

partnership society. Hierarchies maintained by force or the threat of force require defensive habits of mind. In our type of society, the creation of enemies for man begins with his human twin, woman, who in prevailing mythology is blamed for nothing less than our fall from paradise. And for both men and women, this ranking of one half of humanity over the other, as Alfred Adler noticed, poisons all human relations.[3]

Some of Eisler's premises I agree with, others not. As a shaman, for example, I would hardly go along with her statement that human beings have a higher level of growth or 'actualization' than animals. But then perhaps Ms Eisler has worked more closely with the former than the latter. As some of the aforementioned shamans and mystics have so readily attested, the old Goddess religions acknowledged *all* living creatures (and in some cases inanimate objects) as members of the family of Gaia, each fulfilling its destined role in the manner best suited to its type and talents.

There would appear to be just as many men attending the rites and paying obeisance to the tenets of both the old and the new Goddess religions as women, which is a good thing, as it will serve to stimulate their animas and bring out the gentler side of their nature. Weekend seminars, lectures and workshops dealing with the subject of women's mysteries, which help to spread the knowledge and influence of the Goddess far and wide, are becoming more numerous each year. Various feminist-orientated groups and cults, such as Lux Madriana, The Women's Ecology Group, Women for Life on Earth, Women for Animal Rights, The Sophia Network, The British Matriarchal Tradition, and The Rainbow Net are also making their presence felt round and about.

In her book *Man/Woman: the One is the Other*, the French writer and philosopher Dr Elisabeth Badinter emphasizes the resemblances between the sexes, which she refers to in terms of a vertiginous mutation. I see this mutation as crucial to our survival as a species, and essential to our evolutionary progression. Pronounced psychological and somatic differences between the sexes may be indicative of a low position on the evolutionary scale, since the androgyne was always conceived of by the ancients as being the ultimate state of perfection. The androgynous state can, of course, be seen either in terms of a uniting of the anima and animus within the individual, or an eventual union of twin souls — the male and the female. Either way, it would appear to be a fundamental prerequisite to both spiritual and somatic progression. Badinter comments:

> At a time when social reference points are vanishing, when sexual roles are becoming flexible, when women may choose not to become mothers, the specific difference between the One and the Other is becoming more and more difficult to pin down. The growing revelation of our bisexual nature is completing the process of disorientation. Apart from the irreducible chromosomal difference (XX for women, XY for men), we are now reduced to making distinctions between the 'more' and the 'less'. Certainly the One has more male hormones and the Other more female ones, but both sexes produce feminine and masculine hormones. Men have greater muscular strength than women, and greater aggressivity, but these differences vary enormously from one individual to another.
>
> Indeed, if we are definitely differentiated by our hereditary genetic material which is responsible for the sex of the reproductive cells, mental and physical pathology, as well as various cases of intersexuality, oblige us to admit that although the law recognizes two sexes, there does exist a varying number of intermediary types between the well-defined female and the well-defined male. This leads Professor Baulieu to think that there is both 'a great initial similarity and a certain flexibility in the differentiation between the sexes'. In other words, that 'there are no fixed borderlines between the masculine and the feminine.'[4]

The male dominance that has been the norm for so many centuries can hardly be said to have had a good track record. The influence of the Goddess may therefore become a unifying influence between the sexes, which will help us to attain a state of equality where neither factor dominates, but each is acknowledged as *sine qua non* to the other.

The ebbing and flowing tides of religious and cultural emphases prompted me to head the chapter of a book I recently wrote on the subject of Atlantis with the following lines:

> The knowledge and the science of one long-dead age
> Becomes the mystery, the theurgy of the next;
> Until the fires of reason rise to burn the superstitions

That offend their logic.
Yet, from the embers of their holocaust, the Phoenix
    Stretches forth its wings in flight,
Bearing aloft the Gods of future years. [5]

So it was therefore only a question of time before the Goddess returned to us, albeit on a more exalted frequency. But then, perhaps, we are expected to be ready to receive Her at that level, and the scriptures resound with tales of the fate of those who are unprepared for important arrivals, or who refuse genuine invitations.

Chapter 18
Towards the Future

THE feminist and post-feminist movements have so far received little mention in this book. This should not be taken as an indication that I have been impervious to the situation of women worldwide or the work of those admirable women who have laboured against enormous odds to gain a fairer deal for their sisters, but rather that I have been busy doing other things, not the least of which has been observing. Most of my observations have been first-hand, since much of my knowledge and experience has been gathered 'in the field' rather than through other agencies of learning.

It is now 40 years since Simone de Beauvoir's brave and pioneering study of woman's condition, *The Second Sex*, first appeared. The storm it aroused was electric. Words such as priapic, neurotic, repressed, nymphomaniac, lesbian, envious, and embittered were among the abusive epithets levelled at its author, while the Catholic Church promptly placed the book on its blacklist. And yet much of this misogynistic flak can be dated back to a single anatomical fact — women's skulls were observed by Darwin to be somewhat smaller than men's. Herbert Spencer and Carl Vogt, to name but two, were quick to seize upon what they saw to be a god-given opportunity to prove the case for masculine superiority. A series of dubious 'scientific' studies ensued and women's sexuality was suddenly 'discovered' in a Pandora's box of lesbianism, auto-eroticism and many other 'sins' including nymphomania — a term coined in the 1860s. Feminine depravity became for a while a popular subject matter for art and debate, with the Church adding as much fuel as it could lay its hands on to keep the fires of the separatist and dominator factors burning as brightly as possible.

Since then the battle has raged incessantly. The feminist movement has been followed by the post-feminist movement. The mythical bra burners — seen by many as purely a creation of the media — have given way to a more subtle approach to the quest for equality. An article in the American magazine *Time* (4 December 1989) entitled 'Onward, Women!' commented:

- 'The superwoman is weary, the young are complacent, but feminism is not dead. And, baby, there's still a long way to go.'
- 'I reject the feminist label, but I guess I call myself egalitarian.'
- 'I'm feminine, not a feminist.'
- 'I picture a feminist as someone who is masculine and who doesn't shave her legs and is doing everything she can to deny she is feminine.'

These were a few of the comments the interviewer encountered. Countless examples are cited of women who do not consider themselves as feminists but take certain rights for granted. The long, ill-fated battle in the United States for the Equal Rights Amendment to the Constitution appeared to mean nothing to younger women who accept equality without due appreciation of the battles that had raged (and are still raging) along the way. While many professional women are able to enjoy the somewhat meagre harvest of liberation, the majority of women working in the lower echelons of American society have been untouched by its fruits.

Stay-at-home mothers still make up one-third of all American women with children under 18, and many of these feel that their status has been depreciated by feminism. Although it might be tempting to conclude from the wide-ranging complaints that the Women's Movement has failed, breakthroughs have occurred. The explosion of new roles for women, their greater participation in the country's political and intellectual life, and the many viable alternatives that now replace their confinement to the areas of home-making and child-rearing; these and numerous other options may be chalked up as feminist achievements.

The wage gap still leaves much to be desired, however, with women who work full-time still earning only 66 per cent of what a man is paid, a difference that has apparently narrowed by less than 10 per cent over the past two decades. Although in the early 1980s the 'feminization of poverty' became an issue for the Women's Movement, we are informed that the situation has barely budged. The following figures are given in a *Time* article in a table headed: 'The Truth about the Women's Movement':

The movement:	True	Not True
Has helped women become more independent	94%	4%
Has given women more control over their lives	86%	10%
Is still improving the lives of women	82%	12%
Accurately reflects the views of most women	53%	40%
Looks down on women who do not have jobs	35%	57%
Is anti-family	24%	64%
Is out of date in its goals	23%	61%

From the above table it would seem that something is amiss as far as the feminist movement in America is concerned. Let us now take a look at the average woman's choice of priorities:

Which Issues Are Very Important to Women	
Equal Pay	94%
Day Care	90%
Rape	88%
Maternity leave at work	84%
Job discrimination	82%
Abortion	74%
Sexual freedom	49%

When questioned as to whether they considered themselves to be feminists, 33 per cent answered 'yes' and 58 per cent 'no', although 62 per cent considered the feminist movement to have been helpful to women generally, as against 18 per cent who saw it as harmful.

It is interesting to observe the accent on equal pay and the fact that the role of motherhood is still of vital importance to many women, while sexual freedom comes low on the list. How these American figures compare with equivalent European surveys I do not know, since comparative charts are not readily available. However, from various reports I have read from time to time in both the popular press and specialized publications, I would deduce that there is little difference. The majority of women are, like their menfolk, rigidly typecast, although hairline cracks, imperceptible to all but the highly observant, are beginning to appear in the framework of their moulds.

Some thinking women who are more concerned with transcendental values do tend to feel that modern feminism has it wrong by allowing an understandable anger to obscure their real task, which is seen to be to assist with man's spiritual growth. Perhaps it has served to awaken the dormant spirituality in many women, although it has also engendered a nostalgia for a matriarchy, which constitutes as much of an imbalance as the dominant patrism with which we are at present saddled. There are also many women who ache for an equal relationship with a man, but typically find their spiritual insights denigrated or feared by their lovers. Women often contribute to this dilemma by needing men too much and by acting out — often very manipulatively — fantasies of dependence and possessiveness that cramp the masculine spirit.

Brian Magee contributed a lengthy article to the *Weekend Guardian* (11 November 1989) entitled 'Women: The Rights and Wrongs', which he chose to end on a bleak note:

We have already reached a stage where the chief problem is no longer to get the case accepted in theory but to get it put into practice. Before women enjoy real equality of opportunity with men, and genuine equality of consideration by all our social institutions, we have a long way to go.

When that day comes, the differences between the sexes will be much reduced, because they will no longer be reinforced and encouraged by our social arrangements. But they will not disappear.

Even in ideal conditions, with both men and women enjoying complete freedom, and having complete control over their own lives, their spontaneous choices would perpetuate quite a number of those general differences between the sexes with which we are familiar.

On the basis of our evolutionary progress (or regression?) over the past few centuries Magee is probably right, but his assessment fails to take into account those transcendental aspects that could serve as the proverbial donkey's carrot. Most esotericists realize that the spiritually immature tend to cling tenaciously to set dogmas wherein they feel secure, since they lack the temerity to look beyond the obvious and base their selection on a wider sociological or transcendental field. Many metaphysicians are of the opinion that the evolutionary spread on this planet is far too wide, the gap between the spiritually mature and immature being almost unbridgeable, while the majority hover somewhere in the centre, unsure as to which way to jump.

No doubt some who read this book will encounter too much of the metaphysical within its pages for their taste, and I will be accused of stating the obvious without offering viable solutions to the existing problems encountered by both men and women in the environmental and societal estrangements into which they have been programmed. Practical solutions, however, usually come through the hearts and minds of people, and their *wills* to improve matters. They are the overt enactments of the transpersonal enlightenment, or inner awareness, that defies left-brain delineation or rationale.

It is for this reason that I do not see the battle of the sexes as a long, drawn-out, guerilla-like affair, defying logical resolution and extending into perpetuity. Miracles do happen, but the move towards a permanent truce will need to come from both sides, and as yet there may not be a sufficient number of women who want to see the old order changed. And while their free services, both in and out of the home, are still on offer, there is little chance for the rest of us to achieve the equality and respect we hope for, and would, in turn, reciprocate with those men whose animas would allow them to respond to us with the caring and understanding we would so deeply appreciate.

I do not for one moment consider that men are inferior to women, or that we should be dominated by a matrist society, but I do believe in equality and freedom of choice *on both sides*. After all, the spirit or psyche can reincarnate into either sex, and into any time, past or present, so the way we behave towards each other in the 'now' is more than likely to land us with some karmic debts (or credits, as the case may be) in some other place or time. Since individual responsibility goes hand in hand with maturity of spirit, we all too easily advertise who and what we are. In the final analysis our future lies in our own hands. Let us ensure that it is ethically and spiritually orientated, for without doubt as we sow so shall we reap!

At the commencement of this book I speculated as to whether the aberration which causes enmity between the sexes constituted part of the natural evolutionary development of our species, or whether it had been artificially introduced by some agency external to our terrestrial environment. My conclusions are that both processes play a part. There will always be external influences exerted on our planet — some benign, some malign — since it is a part, albeit miniscule, of the greater universe which is, in turn, a living entity in its own right. How we react to such influences will naturally be dictated by the stage of development through which we are passing at any given time. Sometimes we are faced with energies which need to be mastered before we can effect further progress along either our somatic or transcendental evolutionary journeys. Coming to amicable terms with the opposite sex, for example, may be essential to our successful communication with other life-forms we may encounter during the years of space exploration which may well lie ahead.

Growing up is ever a painful process, whether in childhood or the disciplines that will obviously be required if we are to enter the Cosmic Community without feeling that we own the universe. We must first come to terms with the feminine principle within our own kind and learn to understand our *true* position in relation to the other life forms with which we share *this planet*, for until we do we will certainly not have the awareness to comprehend and appreciate the life forms, customs, and beliefs of extra-terrestrial beings.

Among the ancient peoples of Egypt, India, and Celtica, to name but three, a certain aspect of the Goddess received special acknowledgement, that being her role as mistress of demolition and reconstruction, destruction and regeneration, or dispersion and solidification. These were deemed essential to the preservation of the right order of things within the universe. Is it not interesting to observe that it was to a *goddess* rather than a god that this function was allocated? The Egyptians called her Sekhmet, the people of the Indian subcontinent knew her as Kali, while to the Celts she was Morrigan or Cailleach. Many of us are anticipating her return to aid the cleansing and rebalancing of her sister, Gaia. But it will be through the hearts and minds of the peoples of Earth, and the women in particular, that her energies will manifest to help restore the feminine status quo on our planet, thus rendering it once again a true child of the Great Mother.

References

Chapter 1

1 Tomas, A. *Atlantis — From Legend to Discovery*, p.30.
2 Eisler, R. *The Chalice & The Blade*, pp.105-6.
3 Mead, G.R.S. *Fragments of a Faith Forgotten*, p.598.
4 Harding, M.E. *Woman's Mysteries*, p.240.
5 Rush, A.K. *Moon, Moon*, p.99.

Chapter 2

1 Noble, V. *Snake Power*, Vol. 1 Issue 1, p.5.
2 Walker, B.G. *The Woman's Encyclopedia of Myths and Secrets*, p.691.
3 *Ibid.*
4 Scrutton, R. *The Other Atlantis*, p.35.
5 Stone, M. *The Paradise Papers*, p.31.
6 Scrutton, R. *Op. cit.*, pp.28-9.
7 Hope, M. *The Psychology of Ritual*, pp.250-8.
8 Stone, *Op. cit.*, p.87.
9 Walker, *Op. cit.*, p.346.
10 *Ibid.*

Chapter 3

1 Durdin-Robertson, L. *The Goddesses of Chaldaea, Syria and Egypt*, pp.1-2.
2 Bonwick, J. *Egyptian Belief and Modern Thought*, p.115.
3 *Ibid.*, p.114.
4 Aldred, C. *The Egyptians*, pp.68-9.

Chapter 4

1 Badinter, E. *Man/Woman*, p.105.
2 Walker, B.G. *The Woman's Encyclopedia of Myths and Secrets*, p.54.
3 Masters, R. *The Goddess Sekhmet*.
4 Perera, S.B. *Descent to the Goddess*, p.9.
5 *Larousse Encyclopedia of Mythology*, p.57.
6 Perera, S.B. *Op. cit.*, p.11.
7 *Larousse Encyclopedia of Mythology*, p.175.
8 Hope, M. *Elements of the Greek Tradition*, p.85.

Chapter 5

1 Mead, G.R.S. *Thrice Greatest Hermes*, Vol. 1, p.260.
2 *Ibid.*, p.267.
3 Witt, R.E. *Isis in the Graeco-Roman World*, p.203.
4 *Ibid.*, p.165.
5 *Ibid.*, pp.165–6.
6 Hope, M. *The Greek Tradition*, p.59.
7 Mylonas, G.E. *Eleusis*, p.7.
8 Quinn, B. *Atlantean*, pp.169–70.
9 Stone, M. *The Paradise Papers*, p.64.
10 *Ibid.*, p.65.
11 *Ibid.*
12 Eisler, R. *The Chalice and the Blade*, p.106.
13 Crowley, V. *Wicca: the Old Religion in the New Age*, p.9.
14 *Ibid.*, p.172.
15 *Ibid.*, p.174.
16 *Ibid.*, p.179.
17 Walker, B.G. *The Woman's Encyclopedia of Myths and Secrets*, p.51.
18 *Ibid.*, p.1018.
19 *Ibid.*, p.149.
20 Mead, G.R.S. *Fragments of a Faith Forgotten*, pp.333–5.
21 Walker, *Op. cit.*, p.932.
22 *Ibid.*, pp.929–30.

Chapter 6

1 Stone, M. *The Paradise Papers*, pp.51–2.
2 Teish, L. *Jambalaya*, pp.54–5.

3 Begg, E. *Cult of the Black Virgin*, p.1.
4 *Ibid.*, pp.8-9.
5 *Ibid.*, p.14.
6 Pagels, E. *The Gnostic Gospels*, p.26.
7 *Ibid.*, p.77.
8 Begg, *Op. cit.*, p.129.
9 Eliade, M. *Rites and Symbols of Initiation*, p.25.
10 *Ibid.*, p.43.
11 Cameron, A. *Daughters of Copper Woman*, p.125.
12 Rush, A.K. *Moon, Moon*, p.107.
13 *Larousse Encyclopedia of Mythology*, p.447.

Chapter 7

1 Stone, M. *The Paradise Papers*, p.241.
2 Walker, B. *The Woman's Encyclopedia of Myths and Secrets*, p.1095.
3 Stone, M. *Op. cit.*, pp.70-1.
4 *Ibid.*, p.71.
5 Mozart, W.A. *The Magic Flute*, translation by Edward J. Dent, from the score by Boosey & Hawkes, p.158.
6 Vermes, G. *Jesus the Jew*, p.99.
7 Mead, G.R.S. *Fragments of a Faith Forgotten*, pp.75-6.
8 Walker, B. *Op. cit.*, p.776.
9 de Beauvoir, S. *The Second Sex*, pp.120-1.
10 Ashton, J. *Mother of Nations*, p.220.
11 Stone, M. *Op. cit.*, p.241.
12 *World Book Encyclopedia*
13 Stone, M. *Op. cit.*, p.212.
14 Walker, B. *Op. cit.*, p.52.
15 Dale-Green, P. *Cult of the Cat*, p.134.
16 Feldman, C. *Woman Awake*, p.104.
17 Allione, T. *Women of Wisdom.*, p.6.
18 *Ibid.*, p.7.
19 Feldman, C. *Op. cit.*, p.93.
20 *Ibid.*, p.94.
21 Walker, B. *Op. cit.*, p.124.
22 Allione, T. *Op. cit.*, p.25.
23 Walker, B. *Op. cit.*, p.933.

Chapter 8

1 Jung, C. *Archetypes of the Collective Unconscious*, p.175.

2 Harding, M.E. *Woman's Mysteries*, pp.29–30.
3 Eysenck, H.J. and Sargent, C. *Explaining the Unexplained*, pp.66–7.
4 Waite, A.E. *The Occult Sciences*, p.10–11.
5 Walker, B. *The Woman's Encyclopedia of Myths and Secrets*, p.863.
6 Whitmont, E.C. *The Return of the Goddess*, p.124.
7 Cleary, T. *Immortal Sisters*, pp.1–2.
8 *Ibid.*, pp.94–5.
9 *Ibid.*, p.5.
10 *Ibid.*, p.24.
11 *Ibid.*, p.52.

Chapter 9

1 Fraser, A. *The Warrior Queens*, pp.8–9.
2 *Ibid.*, p.9.
3 *Ibid.*
4 *Ibid.*, pp.3–4.
5 *Ibid.*, p.109–10.
6 *Ibid.*, p.131.
7 *Ibid.*, p.294.
8 Walker, B. *The Woman's Encyclopedia of Myths and Secrets*, p.475.
9 Badinter, E. *Man/Woman*, p.120.
10 *Ibid.*, pp.122–3.
11 Stone, M. *The Paradise Papers*, p.250.
12 *Ibid.*, p.253.
13 *Ibid.*

Chapter 10

1 Dally, P. and Watkins, M.I. *Psychology and Psychiatry*, p.132.
2 Badinter, E. *Man/Woman*, p.121.

Chapter 11

1 Bolen, J. *Goddesses in Everywoman*, pp.29–30.

Chapter 12

1 Jung, C.G. *Memories, Dreams and Reflections*, p.163.
2 *Ibid.*, p.199.

3 Kretschmer, E. *A Textbook of Medical Psychology*, p.172.
4 *Ibid.*, pp.192-3.
5 Jung, C.G. *Memories, Dreams and Reflections*, p.259.
6 Hodgkinson, L. *Sex Is Not Compulsory*, p.21.
7 *Ibid.*, p.15.
8 *Ibid.*, p.9.
9 *Ibid.*, p.46.
10 *Ibid.*, p.8.

Chapter 13

1 Harding, M.E. *Woman's Mysteries*, p.239.
2 Jung, C.G. *Aspects of the Feminine*, pp.113-14.

Chapter 15

1 Feldman, C. *Woman Awake*, p.49.

Chapter 16

1 Bancroft, A. *Weavers of Wisdom*, p.vii.
2 *Ibid.*, p.viii.
3 Jamal, M. *Shape Shifters: Shaman Women in Contemporary Society*, p.19.
4 *Ibid.*, p.121.
5 *Ibid.*, p.126.
6 *Ibid.*, p.116.
7 *Magical Blend*, Issue 21, January 1989, pp.64-5.

Chapter 17

1 Aswynn, F. *Leaves of Yggdrasil*, pp.187-8.
2 Eisler, R. *The Chalice and the Blade*, p.186.
3 *Ibid.*, p.190.
4 Badinter, E. *Man/Woman*, pp.153-4.
5 Hope, M. *Atlantis — Myth or Reality?*, Chapter 9.

Bibliography

Aldred, C., *The Egyptians* (Thames & Hudson, London, 1961).

Allione, Tsultrim, *Women of Wisdom* (Arkana Paperbacks, London, 1984).

Anthony, Maggy, *The Goddess Is Alive* (forthcoming).

Anthony, Maggy, *The Valkyries: The Women Around Jung* (Element Books, Shaftesbury, 1990).

Ashton, J., *Mother of Nations* (The Lamp Press, Basingstoke, 1988).

Aswynn, F., *Leaves of Yggdrasil* (Aswynn, London, 1988).

Badinter, E., *Man/Woman: The One is the Other* (Collins Harvill, London, 1989).

Baigent, M., Leigh, R., and Lincoln, H., *The Holy Blood and the Holy Grail* (Jonathan Cape, London, 1982).

Bancroft, A., *Weavers of Wisdom* (Arkana, London, 1989).

Begg, Ean, *The Cult of the Black Virgin* (Arkana, London, 1985).

Berlitz, Charles, *Atlantis* (Macmillan, London, 1984).

Berry, Philippa, *Of Chastity and Power — Elizabethan Literature and the Unmarried Queen* (Routledge & Kegan Paul, London, 1989).

Bolen, Jean S., *Goddesses in Everywoman* (Harper & Row, San Francisco, 1985).

Bonwick, James, *Egyptian Belief and Modern Thought* (Falcon's Wings Press, Colorado, 1956).

Braghine, Colonel A., *The Shadow of Atlantis* (Aquarian Press, Wellingborough, 1980).

Budge, E.A. Wallis, *The Gods of the Egyptians* (Dover Publications, New York, 1969).

Cameron, Anne, *Daughters of Copper Woman* (Press Gang Publishers, Vancouver, B.C., 1938).

Cirlot, J.E., *A Dictionary of Symbols* (Routledge & Kegan Paul, London 1962).

Clary, T., *Immortal Sisters* (Element/Shambhala, Boston & Shaftesbury, 1989).

Crowley, Vivianne, *Wicca* (Aquarian Press, Wellingborough, 1989).

Cumont, Franz, *Astrology and Religion Among the Greeks and Romans* (Dover Publications, New York, 1960).

Dale-Green, Patricia, *Cult of the Cat* (William Heinemann, London, 1963).

Dally, P. and Watkins, Mary J., *Psychology & Psychiatry: An Integrated Approach* (Hodder & Stoughton, London, 1986).

D'Alviella, G., *The Mysteries of Eleusis* (Aquarian Press, Wellingborough, 1981).

de Beauvoir, S., *The Second Sex* (Bantam Books, New York, 1970).

Durdin-Robertson, Laurence, *The Goddesses of Chaldaea, Syria and Egypt* (Cesara Publications, 1975).

Eisler, Riane, *The Chalice and the Blade* (Harper & Row, San Francisco, 1988).

Eliade, M., *Rites and Symbols of Initiation* (Harper & Row, New York, 1985).

Eysenck, H. and Sargent, C., *Explaining the Unexplained* (Weidenfeld & Nicolson, London, 1982).

Feldman, Christina, *Woman Awake* (Penguin/Arkana, London, 1989).

Flaceliere, R., *Greek Oracles* (Elek Books, London, 1965).

Fraser, Antonia, *The Warrior Queens* (Mandarin Paperbacks, London, 1989).

Freud, Sigmund, *The Future of an Illusion* (Anchor Books, New York, 1964).

Gilchrist, C., *The Circle of Nine* (Dryad Press, London 1988).

Graves, Robert, *The White Goddess* (Faber & Faber, London, 1964).

Harding, M. Esther, *Woman's Mysteries* (Rider & Co., London, 1989).

Harding, M. Esther, *The Way of All Women* (Rider & Co., London, 1986).

Heard, Margaret, *The Other Mary Rose* (Women's Hermetic Press, London, 1983).

Hodgkinson, Liz, *Sex Is Not Compulsory* (Columbus Books, London, 1986).

Hope, Murry, *Atlantis — Myth or Reality?* (Penguin/ Arkana, London, 1990).

Hope, Murry, *Olympus — An Experience in Self-Discovery* (Thorsons, Wellingborough, 1990).

Hope, Murry, *The Greek Tradition* (Element Books, Shaftesbury, 1989).

Hope, Murry, *The Psychology of Healing* (Element Books, Shaftesbury, 1989).

Hope, Murry, *The Psychology of Ritual* (Element Books, Shaftesbury, 1988).

Hope, Murry, *Practical Celtic Magic*, (Aquarian Press, Wellingborough, 1987).

Jamal, Michele, *Shape Shifters: Shaman Women in Contemporary Society* (Penguin/Arkana, London, 1987).

Jung, C.G., *Alchemical Studies* (Routledge & Kegan Paul, London, 1983).

Jung, C.G., *Aspects of the Feminine* (Ark Paperbacks, London & New York, 1982).

Jung, C.G., *Memories, Dreams and Reflections* (Routledge & Kegan Paul, London, 1963).

Jung, C.G., *Archetypes and the Collective Unconscious* (Routledge & Kegan Paul, London, 1959).

Kerenyi, C., *The Gods of the Greeks* (Thames & Hudson, London, 1979).

Kretschmer, E., *A Textbook of Medical Psychology* (The Hogarth Press, London, 1952).

Larousse Encyclopedia of Mythology (Hamlyn, London, 1959).

Masters, Robert, *The Goddess Sekhmet* (Amity House, New York, 1988).

Matthews, Caitlin, *The Celtic Tradition* (Element Books, Shaftesbury, 1989).

Mead, G.R.S., *Fragments of a Faith Forgotten* (Theosophical Publishing Co., London, 1906).

Mead, G.R.S., *Thrice Greatest Hermes* Vols. 1, 2 & 3 (Theosophical Publishing Co., London, 1906).

Mead, G.R.S., *Pistis Sophia* (John M. Watkins, London, 1896).

Mooney, Richard, *Colony Earth* (Souvenir Press, London, 1974).

Mylonas, G.E., *Eleusis and the Eleusinian Mysteries* (Routledge & Kegan Paul, London, 1961).

Pagels, Elaine, *The Gnostic Gospels* (Vintage Books, New York, 1981).

Perera, Sylvia Brinton, *Descent to the Goddess* (Inner City Books, Toronto, 1981).

Richardson, Alan, *Priestess* (Aquarian Press, Wellingborough, 1989).

Richardson, Alan, *Dancers to the Gods* (Aquarian Press, Wellingborough, 1985).

Rolleston, T.W., *Myths and Legends of the Celtic Race* (George G. Harrap & Co., London, 1911).

Rush, Anne Kent, *Moon, Moon* (Random House, New York, 1976).

Sagan, C., *Cosmos* (Random House, New York, 1980).

Schwaller de Lubicz, R.A., *Sacred Science* (Inner Traditions International, Rochester VT, 1982).

Scrutton, R., *The Other Atlantis* (Neville Spearman, Jersey, 1977).

Sheldrake, Rupert A., *A New Science of Life* (Granada Publishing, London, 1983).

Shorter, B., *An Image Darkly Forming* (Routledge & Kegan Paul, London, 1987).

Shuttle P. and Redgrove P., *The Wise Wound* (Paladin, London, 1986).

Spence, L., *An Encyclopaedia of Occultism* (Citadel Press, New Jersey, 1960).

Spence, L., *The History of Atlantis* (Rider, London, no date).

Stone, Merlin, *The Paradise Papers* (Virago, London, 1976).

Teish, Luisah, *Jambalaya* (Harper & Row, San Francisco, 1985).

Tomas, Andrew, *Atlantis — From Legend to Discovery* (Robert Hale, London, 1972).

Vermes, Geza, *Jesus the Jew* (SCM Press, London, 1983).

Waite, A.E., *The Occult Sciences* (Kegan, Paul, Trench, Trubner & Co., London, 1891).

Walker, Barbara G., *The Woman's Encyclopedia of Myths and Secrets* (Harper & Row, San Francisco, 1987).

West, John Anthony, *Serpent in the Sky* (Julian Press, New York, 1979).

Whitmont, E.C., *The Return of the Goddess* (Arkana, London, 1987).

Witt, R.E., *Isis in the Graeco-Roman World* (Thames & Hudson, London, 1971).

Wood, David, *Genisis* (The Baton Press, Tunbridge Wells, 1985).

Index